LINGUISTICA EXTRANEA

Studia, 7

STEVEN A. KONOPACKI

THE DESCENT INTO WORDS

Jakob Böhme's Transcendental Linguistics

1979

KAROMA PUBLISHERS, INC.   ANN ARBOR

Publication of this work was supported in part by a grant from the
F. W. Hillis Publication Fund of Yale University

Copyright © 1979 by Karoma Publishers, Inc.
All Rights Reserved

ISBN: 0-89720-018-7 (Cloth); 0-89720-019-5 (Paper)

Printed in the United States of America

yē sātyam mārgayanti sukham vindanti

for

Paul T. Roberge

...Der rechte Grund steckt im Worte verborgen, und ist von dem Menschen niemaln verstanden worden. Denn der Mensch hat seit der Zeit des Falles niemals können die innerliche Geburt begreiffen, wie da sey die himmlische Geburt; sondern seine Vernunft ist in der äusserlichen Begreiffligkeit gefangen gelegen, und hat nicht können durch den Himmel durchdringen und die innerlichste Geburt GOttes schauen, welche auch ist in der verderbten Erden und allenthalben.

Aurora xxi, 10

CONTENTS

Preface xi

Chapter I: The Awakening of Böhme's Linguistic Evolution: The *Aurora, oder Morgenröthe im Aufgang* (1612)..........1

Chapter II: The Code Expands: *Beschreibung der Drey Principien Göttliches Wesens* (1619) and *Hoch und Tiefe Gründung vom Dreyfachen Leben des Menschen* (1619-1620)............41

Chapter III: The Plateau: *De Signatura Rerum oder von der Geburt und Bezeichnung aller Wesen* (1622) and *Von der Wahren Gelassenheit* (1622)........................77

Chapter IV: The Work: *Mysterium Magnum oder Erklärung über das Erste Buch Mosis* (1622)........................97

Chapter V: A New Dawn in the Final Year: *Tafeln* (1624), *Clavis* (1624) and *Betrachtung Göttlicher Offenbarung ... 177 Fragen* (1624)..136

Notes..161

Alphabetic Index...181

Word Index...187

Bibliography...195

PREFACE

Intense spiritual fervor gripped all levels of German society during the early decades of the seventeenth century (Peuckert 1928:1-18). As a massive social force, interest in unorthodox, occult and heretical spiritual movements caught the attention and fancy of not only dukes and nobility, but also shoemakers and common citizens. An abundance of major and minor spiritual prophets proselytized their beliefs against the backdrop of a world intensely attuned to the realities of an oncoming holocaust. Freedom, personal salvation, illumination, astral projection, thought transference, and various benevolent and not so benevolent forms of alchemy were offered to the general public in an organized effort to convert new members to differing modes of thought. Then, as now, much of the true "work," the recruiting, explaining and initiating, took place within the confines of secret conventicles out of public view, if not for the purpose of adding to the mystique of the arcanum, then for self-preservation against the unenlightened sharpened sword of public and orthodox overreaction. Brochures, pamphlets, tracts, and books—for initiates and browsers alike—appeared with great abundance throughout the German-speaking lands. These writings, now generally classified as mystical literature, projected to the reading audience the undeniable conviction that their authors were well seasoned spiritual travellers armed with the necessary mystical credentials: the ability to write a convincing argument. If the argument were well phrased and lucidly stated, then as with Paracelsus, a movement organized itself around the writings, devoted to the care and transmission of the ideas therein. Those who understood and agreed with the writings formed cults, secret societies and even churches around the literature (Schwenkfeld, Paracelsus, Andreä, Böhme). Those who disagreed and misunderstood were persecuted.

The oft cited mystical writer of the German Baroque—although he was completely unaware that a Baroque mode existed—is Jakob Böhme (1576-1624), understood and persecuted, a prophet and a recruiter. His first extant writing, the *Aurora oder Morgen Röte im Auffgang* (1612), offered the contemporary reader "die Wurtzel oder Mutter der Philosophiae, Astrologiae und Theologiae aus rechtem Grunde, oder die Beschreibung der Natur, Wie alles gewesen, und im Anfang worden ist" (Böhme 1715:I). Böhme's quest for the *Wurtzel* 'root of all manifestation' visited great perplexities upon his reading audience for two reasons: first, his thinking was morphemically subarranged and cross-referenced within itself, and secondly, his doctrine was the sum total of his personal path through the thicket of his own conscious effort to obtain knowledge. Modern readers of Böhme are confronted with a wall of unfamiliar terms which perplexed the first circle of faithful students, and more often than not, the pressures of time have intervened between the reader and the manuscript, forcing much semantic association onto the original mystical urge. The purpose of this study is to suggest a simplified method of semantic analysis, whereby the original content of Böhme's unique terminology can be coaxed out of the text without damaging the underlying doctrine. Then the study will diachronically follow Böhme's original linguistic argument to its natural end, rather than its conclusion: Böhme's death interrupts the life's work.

The guiding force behind the few attempts at unravelling the complicated language of German mystical literature begins with the notion of the *Wortfeld* 'word-field' as propounded by Trier (1931). The collection of interrelated words from the articulated (or written) language defines the boundary of the semantic area, or field, of the word under investigation. This concept, long accepted as immutable truth among language investigators, suggests a control mechanism which Trier disregarded "alles was zu diesem rationabilitas-Feld gehört, darf nicht von dem heutigen ratio Begriff aus, entschieden werden" (Trier 1931:24). The difficulty lies, however, in determining the extent to which the present-day *ratio Begriffe* 'rational concepts' have affected the semantic infor-

Preface xiii

mation recorded within the *Wortfelder* of older documents. Since there are no native speakers of Böhmian Silesian, we must analyze the language as it appears on the manuscript page. The semantic values of the *Wortfeld*, dependent upon socioeconomic, political and religious forces of linguistic impact, severely limit the modern attempt to regressively project a semantically neutral consciousness back into the language of older documents, and in effect almost prohibit such an attempt. How can we read Böhme, if not through the matrix of our own linguistic assumptions?

The first step in our linguistic analysis is to identify the paradigmatic extent of the corpus under investigation. Our "language" will assume the form of an entire literary activity, that is, the writings beginning with the *Aurora* (1612) and concluding with the *177 Fragen* (1624). Once the corpus is defined, then the evaluator must read it closely, recording every morphemic entry pertaining to, in our case, language observation. In this manner, the total meaning of the linguistic statement is seen in terms of a number of distinct elements, or semantic components. Factually attestable linguistic information, posited directly by the author, is recorded under each aspect of the linguistic argument. For the sake of the reader's tolerance, I have omitted much of the linguistic feature specifications within the body of this study, referring the reader to Böhme for attestations of veracity. For example, Böhme's description of *Fleisch* 'flesh' can be reduced into components:

> ... Das Fleisch bedeut die Erde, die ist erstarret und hat keine Beweglichkeit; also auch das Fleisch in sich selbst hat keine Vernunft, Begreiffligkeit, allein es wird von der Sternen Kraft, welche in dem Fleische und Adern regieren, beweget (*Aurora* ii, 24).

From this statement, the following features may be posited: *Fleisch* (as revealed solely within *Aurora* ii, 24) + symbolizes the earth, is - reason, - comprehensibility, - motion, but is + moved by the stars. Before a statement as to the linguistic nature of *Fleisch* can be formulated, the lexeme must be diagrammed in detail with respect to the entire section of the linguistic (literary) corpus. Then we need to look closely at what he means by *Sternen* 'stars', *Erde* 'earth', *Begreiffligkeit* 'comprehensibility', and so forth. Once the massive reading through the work is completed in this manner, those points of greatest concern to Böhme elevate above the text and speak their intent to the modern reader. Semantic componency, then, from within the corpus itself, adds much clarity to the nebulous realm of mystical writing, a genre wherein the spatial and temporal dispositions of the evaluator may sharply differ with those of the deceased author. One may believe, for example, that *Gott* 'God' carries the feature + beyond creation, not within elemental matter, whereas another may believe the word signifies a God + within creation. Especially today, the literary scholar is tempted to look askance at the often emotional and hypnotic attraction engendered by the leaders in the consciousness business. Modern audiences are reading massive amounts of transcendental literature, from Vedantic mysticism to Silva Mind Control, written to offer personal freedom, illumination, mental control (of self and others), and a wide array of other possibilities (McDermott 1975:213-40). Although not yet elevated to the status of a literary movement, these "movements" are nonetheless presenting to modern audiences massive amounts of semantic cohesion. In the same way, Böhme's cohesive thought was championed by his followers Franckenberg and Felgenhauer, who unfortunately added to the general lunacy of the period rather than conferred order upon Böhme's logically defined paradigms. Through the following paradigmatic analysis, Böhme the linguist-mystic emerges.

My special thanks to T. L. Markey, P. J. Eldridge, and the F. W. Hillis Publication Fund of Yale University.

Steven A. Konopacki
Yale University, August 1978

CHAPTER I

THE AWAKENING OF BÖHME'S LINGUISTIC EVOLUTION: THE *AURORA, ODER MORGENRÖTHE IM AUFGANG* (1612)

The lengthy and ponderous writings of the Silesian prophet Jakob Böhme (1576-1624) have blessed the world of mystical literature with a corpus of encyclopedic immensity, rich with internal denotation, a fertile ground for connotative interpretation. Overwhelmed with the verbal tonnage encountered in Böhme's literary corpus, his first group of students and interpreters[1] attempted to faithfully adhere to and communicate the particular and complex thoughts entrusted to them. Their explanations of the arcane writings, often minor treatises in themselves, can be comfortably read in a few hours, compared with the several months required to penetrate into their parent source. Their task was not an easy one: rather than engage in a word-for-word reproduction of Böhme, they sought to involve their audience in an active reading[2] through selected details of the entire corpus available to them. While remaining faithful to the Böhmian morphology, each reading represents a unique and novel path through the thicket of interwoven ideas, often not without connotative interpretations proffered as original truth. The second circle of faithful students, the English translators John Sparrow and John Elliston, rather than comment on the manuscripts and first editions in their possession, zealously worked them from 1647 through 1665 into fair English translation. Often clumsy English transformations, these first attempts show themselves to be not entirely free of connotative interpretation.[3] Subsequent generations of Böhme interpreters, each set upon explaining as concisely as possible the entire arcanum, have with one exception (Grunsky: 1956) retained a dependence upon well worn religious, philosophical or historical paths through the corpus. Unfortunately, centuries of labelling Böhme a mystical writer have closed the door to other interpretational possibilities, other readings through the corpus.[4]

A Böhmian encyclopedia charting the paradigmatic extent of each independent thought unit throughout the entire collection of extant manuscripts would entail listing every denotative comment found within the text under consideration. In this manner, a neutral Böhmian message, free from the interpreters' a priori judgments is established, and as a logical sequence, forms the basis of interpretation (via connotative paths). The only danger is that denotation, marking out plainly with a sign, can be short-lived "if the code that institutes it lasts only *l'espace d'un matin*" (Eco 1976:85). The purpose of this investigation is not to construct another Böhmian *Gospel Harmony*, nor to chart the extent of the Böhmian encyclopedia, but rather to focus attention on the morning of his literary creativity, the period of the *Aurora, oder Morgenröthe im Aufgang* (1612). In this *espace d'un matin* 'time of a morning' Böhme develops his most elaborate system of codes: a theory of language which, when applied to the entire literary corpus, transforms itself into a key to deeper understanding.

The code, often alluded to as the *Natursprache* 'language of nature',[5] a term which is presently avoided yet will appear later, develops in its entirety as early as 1612, a period of much inner turmoil and confusion for the young writer in search of an expressive vehicle for his mystical consciousness. Although capable of conveying positions within semantic fields, Böhme's linguistic theory incorporates into itself subtle changes in his perception of his mystical self. The introduction of an alchemical and cabalistic component into the phonology occurs in the early part of the year 1620. This effect upon the entire linguistic system as a whole reveals Böhme as a man deeply obsessed with the idea that somehow, in some manner, the *Geist* 'spirit' behind manifestation and encased within it, can free itself from its material bondage *Begreiffligkeit* 'material palpability as gross matter within the range of the five senses'.

The few scanty facts surrounding the generation of the *Aurora* (1612), facts gleaned from the awestricken Franckenberg report *Gründlicher und wahrhafter Bericht von dem Leben und Abschied Jakob Böhmes* (1651) and the small number of passages within Böhme's collected writings,[6] offer little substantive autobiographical information. As Franckenberg[7] reports, Böhme was to have gazed up from his cobbling one day, whereupon the rays of the sun reflecting in a pewter dish transported him into a different dimension of existence. Lifted out of his body, Böhme felt all of nature within his being. An expansion as large as the universe poured through his consciousness, and in doing so completely changed the simple common shoemaker into a prophetic visionary. The *Aurora*, written as a memorial to this experience,[8] was Böhme's method of recording an indescribable, and singular, experience. The visual impression of this experience upon the young shoemaker (Franckenberg claims it happened three times between 1600 and 1610) is generally accepted as the starting point of his literary career. Steiner (1942), for example, views this supersensual phenomenon as a catalyst to his future development. Without the visions Böhme would have remained in relative obscurity. On the non-Anthroposophic side of the debate, the majority of interpreters unanimously agree that Böhme's following autobiographical statement is nothing more than figurative speech.[9] Böhme's account does not mention the pewter dish, but rather directs the reader's attention to the implications behind the words *Geist* 'spirit' and *Wille* 'will':

> Als sich aber in solcher Trübsal mein Geist (dann ich wenig und nichts verstund was er war) ernstlich in GOtt erhub als mit einem grossen Sturme, und mein gantz Hertz und Gemüthe, samt allen andern Gedancken und Willen sich alles darein schlos, ohne nachlassen mit der Liebe und Barmhertzigkeit GOttes zu ringen, und nicht nachzulassen, Er segnete mich, dann, das ist, Er er-

leuchtete mich dann mit seinem H. Geiste, damit ich seinen Willen möchte verstehen, und meiner Traurigkeit los werden; so brach der Geist durch. Als ich aber in meinem angesetzten Eifer also hart wieder GOtt und allen Höllen Porten stürmete, als wären meiner Kräften noch mehr vorhanden, in willens das Leben daran zu setzen (welches freylich nicht mein Vermögen wäre gewesen ohne des Geistes GOttes Beystand) alsbald nach etlichen harten Stürmen ist mein Geist durch der Höllen Porten durchgebrochen bis in die innerste Geburt der Gottheit, und alda mit Liebe umfangen worden, wie ein Bräutigam seine liebe Braut umfähet... In diesem Lichte hat mein Geist alsbald durch alles gesehen und an allen Creaturen, so wol an Kraut und Gras GOtt erkant, wer der sey, und wie der sey, und was sein Wille sey: auch so ist alsbald in diesem Lichte mein Willen gewachsen mit grossem Trieb, das Wesen GOttes zu beschreiben (*Aurora* xix, 10-13).

What is Böhme saying? The textually attestable denotations arranged under the term *Wille* are: *Wille* differs from *Geist*, *Hertz* 'heart', and *Gemüth* 'the nonmanifested arrangement of man's physical potentials'; it exists within Böhme and God; it is unknown to Böhme if it exists in God alone; it thrives within the light imparted to him by God; it desires to express *das Wesen GOttes* 'the receptive manifested vessel of God'. The related term *Geist* 'spirit' is not understood by Böhme. It exists within the state of his sadness; contains the *Wille*, *Hertz* and *Gemüth*; is able to be affected by the *H. Geist* 'Holy Spirit' through which Böhme can understand the divine will; and it can see through everything, all creatures, herbs and grasses recognizing God within. Random connotative reasoning might lead the reader into realms of interpretation and neighboring semantic fields, wherein terms such as *Wille* and *Geist* frequently appear: theology and philosophy. Since these methodological viewpoints share the same morphology, the features ascribed to them have been allowed to overlap into Böhme's closed semantic system. For an exact reading through Böhme, the precise extent of the meaning, the meaning given by the "enlightened" author to the less awakened reading audience, needs formulation in its own terms in order for the modern perspective to accurately interpret the data.

Looking forward to November 19, 1620, roughly eight years after the completion of the *Aurora* (six of those years were spent in obedient, enforced silence),[10] Böhme in a letter to Paul Kaym mentions the early experience: prophetic urgency is now calm meditative retrospection:

> In solchem meinem gar ernstlichen Suchen und Begehren (darinnen ich heftige Anstösse erlitten, mich aber ehe des Lebens verwegen, als davon ausgehen und ablassen wolte;) ist mir die Pforte eröffnet worden, dass ich in einer Viertheilstunde mehr gesehen und gewust habe, als wann ich wäre viel Jahr auf hohen Schulen gewesen, dessen ich mich hoch verwunderte, wuste nicht wie mir geschahe, und darüber mein Hertz ins Lob GOttes wendete. Dann ich sahe und erkante das Wesen aller Wesen, den Grund und den Ungrund: Item, die Geburt der H. Dreyfaltigkeit, das Herkommen und den Urstand dieser Welt und aller Creaturen, durch die Göttliche Weisheit: Ich erkante und sahe in mir selber alle drey Welte, als (1.) die Göttliche Englische oder Paradeisische; Und dann (2.) die finstere Welt als den Urstand der Natur zum Feuer; und zum (3.) diese äussere sichtbare Welt, als ein Geschöpf und Ausgeburt, oder als *ein ausgesprochenes Wesen aus beyden inneren geistlichen Welten*. Ich sahe und erkante das gantze Wesen in Bösem und Guten, wie eines von dem andern urständete, und wie die Mutter der Gebärerin wäre, dass ich mich nicht allein hoch verwunderte, sondern auch erfreuete (*Sendbrief* xii, 7, 8).

Adjectivally extended, the substantive *Geist* is seen as a feature of *Welten* 'worlds', the origin of the *ausgesprochenes Wesen* 'spoken out being'. A closer examination of the nature of the entities which are spoken out, namely words and sounds, on the one hand disconnects the code from Böhme's theosophy (the origins of the code in *Geist*), and on the other hand reveals the code functioning as a semantic sign vehicle: *Geist, Wille* and *das Ausgesprochene*, as will be seen, function equally within the code. What is the code?

Although Böhme discusses over forty words within the *Aurora*, only sixteen are singled out for linguistic comment: *Barmhertzig* 'benevolence' (*Aurora* viii, 74); *Gib uns unser täglich Brod* 'give us our daily bread' (*Aurora* xiii, 110); *Teuvell* (teu-vell) 'devil' (*Aurora* xiv, 26); *Am Anfang schuf GOtt Himmel und Erden* 'in the beginning God created heaven and earth(s)' (*Aurora* xviii, 48); *sprach* 'spoke' (*Aurora* xviii, 87); and *Tag* 'day' (*Aurora* xix, 84). Within these sixteen words Böhme describes fourteen sounds, categorizing them according to his own specifications: they are *d, t, p, b, k, c* (ich-Laut), *x* (ach-Laut), *sch, m, n, ng, l, r,* and a general vocalic sound.

Böhme differentiates the dental stops *d* and *t* by a feature of hardness operative in the *t* but not in the *d*: "die andere Sylbe Den fasset sich mit der Zungen mit dem obern Gaumen, und lässet das Maul offen am hintern Theil über der Zungen im hintern Gaumen und zittert" (*Aurora* xviii, 69), whereas the *t* "hat seinen Ursprung von dem harten Pochen" (*Aurora* xiv, 26). In the word *Tag* the dental stop is noticeable: "Das Wort Tag ... wenn es aber hervor auf die Zunge kommt, so schleust die Zunge mit dem Ober= Gaumen das Maul zu [apicoalveolar stop]: wenn aber der Geist an die Zähne stösset und will raus [increased aspiration held], so schleust die Zunge das Maul auf, und will vorm Worte raus, und thut gleich einen Freuden=Sprung zum Maule raus [release of aspiration]" (*Aurora* xix, 84, 85).

Böhme accurately identifies the labials *p* and *b* as stops. Concerning the *b* Böhme says "Das Wort Barm ist nur auf deiner

Lippen; und wenn du sprichst Barm, so machstu das Maul zu" (*Aurora* viii, 74), that is, labial stop. In the word *sprach*, Böhme says little concerning the *p* other than it closes the mouth: "Wenn aber der Geist das Wort fasset, so macht er das Maul zu" (*Aurora* xviii, 89).

Böhme understands the velar obstruents *k* and *g* as stops. In the word *GOtt*, Böhme describes the *g* as: it "fasset sich mitten oben auf die Zungen [palatal closure] . . . und schallet aus sich und in sich [voice]" (*Aurora* xviii, 60). The *k* sound is described within the limits of its functional role as the dessonential element in the word *Anfang* where it "fähret schnell vom Hertzen zum Munde raus, und wird auch am hintern Orte der Zungen mit dem Gaumen gehalten, und wenn es losgelassen wird, so thuts noch einen schnellen Druck vom Hertzen zum Munde aus" (*Aurora* xviii, 53). Moulton (1952) argues for the positing of a velar *k* in Böhme's speech by interpreting the phrase *einen schnellen Druck* 'a fast thrust' as the sign of voicelessness. Böhme's linguistic observations as a mental attitude toward the articulated language possess the velar *k* ideationally, although its relation to his actual speech pattern is difficult to determine.

Labiodental fricatives *f* and *v* do not appear within the linguistic explanations of the *Aurora*, although functionally within the code they operate in the same manner as the palatal fricatives *c* (ich-Laut) and *x* (ach-Laut). Böhme notices that the *c* sound holds the word (Barmhertz+ig) together: "Wenn du aber sprichst IG, so fängest du den Geist mitten in den andern zwey Qualitäten, dass er muss drinn bleiben und das Wort formiren" (*Aurora* viii, 77). Since not only the two qualities but also the *Geist* are held within, Böhme's *IG* seems more like a stop than a fricative ich-Laut. He is aware of a feature of depth within the ach-Laut: it "spreutzet im hintern Gaumen in der Höle auf der Zungen [velar with the back of the dorsum raised forming the *Höle* 'cavern'], und behält sein Recht für sich, und bleibet an seinem Orte sitzen, und läst den sanften Geist aus dem Hertzen durch sich aus, und donnert mit seinem Kirren hernach [fricative]" (*Aurora* xviii, 90).

Böhme characterizes the nasals with descriptive accuracy. His bilabial *m* has the features of labiality, voice and nasality: it "fähret bis auf die Lippen [labiality], da wird es gefangen und gehet schallende [voice] wieder zurücke [nasality] bis an seinen ausgegangen Ort" (*Aurora* xviii, 48). The alveolar *n* appears in four passages in the *Aurora*: "wenn sichs aber ausspricht so schleust sichs mitten in seinem Sede mit dem obern Gaumen zu [alveolar closure] und ist halb draussen und halb drinnen" (xviii, 50). In the word *und*, the *n* is "mit der Zungen im obern Gaumen gehalten [alveolar closure]" (xviii, 67). In the word *Nacht* 'night' "so schleust die Zunge das Maul darweil zu [alveolar closure], bis der Geist kommt, und fasset sich auf der Zungen: dann macht sie das Maul geschwinde auf, und lässet den Geist hinaus [alveolar closure opening for vocalic onset]" (xix, 110). The velar nasal *ng* appears only once. Böhme notices that the position of the dorsum is relative to the velum (soft palate) in the syllable *-fang* (An+fang): "Das Wort fang fähret schnell vom Hertzen zum Munde raus, und wird auch am hintern Orte der Zungen mit dem Gaumen gehalten" (*Aurora* xviii, 53).

Böhme accurately describes the voiced lateral *l* as the closure along the median line in the mouth where the breath stream flows freely along the sides of the dorsum. In the word *Himmel* 'heaven' the *l* sound "macht die Lippen wieder auf, und wird mitten auf der Zungen gehalten, und fähret der Geist auf beyden Seiten der Zungen aus dem Maule" (*Aurora* xviii, 62). The dorsal position describes the *l* sound in the syllable *-mel* (Him+mel), offering Böhme a neat transition from language observation to theosophy:

> Dass sichs aber mit dem Wort Mel auf der Zungen mit dem obern Gaumen wieder fasset, und feste hält [bilabial closure], und der Geist auf beyden Seiten ausgehet [lateral position], dass bedeutet, dass GOtt diesem verderbten Königreiche oder Loco in GOtt, wolte wieder einen König und Gross=Fürsten geben, der die innerste Geburt der klaren Gottheit solte wieder

aufschliessen (*Aurora* xviii, 65).

The most significant sound in the entire code is the *r*. Böhme equates this sound with the primary and crucial force underlying manifestation, a force he calls astringency.[11] So important is the idea of astringency, that Böhme devotes a substantial portion of the linguistics of the *Aurora* to explain it. Overlooking the ramifications involved within the Böhmian perspective of the *r*, Moulton (1952), in seeking to prove that Böhme spoke with a uvular *r*, collapses the linguistic data of the *Aurora* into one affirmative statement. Böhme, though, says:

> Das ist ein gross Geheimnis: Das Wort Er bedeutet die angezündete herbe und bittere Qualität, den ersten Zorn GOttes, der zittert im hintern Gaumen, davor fürchtet sich die Zunge, und schmäuget sich im untern Gaumen, und fleucht als vor einem Feinde (*Aurora* xviii, 71).

The trembling feature in the *r*, attesting to the physical vibration of the uvula against the back of the velum, is the main feature by which Böhme elsewhere characterizes the sound: "Dass sich aber das gantze Wort Sprach im hintern Gaumen über der Zungen in der Höhle mitten in der herben und bittern Qualität fasset und kirred" (*Aurora* xviii, 103); "und karrest hintennach" (*Aurora* viii, 74); "so kirret der letzte Buchstabe R, und murret als ein zittender Odem" (*Aurora* viii, 75); and "fasset sich am hintern Theil über der Zungen, im hintern Gaumen, und zittert" (*Aurora* xviii, 69). The importance of the trembling aspect of this sound, while signalling possible spoken uvularity, more importantly signifies a physical reaction within manifestation to the forces of ensuing astringent compaction.

Vocalic sounds hold little interest for the young Böhme. Although he hints at the phonetic description of the vowel *e*, his observations never progress beyond describing the labial opening required to pronounce the sound.[12] Since the dorsum and the points of articulation are not used to the degree they are in the production of obstruent sounds, Böhme is content not to describe the vowels. He remains unimpressed by their presence: "es braucht sich aber die Zunge zu der ersten Sylben Er nicht; sondern sie schmäuget sich in den untern Gaumen hinein, und verkreucht sich als vor einem Feinde" (*Aurora* xviii, 69). Labial opening is important and signals Böhme's later interest in vowels:

> Das Wort GOtt fasset sich mitten oben auf der Zungen und stösset aus dem Hertzen dahin, und lässet das Maul offen und bleibet auf seinem königlichen Sessel sitzen und schallet aus sich und in sich: wenn es aber ausgesprochen ist, so thut es noch einen Druck zwischen den obern Zähnen und Zungen heraus (*Aurora* xviii, 60).

The vocalic function barely surfaces. In the word *Tag* 'day' Böhme realizes that the *t* is voiceless and that the onset of voice commences with labial opening anticipating the vowel: "Das Wort Tag ... macht sich das Maul inwendig weit auf, und das Wort fasset sich mit seinem Schallen hinter der herben und bittern Qualität noch einmal, und wecket dieselbe als einen faulen Schläffer in der Finsterniss auf, und fährt jähling zum Munde aus" (*Aurora* xix, 84-86).

In the word *Barmhertzigkeit*, Böhme inspects the *r* with a close eye on its astringent nature: "das ist die herbe Qualität, die umschleust das Wort, das ist, sie figuriret zusammen das Wort dass es harte wird oder schallet; und die bittere Qualität zerscheidet es" (*Aurora* viii, 74). Before losing Böhme in his terminology, the terms astringent and bitter need further clarification.

Within the vastness of God, a vastness encompassing all dimensions with its dark uniformity, Böhme envisions God's eternity as an all-powerful, omnipresent force desiring to experience itself. Since he is everywhere, God cannot simply reach into himself, for he is himself. Böhme interprets God's will toward objectively extending himself into palpability as a force of contraction, compaction, hardening, and binding together: a mechanism which he assigns the name *die Herbigkeit*[13] 'astringency'. Divine compaction, in congealing divinity within a centripetal astringent nucleus, is a hard, dark sheath surrounding God's will toward feeling himself objectively. Realizing the results of that which it has effected, the encased spirit desires freedom from its prison of dark contraction. Breaking through the dark coagulated compaction requires an enormous centrifugal expansion, a mechanism which Böhme calls *die Bitterkeit*[14] 'bitterness'. As centrifugality breaks away from centripetality, more astringency tries to smother the escaping bitterness, which only increases the intensity of bitterness, and so on into all eternity. Frictional interaction gives rise to motion, which through the collisions of astringency and bitterness generates an atmosphere wherein an immense explosion followed by a flash of fire appears. The process of ensuing manifestation, while too lengthy to adequately describe in the *Aurora*, abbreviates within the linguistic code, and develops as a common denominator throughout the entire corpus. In the above example, *Barmhertzigkeit*, the *r* is singled out as the astringent agent of manifestation, while the general category of bitterness later subdivides the hardened word into syllabic, then phonetic, units. Likewise, in the word *Erden* 'earth', the *r* signifies the dominant point of astringent centripetality, the nucleus around which the outer phonological shape of the word adheres, at the same time reflecting the presence of the bitter centrifugal aspect. With this in mind Böhme describes the tongue crouching in fear as these qualities do battle within the mouth (*Aurora* xviii, 71).

The voiceless velar *k* represents a state of eternal destruction, a form of palpability far removed from the original state of undivided unity. Bohme sees the physical vehicle of the *k* as severed from its state as *Geist* through the astringent hardness created by the plosive stop:

> Das bedeutet, dass die verderbte Grimmigkeit ewig aus dem Lichte GOttes verstossen ist; aber der innerliche

> Geist, der wieder seinen Willen damit beladen ist, wieder in sein erstes Haus soll gesetzt werden (*Aurora* xviii, 55).

There is hope, however, since the inner *Geist* contained within the *k* will somehow evolve back to its original state, here the *erstes Haus* 'first house'.

The apicoalveolar closure *n* is very important even though it is not as astringent as the uvular *r*:

> Dass bedeutet, dass das Hertze GOttes einen Eckel an der Verderbung hat gehabt, und das verderbte Wesen von sich gestossen; aber in der Mitten beym Hertzen wieder gefasset und gehalten (*Aurora* xviii, 51).

The *verderbte Wesen* 'ruined being', a *Wesen* 'being' which at this point is ruined but not yet *ausgesprochen* 'spoken out', is a unique Böhmian category. *Geist* is projected into the material of the heart; there in a state of partial manifestation, it collides with the second wall of material matter, the apicoalveolar closure:

> Gleichwie die Zunge das Wort zubricht, und hält es halb draussen und halb hinnen; also auch wolte das Hertze GOttes nicht den angezündeten Salitter gar verwerfen, sondern die Bosheit und Sucht des Teufels: und das andere solte nach dieser Zeit wieder erbauet werden (*Aurora* xviii, 52).

The apicoalveolar closure in particular, and the points of articulation in general serve as the final stage in the compaction of human language into words, a process etymologically derived (within the Böhmian methodology) from *Geist*.

The last sound Böhme describes is the voiceless alveopalatal fricative *sh*. In the word *schuf* 'created' this sound "fasset sich über und unter der Zungen und macht die Zähne in beyden Gaumen zusammen, und drückt sich also zusammen [raised apex allowing the breath stream to pass over the dorsum through the dental closure as a fricative]" (*Aurora* xviii, 57). In the word *sprach* 'spoke' the *sh* sound "fasset sich zwischen den Zähnen [origin of the fricative sound near the teeth] und zischet der Geist durch die Zähne raus, und die Zunge beuget sich in der Mitten [tongue in a cupped position] und vorne spitzet sie sich [raised apex], als ob sie hörete was da zischete und sich fürchtete" (*Aurora* xviii, 88).

The descent of *Geist* into the confinements of astringent compaction is mirrored in the *sh*:

> Dass aber die Lippen offen stehen, wenn Er (der heilige Geist) durch die Zähne zischet, bedeutet, dass Er mit seinem Ausgange aus dem Hertzen GOttes in der Schöpfung dieser Welt hat die Himmels=Porten wieder aufgeschlossen, und ist durch die Porten des Zorns GOttes gegangen, und hat den Zorn GOttes feste verriegelt und zugelassen, und dem Teufel sein ewig angezündet Zorn=Haus feste zugeschlossen, daraus er ewig nicht kommen kan (*Aurora* xviii, 100).

The hissing feature (*zischt*) of the alveopalatal fricative suggests the point within the *Geist-Begreifflichkeit* spectrum where *Geist* embraces the aspects of created corporeality: on the outside of the mouth. Here within the expanding realm of created nature, Böhme places the devil.[15] The points of articulation are doorways through which God, by the vehicle of *Geist*, effects manifestation, but through which manifestation cannot reverse itself in an attempt to recapture *Geist*:

> Weiter bedeuts, dass der H. Geist gleichwol eine offene Porten in dem Zorn=Haus dieser Welt habe, da Er sein Werck treibe, der Höllen=Porten unbegreifflich, und da Er Ihm einen heiligen Samen samle zu seinem ewigen Lobe, ohne Willen der festen höllischen Porten, und der-

selben auch gantz unbegreifflich (*Aurora* xviii, 101).

The reversal from manifestation back into undivided spirit occurs, but not in a manner comprehensible to the *festen höllischen Porten* 'firmly closed hellish gates'. Even though the *Höllen= Porten* 'gates of hell' notice all movements of *Geist* through matter, they fail to understand the manner by which the holy seed (*heiliger Samen*) can be extracted. To the mystically attuned audience, Böhme offers the extraction of this metalinguistic device as the most serious aspect of his code. The code is a temple of divinity in the world:

> Gleichwie der Geist seinen Ausgang und gefasten Willen durch die Zähne verrichtet, und sich die Zähne doch nicht bewegen, oder des Geistes Willen begreiffen können; also bauet Ihm der H. Geist ohne Begreiffung des Teufels und des Zorns Gottes, ohn unterlass einen heiligen Samen und Tempel in dem Hause dieser Welt (*Aurora* xviii, 102).

As seen, Böhmian phonetic elements, especially the obstruent sounds, are semantic units posited as a precise space within that range of Böhme's thought which confronts the problem: what is the operative principle behind *Geist* becoming *Begreiffligkeit*? The words Böhme selects to express his theosophy connotatively imply semantic agreement with Silesian morphology during the early decades of the seventeenth century. His system of direct denotations, on the other hand, is individual and innovative: through a system of positions and oppositions he establishes a complex network of interrelationships whereby each obstruent sound plays a role in the creation, maintenance and dissolution of *Begreiffligkeit*. Although the idea of letters and alphabets somehow reflecting the creation of the world puzzles the young Böhme, he attempts to find the connecting channel in prophecy:[16]

> Obgleich der Geist in den Schriften Mosis die tieffesten Geheimnisse im Buchstaben hat verborgen gehalten gleichwol ist alles so gar ordentlich beschrieben, dass an der Ordnung kein Mangel ist (*Aurora* xxi, 1) ... Dis muss ich aber sagen, dass Moses wol recht geschrieben hat; aber der rechte Verstand, woraus die Erde worden sey, ist beydes dem Mosi und auch seinen Nachkömmlingen im Buchstaben verborgen blieben, und hat es der Geist bis auf diese Zeit verborgen gehalten. Es ist auch Adam, weil er noch im Paradeis gewesen, verborgen gewesen: nun aber wird es gantz offenbar ... (*Aurora* xxvi, 117-18).

What is it that has been hidden within the letters (*Buchstaben*) up until this period of time? What is about to be revealed? The code.

In the word *Tag*, the role of the astringent force of centripetality and the bitter force of centrifugality are personified:

> Das Wort Tag fasset sich im Hertzen und fährt hervor zum Munde, und fährt durch die Strasse der herben und bittern Qualität, und wecket die herbe und bittere Qualität nicht auf, sondern gehet starck durch ihren Locum, welcher am hintern Gaumen über der Zungen ist, hervor gantz sanfte und der herben und bittern Qualität unbegreifflich (*Aurora* xix, 84).

The *Wort* 'word' originating in the heart, enters the breath stream silently passing over the street of the astringent and bitter qualities (the back part of the mouth). As there has been no vocal vibration, neither the astringent nor the bitter forces have awakened. The *Geist* behind the physical word *Tag* is not yet encased in astringent compaction. The tongue is instrumental in directing the breath stream toward the articulators, directing the *Geist* towards *Begreiffligkeit*:

> Wenn es aber hervor auf die Zunge kommt, so schleust die Zunge mit den Ober=Gaumen das Maul zu: wenn aber der Geist an die Zähne stösset, und will raus, so schleust die Zunge das Maul auf und will vorm Worte raus, und thut gleich einen Freuden=Sprung zum Maule raus (*Aurora* xix, 85).

The labial opening anticipating the outward explosion of the initial *t* sound is a time of great joy for both the tongue and the *Geist*. The nature of forces in control within the mouth dominates the tongue since it has no individuality as an expressive agent: "Die Zunge aber bedeutet die Seele, die wird von den 7 Geister der Natur geboren, und ist ihr Sohn; wenn nun die 7 Geister wollen, so muss sich die Zunge nach ihrem Gefallen bewegen, und muss ihre Sache fördern" (*Aurora* xviii, 118). The *Geist*, meanwhile, seeks escape from its potential manipulators, the forces of astringency; and the tiny labial opening is the door through which it hopes to escape corporeality. Vocalic onset, coupled with a wider labial opening, thwarts this escape:

> Wenn aber das Wort durchbricht, so macht sich das Maul inwendig weit auf, und das Wort fasset sich mit seinem Schallen hinter der herben und bittern Qualität noch einmal, und wecket dieselbe als einen faulen Schläfer in der Finsternis auf, und fährt jähling zum Munde aus (*Aurora* xix, 86).

The awakening of the centripetal and centrifugal forces as a result of their *Schallen* 'resonance' (from the vowel *a*), and their rushing toward the front of the mouth signal the onset of corporeality for the *Geist*:

> Alsdann zarret die herbe Qualität hernach als ein schläffriger Mensch der vom Schlaffe aufgeweckt wird: aber der bittere Geist, welcher vom Feuer=Blitz ausgehet,

The Awakening of Böhme's Linguistic Evolution 17

> bleibet liegen und höret nichts, beweget sich auch nicht.
> Dieses sind nun gar grosse Dinge, und nicht so schlechte
> wie der Bauer wol vermeinet (*Aurora* xix, 87).

Astringent domination within the word *Tag* overshadows the sleeping bitter quality, and as an intense field of darkened centripetality is unable to perceive the divine light shining within *Geist*:

> Dass sich nun erstlich der Geist im Hertzen fasset, und
> bricht durch alle Wachen bis auf die Zunge unvermerckt,
> das bedeutet, dass das Licht aus dem Hertzen GOttes ist
> hervorgebrochen durch die äusserste, verderbte, grimmige, todte, bittere und herbe Geburt in der Natur
> dieser Welt, dem Tode und Teufel, samt dem Zorne
> GOttes unbegreifflich, wie dann geschrieben stehet im
> Evangelio St. Johannis c. 1:5. Das Licht schien in der
> Finsterniss und die Finsterniss habens nicht begriffen
> (*Aurora* xix, 88).

The light shining in the darkness, the spark of *Geist* moving away from its source into manifestation, passes unnoticed by and through externality, corruption, death, bitterness, and astringency into form. Böhme, in witnessing this spectacle, does not include himself among *dem Tode und Teufel samt dem Zorne GOttes* 'the death and the devil including the fury of God' and is thereby able to relate additional information concerning the prime manipulator, the tongue. It "bedeut das Leben der Natur, in welchem die animalische[17] oder heilige Geburt stehet; denn sie ist ein Vorbild der Seelen" (*Aurora* xix, 89). It rejoices in the realization of its role as a divine channel (*Aurora* xix, 90).

The dental opening of the vocalic *a* (T+a+g) allows the spirit— made joyful by the dorsum—to pass through the lips into nature. Böhme envisions divine life and divine will influencing the vocalic emanation as it slowly glides from the opened mouth into manifestation:

> Dass sich aber die vordern Gaumen inwendig erweitern, und dem Geiste Raum geben nach seinem Gefallen, bedeutet, dass sich die gantze siderische Geburt gantz freundlich in des Lichtes Willen gegeben hat, und den Grimm in ihr nicht aufgewecket (*Aurora* xix, 91).

The vocalic outburst of joy is short-lived since with the awakening of the astringent force, and its chase after the vocalic noisemaker, the form and shape of the word *Tag* is compressed by the final centripetality of the velar *g*:

> Dass sich aber der Geist, wenn er zum Munde ausfähret, erst noch einmal hinter der herben Qualität auf der Zungen im hintern Gaumen fasset, und wecket die herbe Qualität als einen Schläffer auf, und fähret schnell zum Munde aus, bedeutet dass der herbe Geist zwar alles in der gantzen Natur muss halten and bilden, aber allererst wenn es der Geist des Lichts hat formiret; dann weckt er erst den herben Geist auf, und gibts ihme in die Hände, dass ers hält (*Aurora* xix, 92).

Words—bundles of astringency—would not exist within external manifestation[18] unless the astringent principle were operative: "Und das muss seyn von wegen der äussersten Begreiffligkeit, die muss im herben Grimme gehalten werden; sonst bestünde nichts im Corpus" (*Aurora* xix, 93).

In the word *Barmhertzigkeit* 'benevolence', astringency enables the syllable *Barm-* not only to resound, but to resound within manifestation:

> Siehe das Wort Barm ist nur auf deiner Lippen; und wenn du sprichst Barm, so machst du das Maul zu, und karrest hintennach; und das ist die herbe Qualität, die umschleust das Wort, das ist, sie figuriret zusammen das Wort, das es harte wird oder schallet, und die bittere

The Awakening of Böhme's Linguistic Evolution

Qualität zerscheidet es (*Aurora* viii, 74).

The astringent nucleus of this syllable, the uvular astringent *r*, is of such a high centripetal compaction, that when combined with the inner bitter quality, nothing but hardness, darkness, cold, and bitterness result: their frictional interaction is aimless and leads nowhere. Böhme says:

> Nun ist aber das Wort Barm ein todt, unverständig Wort, das niemand verstehet: das bedeutet, dass die zwey Qualitäten Herbe und Bitter, ein hart, dunckel, kalt und bitter Wesen sind, die kein Licht in sich haben; darum kan man ihre Kraft ausserhalb des Lichtes nicht verstehen (*Aurora* viii, 75).

Unable to identify the syllable *Barm-* within the corpus of his Silesian, Böhme feels safe in positing its nonexistent semanticity within the language as due to an overabundance of astringency in the syllable. It is so compact that the light of *Geist* cannot shine through it. Polysyllabic words, words which to Böhme's thinking are linguistic stories, theosophic *Erzählungen*, offer a wider field within which the forces of creation interact before becoming *Begreiffligkeit*. The onset of the second syllable *-hertz-* brings light into the entire word thus far (Barm+hertz-) at the same time increasing the astringent compaction: the astringency of the *r* + the dental stop *t* (a formidable obstacle to *Geist*) + the hissing of the sibilant *s* (-hertz > herts > hert+s) as an extension of the fricative *sh* (schuf > s+chuf). The word is finalized within matter with the ich-Laut of the last syllable *-ig*:

> Wenn du aber sprichst Hertz, so fähret der Geist in dem Wort Hertz geschwind wie ein Blitz heraus, und gibt des Worts Unterschied und Verstand. Wenn du aber sprichst IG, so fängest du den Geist mitten in den andern zwey Qualitäten, dass er muss drinn bleiben und das Wort

formiren (*Aurora* viii, 77).

Böhme's analysis of the first line of Genesis, *Am Anfang schuf GOtt Himmel und Erden,* reveals concern for the localization within each syllable wherein astringent manifestation ensues. It is of little importance what these words actually mean within their social context; rather their deeper, more crucial significance purposefully hides within the code:

> Davon schreibet nun Moses: Am Anfang schuf GOtt Himmel und Erden Gen. 1:1. Diese Worte muss man eigentlich betrachten, was sie sind; denn das Wort Am fasset sich im Hertzen und fähret bis auf die Lippen, da wird es gefangen, und gehet schallende wieder zurücke bis an seinen ausgegangenen Ort (*Aurora* xviii, 48).

Am 'in the' exhibits the typical Böhmian features: generation of the word through the heart, projection of the *Geist* into the breath stream, labial blockage from the *m*. Here, however, the bilabial closure ensures that the *Geist* does not enter nature, but rather returns mysteriously to the heart. It returns, Böhme says, since it finds the place of this world evil:

> Das bedeutet nun, dass der Schall von dem Hertzen GOttes ist ausgangen, und hat den gantzen Locum dieser Welt umfasset; als er aber böse befunden worden, so ist der Schall wieder in seinen Locum getreten (*Aurora* xviii, 49).

At this point, Böhme does not explain how the bilabial *m* can bring about such a reversal of the *Schall* 'resonance', although as will be seen toward the end of the sequence, the analysis of the word *Himmel* 'heaven' offers greater possibility.

Apicodental closure is different from bilabial closure. Böhme uses the syllable *An-* (An+fang) to make this point clear:

The Awakening of Böhme's Linguistic Evolution

> Das Wort An das stöst aus dem Hertzen zum Munde aus, und hat einen langen Nachdruck: wenn sichs aber ausspricht so schleust sichs mitten in seinem Sede mit dem obern Gaumen zu, und ist halb draussen und halb drinnen (*Aurora* xviii, 50).

Since Böhme envisions the bilabial *m* holding the outward expanding *Geist* more firmly within the mouth, the description of the *n* as held in check by the *obern Gaumen* 'upper gums' rather than the lips takes on another dimension. The *n* is a fence; on one side, God expresses his wrath with creation, and on the other, he holds *Geist* close to himself:

> Gleichwie die Zunge das Wort zubricht, und hält es halb draussen and halb hinnen; also wolte das Hertze GOttes nicht den angezündeten Salitter gar verwerfen, sondern die Bosheit und Sucht des Teufels: und das ander solte nach dieser Zeit wieder erbauet werden (*Aurora* xviii, 52).

On the *halb draussen* 'half externalized' side of the apicodental closure, Böhme places not only the continuation of the word, the second syllable -*fang*, but also the entire destroyed *Salitter*.[19] The relaxation of the dorsal pressure necessary to produce the dorsovelar nasal stop *ng* is important as another barrier in the same network of walls encountered in the *n* in the first syllable:

> Das Wort fang fähret schnell vom Hertzen zum Munde raus, und wird auch am hintern Orte der Zungen mit dem Gaumen gehalten, und wenn es los gelassen wird, so thuts noch einen schnellen Druck vom Hertzen zum Munde aus (*Aurora* xviii, 53).

The expulsion of the *schnellen Druck* 'fast pressure' into and out of the mouth represents the *Geist* thrusting the devil's field of influence away from itself, away from its own purity:

> Denn der starcke und schnelle Geist stösset den Odem starck von sich, und behält den rechten Ton des Worts oder den Ausspruch am hintern Gaumen bey sich, das ist, den rechten Geist des Wortes (*Aurora* xviii, 54).

The dorsovelar stop cannot be penetrated by the destroyed *Salitter* (*Aurora* xviii, 55).

The cupped dorsal position of the alveopalatal fricative *sh* is the first obstruent modifier of *Geist* in the next word *schuf* 'created'. Dental closure at the onset and relaxed labial pressure on the upper teeth demarcate its first physical boundaries:

> Das Wort Schuf fasset sich über und unter der Zungen [cupped dorsal position] und macht die Zähne in beyden Gaumen zusammen [dental closure] und druckt sich also zusammen: und wenn es zusammen gefasset und ausgesprochen ist, so macht es das Maul schnelle wie ein Blitz wieder auf (*Aurora* xviii, 57).

The teeth hold the word captive within the mouth in the same way that the astringent force of compaction holds the stones, rocks and dirt of the earth together. Both the *Geist* behind the word and the *Geist* underlying astringency issue forth through their captors (articulators) into an atmosphere which Böhme calls "die Tieffe über der Erden" (*Aurora* xviii, 59).[20] Man speaks words into the air, above the astringent floor upon which he stands. That the mouth remains open after the projection of the word *schuf* into the airy depths signals that the following word *GOtt* 'God' demands labial opening for the *g* sound. Böhme notices regressive assimilation within the movements of the articulators. He describes *GOtt* as:

> Das Wort GOtt fasset sich mitten oben auf der Zungen, und stösset aus dem Hertzen dahin, und lässet das Maul offen, und bleibet auf seinem königlichen Sessel sitzen,

und schallet aus sich und in sich: wenn es aber ausgesprochen ist, so thut es noch einen Druck zwischen den obern Zähnen und Zungen heraus (*Aurora* xviii, 60).

Mitten oben auf der Zungen 'medially upon the top of the tongue' (palatal closure) holds the *Geist* captive between the heart and the articulator. The voice associated with the *g* resonates back and forth within this chamber (*schallet auss sich und in sich* 'resounds out of and within itself'). The relaxation of the velar stop *g* allows the breath stream to pass unhindered into its vocalic aspect (*o*) only to be stopped by the articulators of the dental stop *t* (the upper teeth and the tongue). Again, the astringency inherent within the final *t* leads Böhme to conclude that "der letzte Druck bedeutet die Schärfe seines Geistes, damit Er augenblicklich alles ausrichtet in seinem gantzen Corpus" (*Aurora* xviii, 61).

The bisyllabic nature of the next word *Himmel* 'heaven' suggests to Böhme the same divisional relationship between realms of linguistic manifestation as mentioned above. The closure in the middle of the word creates two distinct realms: the first is introduced with a vocalic *h* extension of *Geist* into matter; the second is concluded with the *Geist* sliding around the lateral *l*:

Das Wort Himmel fasset sich im Hertzen, und stösset bis auf die Lippen, da wird es verschlossen: und die Sylbe Mel macht die Lippen wieder auf, und wird mitten auf der Zungen gehalten, und fähret der Geist auf beyden Seiten der Zungen aus dem Maule (*Aurora* xviii, 62).

The adhering of the tongue to the alveolar ridge in the pronunciation of the *l*, in allowing the *Geist* to pass equally unhindered around it into manifestation, is a sign to Böhme that God shall give man new rulers. These *König und Grossfürsten* 'king and granddukes' (*Aurora* xviii, 65) will once again open the innermost divine secrets allowing the original *Geist* to exit around the Father and Son (the prototypes of the tongue) into this world (*Aurora* xvii, 64, 65).

The conjunction *und* 'and' puzzles Böhme. In spite of its observable vocalic onset + nasal stop + dental stop, he feels that the word, like *Barm-*, is "stumm und hat keinen Verstand, und wird nur zum Unterscheid gebrauchet" (*Aurora* xviii, 68). Even though it is held in the upper gums by means of the tongue (*Aurora* xviii, 67), Böhme is at a loss to describe its theosophic content, other than to allude to its possible bitterness (the separating device). It is connected, though, directly to the heart: "Der letzte Druck aus dem Hertzen bedeutet, dass sie wol mit der innersten Geburt in ihrer Sönlichkeit inqualieren werde, aber in ihrer Vernunft nicht ergreiffen" (*Aurora* xviii, 68).[21]

The final word *Erden* 'earth' exhibits the complete range of Böhme's linguistic awareness: the uvular *r*, the hindering of the breath stream by the second syllable *-den* (dn) and its subsequent detour through the nasal passages out into manifestation (*Aurora* xviii, 69, 70). This is all *ein gross Geheimniss* 'a great secret' (*Aurora* xviii, 71). The flowing of the breath stream into the nasal cavity forces the *Geist* to pass into the brain, coming before the seat of the discriminating senses:[22]

> Das Wort Den fasset sich wieder auf der Zungen, und der Geist zeucht die Kraft aus dem Wort, und fähret einen andern Weg damit zur Nasen raus, auch so fähret er damit hinauf ins Hirn vor den königlichen Stuhl (*Aurora* xviii, 72).

The linguistic information of the *Aurora* exhibits three layers of meaning: the first, and most easily accessible, is the Silesian German layer;[23] the second is the phonological layer of alphabetic interaction;[24] and the third is the theosophic level of the code.[25] Unravelling each layer from the other within the above passage from Genesis uncovers the direction in which Böhme's linguistic thinking is progressing. The first layer is the literal meaning

The Awakening of Böhme's Linguistic Evolution 25

associated with each word: *Am* 'in the' *Anfang* 'beginning' *schuf* 'created' *GOtt* 'God' *Himmel* 'heaven' *und* 'and' *Erde* 'earth'. The descriptive phonological layer reveals the following chain of information, in no way divorced from the first layer, rather more indicative of the interpretational possibilities to be encountered in the third: *a* (a sound which moves from the heart to the *m*) + *m* (labial closure) + *a* (a sound which moves from the heart to the *n* sound, with posited length) + *n* (a closure wherein the sound is half out and half in) + *fa* (an indistinct designation of a sound which originates in the heart and moves to the mouth) + *ng* (a sound caught by the gums as a stop) + *sch* (described as a fricative) + *uff* (no mention of its layer 2 designation) + *g* (voice is posited) + *o* (no mention) + *t* (a closure between the lower and upper teeth) + *h* (the emanation of the exhaled *Geist*) + *i* (no mention) + *m* (the labial closure) + *e* (no mention) + *l* (described as a lateral) + *u* (no mention) + *nd* (identified as a stop) + *e* (no mention) + *rdn* (marked with astringency, hence vibration against the uvula). Vowels vanish under investigation. The third layer, the theosophic code layer, reduces even more drastically. Only the most crucial consonantal clusters can signify: *m* (labial barrier between realms) + *n* (another barrier) + *ng* (barrier) + *sch* (hissing forth into manifestation) + *t* (astringency and multiplicity within manifestation) + *h* (*Geist* becoming matter within manifestation) + *m* (the barrier between realms) + *l* (the *Geist* exiting around the Father and Son into manifestation) + *r* (astringency) + *dn* (nasal blockage, a barrier rerouting the message to the discriminative centers in the brain, a movement back to God). Thus, the schemata are revelations only for those careful readers in 1612 patient enough to follow the imprecisions of an early linguistic system to its mature conclusion: *Am Anfang schuff GOtt Himmel und Erde* $>$ $A+m$ $A+n+(fa)+ng$ $sch+(uff)$ $G+(o)+tt$ $H+(i)+mm+(e)+l$ $(u)+nd$ $(e)+rd+(e)+n$ $>$ $M + N + NG + SCH + T + H + M + L + R + DN$.

Individual sounds, their relations with larger systems of meaning generated under the auspices of astringency and bitterness, the role of *Geist* in its descent into manifestation, and the germinal theosophical extensions seen within these early comments, form the entirety of the linguistic basis of the Aurorean code. Böhme, however, plans to expand this workable linguistic thesis into a more encompassing linguistic exegesis. The project, an explication of the *Vater Unser* 'Our Father' does not materialize until seven years later, in 1620. Böhme mentions the project in the *Aurora*:

> Und darum beten wir auch im Vater=Unser: Gib uns unser täglich Brod, Matth. 6:11. Dass also derselbe Ton oder Wort Gib, welches wir aus unserem Centro des Lichts durch den animalischen Geist aus dem Munde von uns stossen in die Göttliche Kraft, soll in der Göttlichen Kraft, als eine Mitformung oder Mitgebärung helfen unser täglich Brod bilden, welches uns hernach der Vater zur Speise giebet. Und wenn denn also unser Ton in GOttes Ton incorporiret wird, und wird also die Frucht gebildet, so muss es uns ja gesund sein, und wir in GOttes Liebe seyn; und haben die Speise als für Natur=Recht zu gebrauchen, dieweil unser Geist in GOttes Liebe hat dieselbe helfen bilden und formen. Hierinnen steckt die innerste und gröste Tieffe GOttes: O Mensch, bedencke dich! An seinem Orte will ichs ausfürlich erklären (*Aurora* xiii, 110-12).[26]

The prayer, especially the word *Brod* 'bread', when articulated correctly becomes a source of nourishment from the Father. It is man's *Natur=Recht* 'right based on his material affinity to nature' to provide for himself in this secret manner. In this way man exercises the potential of his *Geist* (which is eternally unified with God's *Geist*) toward physically sustaining a *Begreifflichkeit* (here, his body). Is this a form of spiritual alchemy[27] or merely a wish couched in metaphoric language? The promise to explain this process in writing is not executed until 1620 in the *Hohe und tiefe Gründung von dem Dreyfachen Leben des Menschen, Nachdem Geheimniss der Dreyen Principien Göttlicher Offenbarung*. As will be seen, although the promise is fulfilled, Böhme's linguistic thinking moves in the direction of personal emancipation within the third layer of language.

Prayer, fasting and the correct preparations required for a direct entry into the Kingdom of God seem to concern Böhme in the sixteenth chapter of *Hohe und tiefe Gründung von dem Dreyfachen Leben des Menschen*. He blesses the chapter with a promising subtitle "Vom Beten und Fasten, auch rechter Zubereitung zum Reiche GOttes: Was das Beten sey oder verbringe; was seine Kraft und unendlicher Nutz sey," although as with all of his writings, he lets his ideas wander freely under these first-layer designations. The analysis of the *Vater Unser*, mentioned in the subtitle, and promised in the *Aurora*, employs the Aurorean code, a code implemented with alchemical and theosophical associations borrowed from the first layer.

Böhme disconnects the prayer into seven requests, breaking each request into syllables, and in a few cases the syllables reduce further to constituent phonological components. Böhme predicts that the audience will have difficulty comprehending:

> Weil wir aber schwer möchten zu verstehen sehen, so wollen wir nur einen summarischen Inhalt und Verstand setzen, und fürter das Werck der höchsten Zungen, dem Geiste GOttes in ieder Seelen empfehlen (*Dreyfach* xvi, 29).

After the general exhortation "Unser Vater im Himmel" (*Dreyfach* xvi, 30), Böhme utters the first request: "Dein Name werde geheiliget" (Dein Na+me wer+de ge+hei+li+get) (*Dreyfach* xvi, 31). The second and third requests complete the Dein-Trinity: "Dein Reich komme" (Dein Reich kom+me), "Dein Willen geschehe wie im Himmel also auch auf Erden" (Dein Wil+len ge+sche+he wie im Him+mel al+so auch auf Er+den) (*Dreyfach* xvi, 32, 33). The fourth request "Gib uns unser täglich Brot heute" (Gib uns un+ser täglich Brot heu+te) (*Dreyfach* xvi, 34) includes a parenthetical remark on the linguistic nature of the Hebrew words *Tetragrammaton* and *Adonai*. These remarks are abbreviated comments, strangely put aside for a few years. Had Böhme not wanted to finish the explication of the *Vater Unser*, in itself a major unified effort, these remarks could have developed into another full-scale treatise. The fifth and sixth requests begin with the nebulous conjunction *und*: "Und verlass uns unser Schuld als wir verlassen unsern Schuldigern" (Und ver+lass uns un+ser Schuld als wir ver+lass+en unsern Schul+di+gern), "Und führe uns nicht in Versuchung" (Und füh+re uns nicht in Ver+such+ung) (*Dreyfach* xvi, 35, 36). The final request "Sondern erlöse uns vom Übel" (Son+dern er+lö+se uns vom Ü+b+e+l) (*Dreyfach* xvi, 37, 40-43) concludes the prayer. The final "Amen" (A+men) (*Dreyfach* xvi, 44, 45) followed by the unsyllabified "Dein ist das Reich und die Kraft und die Herrligkeit in Ewigkeit" (*Dreyfach* xvi, 52) are the ninth and tenth exhortations to the Divine.

By means of the outward vehicle of the first layer of language, Böhme calls to his *Vater im Himmel* 'father in heaven' invoking his presence within manifestation. The component phonological units reveal divinity in the process of becoming manifestation, divinity sliding down into the realms of *Begreifflichkeit*. The first syllable *un-* (un+ser) is "der ewige Wille GOttes zur Natur" (*Dreyfach* xvi, 30), whereas the second syllable *-ser* "hält inne das erste Principium" (*Dreyfach* xvi, 30). Passing through the heart into the breath stream, then into the word by means of the vocalic *u*, *Geist* is modified by the *n*, the *s* and the *r*. All offer a high degree of dark astringency to the *Geist*. Contrasted with the darkness of the first word, *Vater* (the second) contains images of light: "dann Va ist die Mutter ausm Lichte, welche Wesenheit gibt: und Ter ist die Mutter des Feuers=Tinctur, welches das grosse und starcke Leben giebet" (*Dreyfach* xvi, 30). The bisyllabic construction Va+ter is a direct result of the Father's assuming the aspects of both the male and female principles within created nature. The eternal propensity towards becoming, *Va+ter* becoming *Wesen*, is hindered by the bilabial stop *m* in the next word *im*: "die Sylbe gehet aus dem Hertzen, schallet durch die Lippen, und die Lippen behalten das Hertze im innern aufgeweckt" (*Dreyfach* xvi, 30). The awakened heart is waiting to burst forth within *Himmel. Im* reflects the semantic energy of the following word: the encased and protected will towards manifestation through the bisyallbic *Himmel*. Böhme says "und mit dem Worte Him (ist die Seele) zu einer Creatur geschaffen, als zum Mel: Dann Him ist Mels Wohnung" (*Dreyfach* xvi, 30). As seen in the *Aurora*, the confinement of *Geist* behind the labial barrier represents the first stage of manifestation. The *Geist* moves away from the heart, existing in a suspended state of partial manifestation. Full compaction ensues only when this *Geist* exits around both sides of the dorsum (mel). As *Him-* is the residence of *-mel*, so also *Geist* is the home, the origin of *Begreifflig-keit*. Through the correct deliverance of this invocation, divinity descends into matter, and Böhme presents a list of *Bitten* 'requests' to this mystical God.

Called *die erste Bitte* 'the first request', Böhme uses the phrase "Dein Name werde geheiliget" (*Dreyfach* xvi, 31) to further delineate the movements of the *Seele* 'soul' from the uncompressed realms of *Geist* towards the grosser realms of manifestation: *Seele* acquires the attributes of compaction, hardness and palpability. In the syllable *dein* 'your', Böhme sees the soul becoming part of a larger vibratory family: that of *GOttes Stimme* 'God's voice' (*Dreyfach* xvi, 31). Since this is a new realm for the soul, the bisyllabic *Na+me* offers it a new milieu: astral (between God and matter, not yet manifested) corporeality. Not yet substance, the soul, having absorbed into itself features of a grosser vibration, becomes what Böhme calls *die gantze Creatur* 'the complete created being' (*Dreyfach* xvi, 31). This aggregate of features, the *Creatur*, willfully lowers itself into a denser compaction of itself, a submission Böhme calls *Wille* 'will'. It is at this point in the genesis of creation that Lucifer refuses to resign himself to the divine process. Instead, he fights against the process of becoming nature (*Naturwerdung*):

> Und wenn wir sagen Wer, so fähret die gantze Creatur in
> Willen: dann Wer hat das gantze Centrum; Und mit der
> Sylbe De leget sich in Gehorsam in der Sanftmuth, und
> will das Wer im Feuer nicht entzünden, wie Lucifer
> gethan hat (*Dreyfach* xvi, 31).

In spite of the high level of astringency in the syllable *wer-*, Böhme sees the *Seele* attracting to itself heavenly corporeality (*himmlische Wesenheit*) but quietly "als ein stilles Kind ohne Zorn" (*Dreyfach* xvi, 31). The final word of the request *geheiliget* 'made holy' (ge+hei+li+get) reveals a close association with the first layer of Silesian German. The first syllable *ge-* expresses the verbal action within the root of the first-layer verb *gehen* 'to go' with the modification that subjects and objects, not seen in the colloquial uses, appear posited within Böhme's code. The syllable is the soul going into manifestation: "Und wenn wir sagen Ge, so gehet die Seele in der himmlischen Wesenheit" (*Dreyfach* xvi, 31).[28] The verbal expansion of the soul, once modified by the velar stop *g*, passes unhindered through the next four vocalic sounds *e, h, e,* and *i*,[29] called here trinity. Again, the vowels do nothing. The syllable *-li-*, armed with the lateral obstruent *l*, is the point of interchange. The soul drops further into manifestation, leaving behind its more subtle aspects in the process of becoming. At the same time, though, the Father/Son aspect of the lateral accepts the Holy Spirit into the feature specification: "Mit der Sylbe Li hat der Seelen Wille den H. Geist gefasset" (*Dreyfach* xvi, 31). The final syllable *-get*, with the two obstruents *g* and *t*, concludes the word and marks the point where the "Seelen Willen mit dem H. Geiste ausgehet" (*Dreyfach* xvi, 31).

The soul, localized within the features of the will, exercises this potential by opting for the divine, merging itself within divine will in the word *Dein* (*Dreyfach* xvi, 32). The next word *Reich* 'kingdom' (*Dein Reich komme*) shows the soul desiring liberation from its astral existence, an existence severed from the pure unity of God. This desiring (*begehren*) manifests itself in the astringency of

The Awakening of Böhme's Linguistic Evolution 31

the *r*: by drawing into itself it expands. In the last word *komme* 'may come', the soul races outward through the first syllable *kom-* in an attempt to control *Kraft* 'power'. Jumping over the bilabial wall, the soul extends itself into the world of manifestation as an object. The divine subject verbally extends itself into manifestation, becoming objective corporeality:

> Mit der Sylbe Me machet sie ihren Himmel auf, und gehet mit der gefasseten Kraft aus im Reiche, als ein Gewächse; Dann das Me machet die Lippen auf, und lässet das Gewächse des Willens ausgehen, und langsam sanfte wachsen (*Dreyfach* xvi, 32).[30]

In the next request, "Dein Willen geschehe wie im Himmel also auch auf Erden," Böhme moves quickly to the second word, having already worked *Dein* into a plausible linguistic statement. He says that the syllable *dein* "wirft sich in GOttes Willen ein" (*Dreyfach* xvi, 33). The next word *Willen* 'will' reaffirms the soul's desire to intermingle and wander with the Holy Spirit. The first syllable *wil-* signifies the desire towards incorporation within *Geist, -len* strengthens this notion:

> Mit dieser Silben nimt sie den Geist mit dem Willen ins Centrum ein, als ins Hertze, und will dass ihr Wille im H. Geist soll im Hertzen wallen (*Dreyfach* xvi, 33).

The overabundance of lateral sounds mixed with the word play *willen/wallen* (< w+l+n) explains Böhme's multilevel linguistic thinking: the lateral *l* in both words affords the *Geist* and the soul (now with the feature of *Wille*) a relatively unobstructed and astringent-free area within which they can intermingle (*wallen*) on both sides of the dorsum. *Geschehe* (Ge+sche+he), like *geheiliget*, is related to the German verb *gehen*: "Ge, mit dieser Sylbe gehet sie in Willen" (*Dreyfach* xvi, 33). The next syllable *-sche-* (alveopalatal fricative + vowel) expresses the function of the coming into existence of manifestation, although in this instance Böhme chooses the verb *wircken* 'to effect, to bring about within action' to pattern with this syllable: "Sche, mit dieser Sylbe wircket sie GOttes Wercke; Dann da thut sie, was des Vaters Rath ist, was das Hertze GOttes will' (*Dreyfach* xvi, 33). God effectuates through the *-sche-* objectively leading himself into manifestation, a process which the syllable *-he* patiently accepts. Since *-he* is purely vocalic and nonobstruent, it cannot do anything but accept that which is flowing into it. The soul, in obedience to the dictates of God, "bücket sich als ein Kind" (*Dreyfach* xvi, 33) in exactly the same manner as the dorsum medially bows to the hissing sound of the Aurorean alveopalatal fricative (*Aurora* xviii, 88). The next word, *wie* 'as', being completely voiced, elevates linguistic observation into theosophic explication: "wie, da gehet sie abermal in die Stimme der hohen Majestät" (*Dreyfach* xvi, 33). The next word *im* 'in the' is the heart of God (*Dreyfach* xvi, 33) through which the soul passes into creation. The opening of the bilabial closure (*im*), anticipating the vocalic onset of the following word *Himmel*, stresses again the idea of creation: "Him ist abermal die Schöpfung der Creaturen: Mel ist die Seele" (*Dreyfach* xvi, 33). The lateral *l* in the next word *also* 'as' gives the soul power with which to grab the divine will (towards manifestation) forcing it through the hissing (hence vibratory) aspect of the syllable *-so* into corporeal manifestation. This state of affairs, termed the *äussere Principium* 'external created realm or principle' is so powerful that in the following word *auch* 'also' the soul yields to it "alles was sie in sich hat, heraus ins äussere, ausser sich in diese Welt" (*Dreyfach* xvi, 33): the final *o* (als+o) is the unobstructed escape passage, leading into the *auch*. Here, the earlier Aurorean phonology supports this observation. The conclusion of the word *auch* with the *x* (ach-Laut) in speech, but with the vocalic *h* in writing (that is, viewing *auch* as completely nonobstruent) allows the soul to slip through its casing into the next word *auf*, where the vowel + obstruent fricative checks the dissipation of the soul:

The Awakening of Böhme's Linguistic Evolution 33

> Auf, mit dieser Sylbe fasset sie das wieder, und will dass ihr Wesen nicht soll zerstreut werden: Dann sie lässet nur den Willen vom Wesen durch die zugethane Lippen an die Zähne ausgehen, und will, dass die Form des Willens als ein figürlich Wesen soll ewig bleiben (*Dreyfach* xvi, 33).

Böhme directs the entire cosmic process toward the earth, toward molecular configuration and substance within the last word *Erden* 'earth'. Within the structure of the first syllable *Er-*, the strong astringency which creates stones, rocks and earth is the *r*. This sound allows the soul to imprint its special miraculous mark onto the barrier or matrix of the world of manifestation. The final syllable *-den* is the gate which finalizes the soul's migration into matter, a gate which also prohibits the devil from trying to return through it back into spirit. The components of *-den*, as seen (*Aurora* xviii, 70), reroute the path of the *Geist* through the nose. Fortunately, the devil has not thought of reentering through the nostrils.

The fourth request "Gib uns unser täglich Brot heute" (*Dreyfach* xvi, 34) brings the reader back to the Aurorean promise. The emanation of divine energy out of the mouth will help man provide physical sustinence for himself (*Aurora* xiii, 111). The features associated with food, the *Brot* 'bread', extend forward in the request from the penultimate word to the first word: *gib* becomes food for the soul. Here the third layer of language operates:

> Gib, da stecket der Wille im Hertzen, und dringet heraus, und das Maul fänget ihn: Das ist, die Seele will gespeyset seyn; was das Wort aus sich gibt, das fasset die Seele, denn es ist ihr, sie wils haben (*Dreyfach* xvi, 34).

"Was das Wort aus sich gibt," manifestation, linguistic phonological form, is the goal of the desiring soul (will). It desires a more compact form of *Wesenheit* 'being within a vessel', a denser

Begreiffligkeit. The syllable *uns* 'us' offers the soul (will) the opportunity to "zeucht das mit aller Begierde zu sich ... sie will es zugleich haben, und nicht alleine im Geitze, wie der Teufel thut" (*Dreyfach* xvi, 34). *Unser* 'our' (un+ser) clarifies the union of two important principles: the unseen, uncreated and unmanifested *Samen* 'seed' on the one side of the nasal *n*, and the seen, created and manifested generation of nature on the other. That this is important to the soul (will) coming into manifestation is revealed in the following:

> Dann das [the un+ser] ist der Seelen Band, dass sie ewig lebe und bestehe; Das begehret der Wille der Seelen, sonst zerbräche sie, dann ein Geist begehret nichts mehr als sein Band zu erhalten, und das mit Kraft zu erfüllen, dass es quelle (*Dreyfach* xvi, 34).

The soul (will) is comforted along its path by the sign of the trinity, which Böhme sees represented in the syllable *täg-*: the cross shape of the *T* along with the three (trinity) letters comfort the soul. The second syllable *-lich* offers the soul (will) nourishment by means of a light radiating from the syllable: the addition of a final *T* to the syllable strengthens its position within the first layer as *Lich+t* 'light' to the exclusion of interpretational possibilities allowable within the second and third layers of lateral + vowel + obstruent fricative. *Brot*, representing physical sustinence on the first layer, is the common interpretation of the labial stop + uvular *r* + vowel + dental stop. Böhme is quick to remind the reader that he is referring to heavenly bread, not to common table bread, since the final letter is the crucifix-shaped T, and as such carries meaning within the third layer: "Wiewol es der letzte Buchstabe in der Sylbe Brot ausspricht, das es paradeisisch Brot sey, dann das Creutz führet in seinem Character + in der Natursprache den schweren Namen GOttes" (*Dreyfach* xvi, 34). *Heute* 'today', in concluding the phrase, concludes the migration of the soul (will): here it enters into *Wesenheit*, but an eternally redemptive container, a manifestation wherein the path back to original divinity is possible. *Heu-* is the invisible aspect of *Wesenheit, -te,* the corporeal. Both types of sustinence, types of bread are necessary: "Dann die Seele begehret zweyerley Brot, eines dem Bauche, und das ander ihrem H. himmlischen Leibe" (*Dreyfach* xvi, 34).

The fifth request, "Und verlass uns unser Schuld als wir verlassen unsern Schuldigern" (*Dreyfach* xvi, 35), shows the soul (will) contained within the first word *und* passing through the wrath and anger of the astringent syllable *ver-* "als ein aufwachendes Wesen, gleich einer Blumen" (*Dreyfach* xvi, 35). In penetrating the *ver-* the soul becomes dark and impure; it must be cleansed if it is to retain its identity as *Geist*. The cleansing bath occurs in the following syllable *-lasse*: "In der Sylbe Lasse ist das Bad, darinnen das Ver muss gewaschen werden, oder bestehet nicht in GOttes Reich" (*Dreyfach* xvi, 35). The separated elements (elements broken apart as in the alchemical dissolution) are coagulated anew in the following word *uns*. The dross is further refined from the soul (will) in the bisyllabic *un+ser*, with the expulsion of *Schuld* 'guilt' from within: "Schuld, das ist das rechte Register das der Zorn in die Seelen hat eingeführet, das begehret der Wille gar weg zu werfen" (*Dreyfach* xvi, 35). The hissing sibilant in *Schuld* magnifies the desire towards matter into *Wesen*, a *Wesen*, however negative, which stands in object relation to God (*Dreyfach* xvi, 35). In the next word *als* 'as', the soul (will) gathers everything with the feature +soul in an attempt to reconstruct its original essential unity. It has erred, for in collecting features, it unwittingly attracted into the features those negative qualities of *Angst* 'fear', *Qual* 'torture', and *Unruh* 'disquiet' as seen in the word *wir* 'we'. The centripetal aspect of astringency comes to the soul's assistance in the following syllable *ver-* where it acts as a collection and disposal agency for these negative features: *ver-* is the framework wherein the soul (will) "will aller Seelen Grimm auf einen Hauffen unter sich in Abgrund drucken" (*Dreyfach* xvi, 35). The final syllable *-lassen* (lass+en) reflects the hissing of the cleansing process, the bath appears again: "Dann die Sylbe Sen behält die Form der Wunder, aber sie müssen im Lassen gewachsen [gewaschen] seyn, dann Lassen ist das Bad" (*Dreyfach* xvi, 35). Again, the following syllable *un-* (un+sern) carries the soul (will) back through divine love, changing it into a good child. The second syllable *-sern* is the vessel in which the soul reposes after passing through the purifying bath of *-lassen*. Böhme understands this mystery as "es stellet das dar, was aus des Feuers=Tinctur in der Seelen ist zum Wunder kommen" (*Dreyfach* xvi, 35). The next word, *Schuldigern* 'guilty ones', expresses his negative opinions of formal academic education. *Schuldigern* contains the root *Schul-* (*Schule* 'school'), a term he frequently equates with useless words, futile acts and unadulterated ignorance:[31] the syllable *Schul-* "zeiget an das unnütze Werk dass eine Seele gegen der andern aus des Feuers=Tinctur gewircket hat .... Und ist eine Darstellung des Übels" (*Dreyfach* xvi, 35). The conglomeration of useless works of souls occurs in the following syllable *-di-* as a *böses Kind* 'bad child' and concludes in the syllable *-gern* (*Dreyfach* xvi, 35).

The sixth request "und führe uns nicht in Versuchung" shows the soul (will), now free of its negative baggage, able again to enter into the love and meekness of God. It must first humble itself before the trinity, the three letters of the first word *und* (u+n+d). The nebulous conjunction finally takes on meaning within the code. Sufficiently traumatized from its experiences with negative manifestation, the soul (will) implores the Holy Spirit in the syllable *füh-* (füh+re) not to abandon it within the realm of devilish beguilements within the world of matter. The soul (will) cannot trust itself: "So flehet sie nun dem H. Geiste, dass Er nicht mit ihrem Willen soll in die Proba eingehen: dann sie trauet ihr nicht vor dem Teufel zu bestehen, wann er sie sichten soll" (*Dreyfach* xvi, 36). The next word *uns* offers the soul (will) another reunion within divine majesty before it is forced to descend into the wrathful aspect of manifestation for "in dieser Sylbe reisset der Wille schlechts aus der Zorn=Wurtzel aus" (*Dreyfach* xvi, 36). While the soul (will) appears as resonance, *Klang*, within the next word *in*, it is nonetheless compacted *Wesen*. It can break away from this bondage and does so within the structure of the following word *Versuchung* 'temptation'. The raging, burning, fiery aspects of manifestation must be tempered and cooled, a process achieved through the application of the features of coolness and darkness seen in the uvular *r* in *Ver-*: "da muss sie mit dem Willen durch den Grimm gehen und ihn sänftigen, sie muss ihn erkühlen dass er sie in ihrem sanften Leben nicht anzünde" (*Dreyfach* xvi, 36). After extinguishing the raging, grim aspects of manifestation, the triumphant soul (will) passes through matter reigning over the seven powers in nature.[32] The soul (will) is "als ein König über sein Reich" (*Dreyfach* xvi, 36).

The purified, majestic soul (will) appears in the first syllable of the next request "sondern erlöse uns vom Übel" as a power and splendor outside the heart. Böhme describes this power as existing in a unique relationship with the omniscient divine, a relationship which he calls "ein eigen Principium' (*Dreyfach* xvi, 37). The soul (will) emanating this principle power holds the eternal natural manifested tendency towards wrath (*Grimm*) in check within the syllable *-dern* (son+dern); the high frequency of astringent obstruents forces wrath to be self-contained. Having overcome *Grimm*, the soul (will) employs the astringency of the *r* in the next word (e+r+lö+se) as a creative mechanism; flowers, shapes of all dimensions and the wonders of God spring forth from this relationship. The plant image develops within the syllable *-lö-* where it "ist das Gewächse, so aus dem Grimm aus der Natur wächset, ist nun lieblich und gut, und taugt in GOttes Reiche" (*Dreyfach* xvi, 37). The final syllable *-se* represents the fruit of the plant, which Böhme tells the reader is *vom Zorn los* 'wrathfree' (*Dreyfach* xvi, 37), the cleansing feature of the *s* having operated within the prescribed manner. *Uns* and *vom* show the soul (will) jubilantly rejoicing in a reunion with all souls realizing that "sie sey eine Wurtzel in GOttes Reich vor ihrer Schöpfung gewesen" (*Dreyfach* xvi, 37). The desire to be eternally free from wrath, to be *vom Zorn los* is seen in the complete phrase *Erlöse uns vom Übel* 'deliver us from evil':

> Darum flehet die Seele, so sie noch unwiedergeboren ist, und noch im irdischen Leibe alleine stecket, und spricht: Erlöse uns vom Übel! Sie begehret vom Zorn ledig zu seyn (*Dreyfach* xvi, 39).

Böhme breaks the word *Übel* apart into its constituents. The umlauted vowel *ü*, for unknown reasons, becomes the *Feuer=Kind* 'fire child' (*Dreyfach* xvi, 40). The outer perimeter of manifestation, the shell of its materiality, "das äussere Regiment" (*Dreyfach* xvi, 40) is the *b*. The last two letters are one unit *-el*, the angel (<*Eng+el* 'angel') desiring to be free from the first two letters: "des Engels Wille will frey seyn von der Falschheit, er will über das Übel herrschen" (*Dreyfach* xvi, 40).

The body of the prayer concludes with a description of the word *Amen* (A+men). The letter *a* as an undesignated vowel relates several semantically valid statements: as all sounds, it "dringet ausm Hertzen aus" (*Dreyfach* xvi, 44), as a vowel it "hat keine Natur" (*Dreyfach* xvi, 44). It is born "aus dem ewigen Willen" (*Dreyfach* xvi, 45) and through obstruent modification and blockage becomes "das gantze Alphabeth mit 24 Zahlen" (*Dreyfach* xvi, 45). The final syllable *-men*, due to the two points of astringent obstruency, symbolizes the entirety of the physically created alphabet: the vocalic stream cannot pass unmodified around the syllable (*Dreyfach* xvi, 45). Böhme summarizes the significance of the prayer:

> Das Vater unser ist GOttes Wort und hat sieben Bitten, und einen Eingang, und Amen: Das ist zusammen Neun=Zahl, und die Zehen=Zahl ist GOtt selber. Mit dem Eingange des Vatere Unsers gehet der Seelen Wille in Vater, und mit den sieben Bitten nimmt sie, was des Vaters ist, dann davon wird sie wieder ein Engel; dann sie krieget in den sieben Gerichten Centrum Naturae himmlisch, Göttlich, und im Amen fasset sie das alles zusammen, und wohnet darinnen, denn es ist ihr

Leib, es ist Christi Fleisch, GOttes Leib (*Dreyfach* xvi, 49).

The concluding phrase "Dein ist das Reich, und die Kraft und die Herrlichkeit in Ewigkeit" (*Dreyfach* xvi, 52) becomes one morphemic unit: the major components *Reich* 'kingdom', *Kraft* 'power', and *Herrligkeit* 'splendor' symbolize God's triune domination over all material and uncreated things. Rather than analyze the phrase with regard to the plight of the soul (will), Böhme lets linguistic analysis rest awhile. The next line of text begins the nineteenth chapter entitled "Vom Segen GOttes in dieser Welt, eine gar sehr gute Offenbarung für den schwachgläubigen Menschen," an interesting topic which unfortunately does not employ the linguistic code.

The promise to explain the *Vater Unser* "an seinem Orte" (*Aurora* xiii, 111) within a major writing some seven years after the promise was made, and then to interpret this within a linguistic system of comprehension levels, marks the beginning of Böhme's linguistic career. Böhme's man perceives God only after the film of astringency is removed from his sight, after the wall of materiality is realized as a wall, and after language is understood as a process wherein God the subject is realizing himself as God the object. To this end, Böhme implores the reader to allow himself the inner freedom to burn away the astringent dross from the word, thereby revealing the shimmering light:

> Die gantze GOttheit mit allen Kräften und Wirckungen, mit samt ihrem instehenden Wesen, sowol ihr Auffsteigen und Durchdringen und Veränderung, das ist, das gantze Gewircke oder die gantze Gebärung, wird alles verstanden im Geiste des Worts. In welcher Proportz oder instehenden Gebärung der Qualitäten der Geist das Wort fasset und formet, und damit ausfähret, eben eine solche instehende Geburt, Durchdringen, Auffsteigen, Ringen und Siegen hats auch

in der Natur (*Aurora* xix, 72, 73).

Even though Böhme uses the second linguistic layer with greater frequency in the *Aurora*, his reliance upon the third layer grows stronger with each passing year. This does not deemphasize the first two layers in favor of the third; rather it explains to a reading audience trained in the application of the nuances of the first two levels the more advanced linguistic possibilities of the third. Should none of his words make sense to the reader, then Böhme reminds the reader that in spite of the linear progression of his words, his thinking is nonlinear. Although reflected within linear word chains, which many assume to be the only level of language, Böhme's concentration is on the third layer of the code. The reader, he concludes, rather than the words, is at fault:

> Ja wenn ich eine Engels=Zunge hätte, und du einen Engels=Verstand, so wolten wir wol sein davon reden; aber so sihet es nur der Geist, und die Zunge kans nicht erheben, denn ich kan keine andere Worte als die Worte dieser Welt; so aber nur der H. Geist in dir ist, so wirds deine Seele wol begreiffen (*Aurora* iv, 29).

CHAPTER II

THE CODE EXPANDS: *BESCHREIBUNG DER DREY PRINCIPIEN GÖTTLICHES WESENS* (1619) AND *HOCH UND TIEFE GRÜNDUNG VOM DREYFACHEN LEBEN DES MENSCHEN* (1619-1620)

The progression of human thought through spoken linguistic phrases—phonetically linear channels of syntactic arrangement—rather than through nonverbal esoteric images,[1] qualifies Böhme's linguistic approach as well as his prophetic frustration in *Beschreibung der Drey Principien Göttliches Wesens* (1619). Written after seven years of censured silence, Böhme adds the newly formulated three principles to the linguistic anchor of the *Aurora*. What are the three principles?

Underlying every extensional expression of manifestation, Böhme envisions a tripartite apportionment of divine will: pure unmanifested energy (Father), reflected energy within matter (Son) and matter itself (Holy Spirit). The absence of *Begreiffligkeit* characterizes the first two expressions, called *Principien* 'principles'; its presence, the third. The first principle, centripetal astringent compaction, functions as a primum mobile assuring the perpetuation of the other two principles. As seen in the *Aurora*, astringency, wrath, and anger inwardly projected into each other characterize this first principle. The outward disconnection from within the hardened, dark, and compacted mass of centripetal force characterizes the second principle. An outward expression as manifested light occurs simultaneously with an inward self-consumptive astringent urge toward darkness. The delicately measured balance between these principles enables the third principle, manifestation, to become apprehensible, thereby *begreifflich*.[2]

The first principle is an emanation of divine energy, subtly vibrating and alone, within itself and unreflected. The second principle is seen only through the matrix of the third, matter. Just as a beam of light (first principle) cannot be seen until particulate matter (third principle) enters the vacuum, reflecting its presence (second principle), so too, Böhme's Father cannot realize himself as Son except within matter, *Begreiffligkeit*. It is here, within the third principle, that the Father reaches out (<*greiffen* 'to grab, reach') realizing himself as objectified reality.

Unable to linguistically control a syllogistic argument by means of syntactic structures, Böhme integrates the expressive features of the *Drey Principien* into his analysis of the syllables and words which intrigue him. As earlier, each syllable is a reduced Böhmian phrase, with some letters disclosing a close affinity to the principles. He begins the linguistics of the *Drey Principien* with an etymology of the word *Mercurius*:

> Nun verstehe recht, wie dis Mercurius sey: Das Wort Mer ist erstlich die strenge Herbigkeit; Denn im Wort auf der Zungen verstehst du es, dass es aus der Herbigkeit karret, und verstehst auch, wie der bitter Stachel darinnen sey. Denn das Wort Mer ist herbe und zitternd und formet sich ein iedes Wort von seiner Kraft, was die Kraft thut oder leidet. Das Wort Cu verstehst du, dass es sey des Stachels Reibung oder Unruhe, der mit der Herbigkeit nicht zu frieden ist, sondern sich erhebet und auffsteiget: Denn die Sylbe dringet mit Kraft vom Hertzen zum Munde aus; also geschicht es auch in der Kraft Prima Materiae im Geist. Weil aber die Sylbe Cu also einen starcken Nachdruck hat vom Hertzen und doch auch alsbald von der Sylbe Ri gefangen wird, und in dieselbe der gantze Verstand verwandelt wird, so bedeutet und ist es das bitter=stachlichte Rad der Gebärung, das sich drehet und ängstet so geschwinde als ein Gedancken. Die Sylbe Us ist der geschwinde Feur=Blitz, dass sich die Materia im geschwinden Drehen zwischen der Herbigkeit

The Code Expands 43

> und Bitterkeit im geschwinden Rade entzündet: da versteht man im Worte gar eigentlich wie die Herbigkeit erschricket, und die Kraft im Worte wieder zurücke aufs Hertze sincket und unmächtig wird, gantz dünne. Der Stachel aber mit dem drehenden Rade bleibet im Blitz, und fähret zum Munde durch die Zähne aus, da dann der Geist zischet gleich einem angezündeten Feur, und sich zurücke im Wort wieder stärcket (*Drey Principien* i, 13).

Mercurius originates within the severe, trembling, and rumbling realm of astringency (first principle). The uvular *r* asserts itself orally *im Wort auf der Zungen* where Böhme invites the reader to pronounce the word in order to feel the interactions to which he is referring. The *r* is the force from which all manifestation, all astringency originates. Since Böhme cannot posit pure astringency anywhere within the entire cosmos, the second syllable *-cu-* contains features of centrifugal expansion:[3] the *Stachels=Reibung* 'stickling friction' expresses itself actively through the verbal *erheben* 'to elevate' and *auffsteigen* 'to ascend', both signifying on the first language layer, expansion away from, rather than movement toward, the point of origin. The high concentration of astringency in the *r* of the next syllable *-ri-* centripetally checks the outward expansion encountered in the previous syllable *-cu-*. In and out, up and down, the principles whirl within one another; they settle into the *Rad der Gebärung* 'the wheel of generative force, the birth of manifestation': an interaction obligatory for matter to exist. The last syllable *-us*, rich with the sibilant *s* hissing into manifestation, is the meeting ground for all the principles: here matter is enkindled (*entzündet*<ent+S+ündet), reflecting not only the interactions of the first and second principles, but through *entzünden* matter will be turned into the residence of man's archenemy, Lucifer. Böhme concludes this etymology with a summary of the entire process: the tumbling interactions begin in the heart, exit through the mouth, then between

the teeth, carrying with them a small splinter of *Geist*. Without this *Geist* language could not exist.

Since non-Germanic words such as *Mercurius* and *Matrix* (*Drey Principien* xi, 17, 18) exemplify the semantics of a closed alien corpus rather than the associative realism encountered in words of a communal Germanic origin, Böhme's kinship with monolingual thinking and writing leads him to create mystical word roots. He derives and justifies the semantic field of his multilayered German by means of these unique roots. He is careful, though, and warns the reader not to equate any of his words with meanings they may have acquired elsewhere (namely from the first layer):

> Nicht verste ich hiermit gäntzlich den Mercurium in dem 3ten Principio dieser geschaffenen Welt, den man in Apothecken braucht, ob er gleich wol auch eben diese Kraft hat, und dieses Wesens ist; sondern ich rede im ersten Principio vom Urkund des Wesens aller Wesen ... Wiewol in beyden im Urkunde keine Abtrennung ist, als nur das äusserste und dritte Principium. Das siderische und elementische Reich ist aus dem ersten Principio erboren, durchs Wort und Geist GOttes, aus dem ewigen Vater, aus dem heiligen Himmel (*Drey Principien* i, 15).

The same is true of the word *Sulphur*:

> Das Wort Sul bedeutet und ist die Seele eines Dinges, denn es ist im Wort Sulphur das Oel oder das Licht, welches aus der Sylbe Phur erboren wird; und ist eines Dinges Schöne oder Wolthun, seine Liebe oder Liebstes: in einer Creatur ist es das Licht, davon die Creatur sihet, und steht darinnen die Vernunft und Sinnen; und ist der Geist, der aus der Sylbe Phur erboren wird. Das Wort oder Sylbe Phur ist die Prima Materia, und hält im 3ten Principio in sich den Macrocosmum, davon das elementische Reich oder Wesen erboren wird. Aber im ersten

The Code Expands 45

> Principio ist es das Wesen der innersten Geburt, aus welchem GOtt der Vater seinen Sohn von Ewigkeit gebieret, und aus welchem der H. Geist ausgehet, (verstehe aus dem Sul und aus dem Phur). In dem Menschen ist es auch das Licht welches aus dem siderischen Geist erboren wird im andern Centro des Microcosmi (*Drey Principien* ii, 7).

Keeping in mind Böhme's lack of interest in vocalic sounds, the first syllable *Sul-* reduces to a consonantal root **sl*, the same root generating through a form of alphabetic mutations, a Böhmian Ablaut, the word *Seele*: "Das Wort Sul(S+[u]+L) bedeutet und ist die Seele(S+[ee]+L+[e])eines Dinges" (*Drey Principien* ii, 7). It is interesting that *Sul-* (<*sl) is also light (*Licht*<L+icht) expanding centrifugally towards positivity: the *Seele* is the second principle as seen above (S+ee+L+e U+nd L+icht>S + (L) + U + L>S + ⌀ + U + L>S + U + L> *sl* >*Sul-* as in *Sulphur*). The first lateral vanishes in view of the final *l*, to make the etymological connection more readily accessible. The penultimate vowel vanishes into the root form, only to reappear within a different word shell. Generation occurs through the astringency of the uvular *r* in the second syllable *-phur*: "Das Wort oder Sylbe Phur ist Prima Materia" (*Drey Principien* ii, 7). Here the root within *Prima*, **pr* receives support from the *r* embedded within the surface form of *MateRia* and qualifies with *Sulphur* (Sul+P+hu+R): astringency, matter, and roots work effectively together within the code. The extension of the second principle through the agency of matter is reflected and refracted light. Through syllabic reversal, a movement toward which Böhme now shows favoritism, the secure timeworn ideas of predominating astringency seem to come to an abrupt end. Or perhaps Böhme attempts to destroy vestiges of linear syllabic thinking within the reading audience by positing astringency in the last syllable *-phur*, and the second (and therewith the third) principle in the first syllable *Sul-*. Has prophetic frustration with linear modes of transmitting divine impulses eclipsed Böhme's powers of logic? Is Böhme involved with a right to left orthography (Hebrew?)? Before dealing with this interesting speculation, the subsequent changes in linguistic thinking through the year 1624 need formulation.

Böhme's Aurorean dependence on the theory of astringent compaction characterizes the most casual reading through the first chapters of the *Drey Principien*. Only twenty-three lines into the work, Böhme's reliance on astringency overpowers the newly formulated theory of the three principles. The syllable *-phur* reflects this relationship:

> [it] . . . ist die innerste Kraft, der urkundliche Quell des Zorns, der Grimmigkeit oder der Beweglichkeit, wie im I. Cap. gemeldet; und hat in ihr viererley Gestalt, als (1) Herbe, (2) Bitter, (3) Feuer und (4) Wasser (*Drey Principien* ii, 8).

The second and third chapters repeat from various perspectives the same commentaries on astringency as encountered earlier: linguistic analyses temporarily vanish until Böhme unexpectedly reminds the reader in the fourth chapter that "Das Wort ist dir nahe, ja in deinem Hertzen und Lippen (Deut. 30:14) und GOtt selber ist das Wort, das in deinem Hertzen und Lippen ist" (*Drey Principien* iv, 10). With the zeal of an enthusiastic new preacher Böhme begins teaching his particular brand of German mysticism: language contemplation gives man a vehicle of transcendence, a path back to spirit.

Seven years after writing about the bilabial closure *m* in the word *Himmel*, Böhme indirectly addresses those readers who have been following what he has been saying by giving them further stages in the linguistic process, an advanced training for the faithful readers. To other newcomers, he imparts the background information orally. Under no circumstances does he wish to throw his pearls of wisdom before the swine (*Drey Principien* vi, 16) but rather before his group of faithful and financially supportive

The Code Expands

adherents. He writes exclusively "Anlangend die Kinder GOttes, welchen dieses alleine gilt, wird der Geist GOttes wol unterweisen und lehren" (*Drey Principien* vi, 16). By regressing further into the more advanced levels of linguistic speculation, Böhme protects himself from the sharpened sword of public and clerical overreaction should his manuscripts surface. In this manner, he continues his discussion.

Basing his argument on accepted Biblical truth, Böhme says "so schreibet Moses davon (Gen. I:16): GOtt habe eine Veste zwischen die Wasser gemacht, und das Wasser unter der Veste von dem Wasser über der Veste geschieden, und die Veste Himmel geheissen: Ist gar recht, aber bisher übel verstanden worden" (*Drey Principien* vi, 15). Here, Böhme focuses the divisionary bifurcation between the sides of heaven seen earlier (*Aurora* xviii, 62ff.) through the lens and semantic network of the three principles. His concern about the features of the materially manifested and the nonmaterial unmanifested sides of heaven is linguistic:

> Nun siehe, der Himmel ist die gantze Tieffe, soweit sich die AEther haben zur Geburt dieser Welt eingegeben: und der ist die Matrix, aus welcher die Erde, Steine, und materialisch Wasser sind erboren (*Drey Principien* vi, 16).

Böhme's geocentricity, which has been cited as a probable source for Newton's theory of gravitation,[4] views man's side of heaven yielding a proliferation of hardened, astringent forms, here the *Erde, Steine* and *materialisch Wasser* 'material water'. He stresses their astringent character, relying on the feature of +dead and a direct connotation of astringency through the uvular *r*:

> Nun hat GOtt das materialische Wasser alda entschieden von der Matrice; und siehet man gar eigend alhier, wie das materialische Wasser gleich wie ertödtet, oder darinnen der Tod ist; denn es hat nicht können in der

schwebenden Mutter bleiben, sondern ist auf die Erd=
Kugel geschaffen worden, und GOtt hat es Meer geheissen: darinnen verstanden wird in der Natur=Sprache als
ein Grünen im Tode, oder ein Leben in der Zerbrechlichkeit. Wiewol ich dem Leser mit diesem stumm seyn
werde, weiss ichs doch wol, lasse mir auch genügen, die-
weil der viehische Mensch solches zu wissen nicht werth
ist (*Drey Principien* vi, 16).

As with the bisyllabic *Himmel*, Böhme equates the monosyllable *Meer* 'ocean, sea' with the second syllable of *Himmel*, the *-mel*. *Meer*, created with a bilabial closure + lengthened vocalic sound + astringent r^5 is an indication of man's side of the firmament, "this" side of the matrix. *Meer* is not only a secondary connotation (on the first layer of language) for the body of material water; it is primarily (on the third layer) a denotation for *ein Grünen im Tode* 'growth within the realm of death'. The *Geist* enters physical form, tumbles from the bilabial closure *m* through the snarling astringent *r*, experiencing *ein Leben in der Zerbrechlichkeit* 'a life within brittleness'. This fractionated limited brittleness characterizes the linguistic spectrum of the third principle. How does this notion expand the code? The acoustical form of the word terminates, the message reaches the recipient, the form then shatters apart (<*zerbrechen* 'to break into pieces') allowing the *Geist* an unrestricted path back to its divine source. As will be seen, *Zerbrechlichkeit* is not without its effects.

Böhme modifies the word *Himmel* by incorporating into it features of division: the heavens are a divisionary firmament between the first two and the third principles. The word *Himmel* can replace *Matrix*:

Nun als der Himmel ist von Erden und finstern Gestieb
in der Zusammentreibung lauter worden, so sind alda in
der Matrice des Himmels gestanden die drey Elementa
Feuer, Luft und Wasser. Dieses sind drey Dinge ineinander

> in einer Mutter, und die Mutter wird alhier der Himmel geheissen, darum werde ich nun im Schreiben für das Wort Matrix das Wort Himmel gebrauchen, denn der Himmel ist die Matrix. Und heisset darum Himmel, wegen der Scheidung ... (*Drey Principien* vi, 17, 18).

What, now of the word (Word)?

The vibrationless realm of divinity, omnipresent behind the interactions of the three principles, is *the* source into which Böhme strives to elevate himself (for he claims to have had access to this ecstacy)[6] as well as the reader. Of prime concern here is not how the Word creates, but how can words (<Word) create rather than add to the abundance of death and destruction, misunderstanding and confusion within human languages? He gives mild advice by summarizing the descending path:

> Denn seine Seele in ihrer eigenen Substanz ist aus dem ersten Principio, welches von Ewigkeit keinen Grund oder Anfang hat; und die ist in Zeit der Schöpfung des Menschen im Paradeis oder Himmel=Reich durch das Fiat auf Geistes=Art recht corporired worden, ist aber mit der ersten Kraft ... blieben stehen, und durch das ander Principium, als durch das Hertze GOttes durchleuchtet ... vom wallenden Geiste GOttes in die Matricem des dritten Principii, in den gestirnten und elementischen Menschen eingeblasen worden ... denn so das Licht in ihme ist, so ist er in allen dreyen Principien geboren (*Drey Principien* vii, 2).

The reader must inwardly realize what Böhme calls a *Licht* 'light'. Once perceived, it must be seen as the reflection of divinity within the third principle before the words man utters through the mouth can take on any divine meaning. Man turns into a channel through which *Geist* becomes *Begreiffligkeit*:

> Darum saget auch Christus: (Matth. 17:20) So ihr Glauben habt als ein Senfkorn, so möget ihr sagen zum Berge: Stürze dich ins Meer, so sols geschehen; und in dieser Macht haben Menschen durchs Wort und Geistes Kraft Todten auferweckt, und Kranken gesund gemacht. Anders hätten sie diesen nicht können thun, so sie nicht in der Macht aller dreyen Principien wären gestanden (*Drey Principien* vii, 3).

Outside of the three principles, beyond where the Word is recognized, Böhme notes that expression using the astringent-laden first level of language is futile and frustrating. Man's language, if solely derived from the qualities of the third principle, is nothing more than a dead, ineffective and astringent shell, borrowed for a time, filled with dull first-layer semantic values, then cast away after use. True words, words the "Evangelist Johannes" (*Drey Principien* viii, 17) describes, are necessary tools through which a distinct multiple world is forged, then explained, on this side of the matrix. They serve a secondary function by promoting human conversation through communication. Böhme relies upon the Apostle John for support in this matter:

> Siehe was Johannes saget: Im Anfange der Schöpfung und vor Zeiten der Welt ist gewesen das Wort, und das Wort ist GOtt gewesen ... und das hat in der Finsterniss geschienen, und die Finsterniss hats nicht können fassen. Da versteht man klar (1) wie das ewige Licht GOtt sey, und verstehest, (2) wie es in der ewigen Kraft seinen ewigen Urkund habe, und verstehest (3) wie das ewige Wort sey, das in der Finsterniss scheine. Weil dann dasselbe Wort an allen Orten hat alles geschaffen, so ists auch an allen Orten gewesen, denn ohne dasselbe ist nichts gemacht (*Drey Principien* viii, 18).

He begins to answer his three questions by introducing a new

The Code Expands 51

interpretation of the *Wort*. He says:

> Nun hat dasselbe Wort keine Materiam gehabt, daraus es etwas gemacht hat, sondern aus der Finsterniss hats alle Ding geschaffen und ans Licht gebracht, dass es erscheine und da sey (*Drey Principien* viii, 19).

The Word is a force. It is matterless, originating within the darkness (astringency). It creates all things from the darkness, brings all creation into the light, causally allowing creation to exist and to reflect (<*erscheinen* 'to appear'). He continues:

> Denn in Ihme war das Leben, und Er gab das Leben ins Geschöpfe: und das Geschöpf ist aus seiner Kraft, und die Kraft ist materialisch worden, und das Licht scheinet darinnen; und die materialische Kraft kans nicht ergreiffen, denn sie ist in Finsterniss (*Drey Principien* viii, 19).

The Word evolves into the *Geschöpf* 'that which has been created, creature' reflecting in due response to its absorption of *Kraft* 'power' a materiality, its existence as a *Wesen*. Without power there would be no matter, no *erscheinen*. The *Wort*>*Geschöpf* takes on the feature of matter, thereby hopelessly sealing all pathway doors back to God. Böhme cannot imagine the complex of material power comprehending the existence of divine power:

> Weil aber die materialische Kraft nicht kan das Licht ergreiffen, das von Ewigkeit in der Finsterniss scheinet; so hat ihm GOtt ein ander Licht gegeben, das aus der Kraft worden ist als die Sonne: die leuchtet in dem Geschöpfe, dass das Geschöpf im Lichte und offenbar sey (*Drey Principien* viii, 19).

Terrestrial sunlight replaces divine light, a requirement in a Böhmian world where illumination is an important adjunct to effective speech.

Out of the dualities of light and dark, each demanding its reality in terms of the presence of the other within, Böhme develops the theory of shadows, a *Schattentheorie*. He says:

> Denn zu dem Ende sind alle Creaturen dieser Welt erschienen, dass sie sollen seyn ein ewig figürlich Gleichniss: nicht dass sie in diesem Geiste in ihrer Substanz bleiben, nein, das ist es nicht; es gehen alle Geschöpfe wieder in ihr AEther, und zerbricht der Geist, aber die Figur und Schatten bleibet ewiglich (*Drey Principien* ix, 21).

The *Geschöpf*, as a *Creatur*, is posited with *Substanz* 'matter'. In this way it eventually disintegrates releasing the *Geist*. It is interesting to watch Böhme first select a non-Germanic word, in this case *Figur* 'figure, shape', then replace it with a Germanic counterpart, *Schatten*. Böhme's penchant for extending semantics between words and syllables expresses itself fully within his definition of *Schatten*:

> Es wird alles im Schatten bleiben, und ein iedes in seiner Quall: darum wird dis den Gottlosen eine ewige Schande seyn, dass sie in Ewigkeit werden alle ihre Wercke sehen, und alle ihre Worte als ein beflecktes Tuch, welche werden voll Zornes GOttes stecken, und brennen nach ihrer Essentia und hier angezündeten Quall (*Drey Principien* ix, 23).

Böhme, in stripping the shell of materiality from the *Geschöpf*, attempts to preach a moral message: the deeds of the godless never vanish. They are recorded on the face of the earth as a fluctuation in the divine vibration, a fluctuation which will always continue to effectuate. *Schatten* being—*Geschöpf*, eternal, and a repository of everything, records man's dismal deeds. Viewed from

The Code Expands

the linguistic perspective, *Schatten*, being without *Geist* (that is, −*Geist*), is therefore not a *Geschöpf*, since *Geschöpfe* are repositories for *Geist* within matter. The good people, Böhme goes on to mention, upon shedding their substance, leave them within the realm of manifestation, vanishing as *Geist* within divinity. This thought leads Böhme into chiliastic tendencies:

> Denn wenn das 3te Principium dieser materialischen Welt wird zerbrechen, und in sein AEther gehen, alsdann bleibet aller Creatur, auch aller Gewächse, und alles des, was ist ans Licht kommen, Schatten, auch aller Worte und Wercke ihr Schatten und Figur; und ist unbegreifflich, auch ohne Verstand und Erkentniss, gleichwie ein Nichts oder Schatten gegen dem Lichte (*Drey Principien* ix, 39).

With mystical maturation, Böhme connects what he understands as *Schatten* with what later evolves as the concept of the *Signatur* 'signature'.

Turning for a moment to the unmanifested, preternatural[7] side of the matrix, Böhme engages the reader in the continuing story of Spirit in search of matter. He addresses man's free, eternal doorway to divinity, the soul (rather than the astringently beclouded *Leib* 'body'), in an attempt to explain the origin of the third principle:

> Nun siehe du vernünftige Seele, mit dir rede ich und nicht mit dem Leibe, du begreiffsts alleine. Wenn die Geburt nun also immer erboren wird, so hat eine iede Gestalt ein Centrum zur Wiedergeburt (*Drey Principien* ix, 35).

What is the nature of the center back to rebirth? The soul and the faithful followers can penetrate the opaque terminology:

> Denn das gantze Göttliche Wesen stehet in steter und ewiger Geburt, aber unwandelber gleich des Menschen Gemüthe, da aus dem Gemüthe immer Gedancken geboren werden, und aus den Gedancken der Wille und Begierlichkeit; und aus dem Willen und Begierlichkeit das Werck, welches zu einer Substanz gemacht wird im Willen; alsdann greiffen zu Mund und Hände, und verbringen das, was im Wille substantialisch ward (*Drey Principien* ix, 35).

Rather than answer the question directly, Böhme resorts to phraseology which leads him closer to the anchor of linguistics: finding the *Centrum zur Wiedergeburt* demands the prerequisite realization of the function of what he calls *Gemüt* '(on the first layer) senses, mood, inclination'. What is this *Gemüt*?

Since thoughts require objects upon which to project their semantic components, they reach out of themselves (*begehren*) toward form. *Gemüt* is the first channel through which the ocean of thought passes, there being directed into different semantic positions: thoughts of possession funnel into word-fields indicative of things or qualities possessed or that possess; thoughts of love channel toward people, objects and qualities loved or loving; thoughts of God are those subtle vibrations within the *Gemüt*, which aided by the concept of external tendencies (*Signatur*), redirect themselves back to the divine source. Man needs only to follow. His *Gemüt* orders and shapes the directions of the divine emanations into grosser channels of perception, depositing them finally within the manifested shell of materiality. He delineates this process:

> Also auch ist die ewige Geburt; da von Ewigkeit ist immer erboren worden die Kraft, und aus der Kraft das Licht: und das Licht ursachet und machet die Kraft (die Kraft und) das Licht scheinet in der ewigen Finsterniss, und machet den sehnenden Willen im ewigen Gemüthe,

The Code Expands

> dass der Wille in der Finsterniss gebieret die Gedancken, und die Gedancken die Lust und Begierlichkeit: und die Begierlichkeit ist das Sehnen der Kraft, und in der Kraft Sehnen ist der Mund, der spricht aus das Fiat, und das Fiat macht die Materiam, und der Geist der in der Kraft ausgehet zerscheidets, und nimt nicht eine Essentia von der andern sondern zerscheidets: und in dem zerschiedenen Wesen, weil iedes gantz ist unzerbrochen, ist wieder in iedem Dinge das Centrum der Vielfältigung, gleich des Menschen Gemüthe mit Ausgang der Gedancken (*Drey Principien* ix, 36).

The *Mund* 'mouth' is the point in the universe through which divinity moves into manifestation (the matrix) as well as the position within the vocal mechanism where the idea becomes speech. Through the astringent manipulations of the mouth, *Fiat*[8] occurs, whereby *Materia*, words and being, follow. Böhme reminds the reader that even though he perceives apparent multiplicity of form, there is underlying unity. Each and every thing has a center which generates its characteristic features, its multiple aspect within matter. In man, the *Gemüt* is one such vital *Centrum* 'center'.

Böhme, in full view of the fact that his reading audience is carefully following his words, no longer scolds them into closer textual readings; rather he demands that they return their contemplations to the origins of language:

> Und ist uns nun treflich zu bedencken vom Urkunde der Sprache, Gemüthe und Sinnen, in welchen der Mensch GOttes Bilde und Gleichniss ist, und in welchem die edle Erkentniss aller dreyen Principien stehet (*Drey Principien* xiv, 55).[9]

Böhme directs the reader's attention to the center of the word, toward the nucleus. Into this center, he posits *Geist* and the feature of division (bitterness). Without division there could be no syllabic distinction; language would resemble animal noises. The key factor, he adds, is *Verstand* 'understanding, comprehensibility' without which the sense perceptors could not perform their language-related function. Concerning the ears, Böhme says:

> Nun was machet dann das Gehör, dass du hörest was tönet und sich reget; wilst du sagen vom Schalle der äussern Dinge, so da schallen? Nein, es muss auch etwas seyn, das den Schall fänget und mit dem Schalle inqualiret, und den Ton unterscheidet was gepfiffen oder gesungen ist: das äussere kans alleine nicht thun, das innere muss den Schall fangen und unterscheiden (*Drey Principien* xv, 67).

Böhme's bilabial thinking, crucial to the word *Himmel*, expands into an internal/external operative mechanism whereby two functioning ears can be seen. A balance between an internal and an external ear—not in the biological sense—with gross vibrations, here *Essentien* 'essence' intervening, is necessary in order for man to hear. Matter is the matrix through which the inner potential for hearing passes to intermingle with external acoustical vibrations. These result from material interaction, the basis of which is the astringency of the hearing apparatus: "Denn das äusserliche Tönen inqualiret mit dem innern, und wird durch die Essentien entschieden" (*Drey Principien* xv, 68).

The *etwas...das den Schall fänget und mit dem Schall inqualiret* 'something...that captures the resonance, qualifying with it' is the same thing Böhme finds operative behind all sense impression: discrimination. He personifies it as a counsellor, who either accepts or rejects that impression placed before him:[10]

> Darum hat der Schmack die Zunge, dass er es soll wegspeyen, so es falsch ist; ist aber ein Gedancke zu einem Worte, so ist die Lippe die Thürhüter, die soll zusperren,

The Code Expands

> und die Zunge nicht mit heraus lassen, sondern soll es in die Region der Luft, in die Blase und nicht ins Hertze führen und erstricken, so ists todt (*Drey Principien* xvi, 18).

The resonance of language, the *Schall*, passes from the counsellors of the eyes, ears, nose, and mouth (*Drey Principien* xvi, 18) to the general sensory mechanism *Fühlung* 'physical awareness'. After analyzing the component features "aus welcher Qualität es ist, obs heis oder kalt, hart oder weich, dick oder dünne" (*Drey Principien* xvi, 19), *Fühlung* passes them to the center of divine light in the body, the heart. Here, the physically-oriented life current penetrates the resonance "in eine grosse Tieffe, und siehet was darinnen ist, wie viel er des Dinges will annehmen und einlassen" (*Drey Principien* xvi, 19). If the outer resonance agrees with the dictates of the inner counsellors, then these features pass onto the tongue for final modification before exiting through the mouth into nature. The air stream is suddenly important:

> Denn die Region der Luft muss alhie das Werck führen durch den Hals, da denn alle Adern im gantzen Leibe hingehen und alda zusammenkommen; und bringen die Kraft der edlen Tinctur dahin, und vermischen sich mit dem Worte, darzu alle drey Regionen des Gemütes kommen, und vermischen sich mit den Unterscheiden des Worts, da ist eine gar wunderliche Gestalt. Denn iede Region will das Wort nach ihren Essentien scheiden: denn der Schall gehet aus dem Hertzen aus allen dreyen Principien (*Drey Principien* xvi, 20).

The vaporous nonmaterialized *Geist* seems to control the entire human mechanism:

> Zum 3ten kommt das 3te Regiment zur Bildung des Worts, der Geist der Sternen und Elementen; und

> vermischet sich im Gehäuse und Sinnen des Gemüths, und will das Wort aus eigener Macht bilden, denn es hat die gröste Macht, denn es hält den gantzen MENSCHEN gefangen, und hat ihn mit Fleisch und Blut bekleidet, und inficiret den Willen des Gemüths (*Drey Principien* xvi, 22).

Man, the matrix through which the Word passes, converts the Word into words, implementing the process by adding understanding and rationality into the new words. Only through man, Böhme adds, can divinity assure itself of existence as apprehensible matter. Animals gape dumbly at the process unfolding before their sense receptors:

> So ist nun zu ersinnen, dass der Schall in der Tinctur des Menschen höher ist als der in Thieren: denn er urkundet und entscheidet alle Dinge was tönet, und weiss wovon es kommt, und wie sichs urkundet; das kann kein Thier thun, sondern es gaffet es an, und weiss es nicht was es ist (*Drey Principien* xv, 69).

Since man possesses a higher sense of rational division than the animals, Böhme understands the nature of divine resonance within the depths of his being. His physical motion toward or away from objects that resound (*tönen*) and the incorporation of their features into the process of mental discrimination, elevate man above all *Geschöpfe*. Were man to gape at language as it passes by, without attempting to extract the *Geist* from beneath the surface, he would never understand his etymological origins within divinity. Language contemplation leads to a direct knowledge of the *Ausgeburt aus dem Ewigen* 'outbirth from the eternal' (*Drey Principien* xv, 69).

Were the process of divine reintegration so clearly understood by his readers, Böhme would have little recourse than to usher the multitudes across the bilabial threshold. Times as they were,

The Code Expands 59

Böhme realized early in his calling that Adam's fall closed the once opened gate. Böhme posits into Adam's falling into matter two features of universal validity, features which hinder man's perception of the higher realms: *Zerbrechlichkeit* 'brittleness' and *Unverstand* 'lack of understanding' (*Drey Principien* xv, 70). If things did not break apart, if they did not expire, and if man understood them in their state of not breaking apart, then Böhme adds, man would be one step closer to understanding the Word. Were *Geist* allowed to tumble freely through the matrix, unchecked by the polarities inherent within the qualities, then a perfect balance between form and content, between *Geist* and *Begreiffligkeit*, would exist. Man, however, living within *Zerbrechlichkeit* and fearing the final death in dissolution, one day succumbs to them. Reacting against nature (+ *Zerbrechlichkeit*) from the perspective of *Unverstand*, man seems hopelessly lost. Böhme's solution is simple: scrutinize not only the inner soul (what he can apprehend of it) but also examine the physical form:

> So wir dann den elenden Fall Adams und Hevä betrachten, so dürfen wir nicht lange dem tollen Anti-Christ nachlaufen, von ihme Weisheit zu forschen: er hat keine ... wir dürfen keinen Doctorem dazu, auch keiner fremden Sprache, es steht in unserem Leibe und Seele geschrieben: und so wir das sehen, erschrecket es uns also sehr, dass wir darob erzittern wie der Hevä und Adam in ihrem Falle geschehen ist (*Drey Principien* xvii, 40).

Neither the learned *Doctores* nor knowledge of exotic foreign languages intimidates the self-reliant Böhme. He calls upon his readers to analyze themselves, and once realizing the nature of the soul and the body, they too shall tremble in humiliation. Aligning his heart within the "Wesen dieser Welt, erschaffen ausm Urkunde aller Dinge" (*Drey Principien* xxi, 11), Böhme calls to the reader from the perspective of the principles: everything is to be found within them. There must be a conduit connector present between man's *Verstand* and the vitality within the principles:

> Seine Seele (ist) ausm ersten Principio mit dem andern durchleuchtet, und sein Leib aus dem Element aus dem Barm oder Geburt aus der Göttlichen Kraft vor GOtt, welcher war eingegangen in die Ausgeburt des Elements, als in die vier Elementa, und gäntzlich in Geist dieser Welt, als ins dritte Principium (*Drey Principien* xxi, 11).

Keeping the above in mind, Böhme attacks the sages of learning, the *Buchstabengelehrten* 'scholars of the letter':[11]

> Als aber die Heiligen ihre Lehre in Schrift fasseten, damit man sie könte abwesende verstehen was sie lehrten, da fiel die Welt zu, und ein ieder wolte ein solcher Lehrer seyn, und dachten nun, die Kunst steckte im Buchstaben: Da kamen sie gelauffen alte und Neue, die ein Theil nur im alten Menschen stecketen, und hatten kein Erkentniss von GOtt, lehreten also nach ihrem Dünckel, nach den aufgeschriebenen Worten, und legten dieselben aus nach ihren Gutdüncken (*Drey Principien* xxvi, 18).

The ability to read the writings of the holy sages, the *Kunst* 'art' (<*können* 'to be able to') necessary to penetrate deeper than the letters, seems lost within time. Böhme hears only the darkened, personally interpreted exegeses of preachers lacking knowledge of God. This closely reflects the human condition which Böhme is trying to liberate. Rather than falling prey to the obfuscation of words, explicated from the realm of the astringent darkness of individual personalities, Böhme offers the readers the option of following him through his own brand of linguistic exegesis. He calls this his *work*:

The Code Expands

> So will ich doch mein Tagwerck nicht so gar übergehen sondern arbeiten auf dem Wege, soviel ich kann: und solte ich doch kaum auf diesem hohen Wege können die Buchstaben zehlen[12] so wirds doch zu hoch seyn, dass mancher sein Lebtage daran wird zu lernen haben; der vermeynet, er wisse es gantz wol, wird noch nicht den ersten Buchstaben vom Paradeis erlernet haben: denn es werden keine Doctores auf diesem Wege in dieser Schule gefunden, sondern nur eitel Schüler (*Drey Principien* ix, 9).

Mensch 'person', *Maria, Himmel, Barmhertzigkeit, Immanuel, Jesus* and *Christus* exhibit obstruent features characteristic of Böhme's newly developed system of matrices. Beginning with *Mensch*, Böhme says that since man is a "vermischte Person" (*Drey Principien* xvii, 16), it would be natural to name him according to the predominant quality: intermixing. The person is a *Mensch* since the bilabial closure *m* draws a dividing line between the realms (second and third principles), seen above in *Himmel* and *Meer*. He extends the semantic root of *vermischt* (ve+r+mi+ SCH+t), the *sch*, into the fricative *sch* found in *Mensch* (Men+ SCH). The hissing interaction, the mixing and blending of the first two principles into the third, brings about man's temptation within the Garden of Eden:

> Als aber die Weisheit GOttes sahe, wie der Mensch lüsternd ward vom Geiste dieser Welt, sich mit den vier Elementen zu mischen; so kam das Gebot und sprach: du solt nicht essen vom Baum des Erkentniss Gutes und Böses (*Drey Principien* xvii, 17).

Böhme describes *Maria* with the following words:

> Also ist in diesem Jahr, wie obgemeldet, der Engel Gabriel kommen zu einer armen aber züchtigen und

keuschen Jungfrauen, von GOtt dem Vater gesandt gen Nazareth, Maria genant. Ihr Name, heisset recht auf teutsch in der Natursprache eine Errettung aus dem Jammerthal (Ob wir wol nicht aus der hohen Schulen dieser Welt sind erboren mit vielen Sprachen; so haben wir doch die Sprache der Natur in unseren Wunder= Schule auch fix, welches Meister Hans in seinem freyen Hütlein nicht gläubet) (*Drey Principien* xviii, 37).

What is the correct interpretation of the letters M+a+r+i+a according to the linguistic rules of the Böhmian code? As seen through an earlier framework, the bilabial closure *m* + vocalic *a* + astringent uvular *r* + diphthong *ia* (actually two vowels each independent of the other *i* + *a*) explain her significance on the second phonological layer, at the same time sharply denoting her physicality as a *Wesen*. Böhme, though, elects to progress further with the etymology: *Maria* functions as the *Errettung aus dem Jammerthal* 'deliverance from the valley of anguish' and the veracity of the statement on the first layer conveniently bears witness to the third-layer alphabetic interpretation. Böhme notes a striking resemblance between the words *Maria* and *Jammerthal* (Iammerthal): the derivation works in both directions (Ia+M+[e]+R > Ia+M+R > M+R+IA > M+[a]+R+IA) with vocalic deletion and syllabic reversal affecting the transformation. As *Mensch* reveals the root **sch* (<vermi+SCH), the above transformation yields the root **m-r* (+ or − Vowel not yet clarified). Böhme is careful not to hastily overextend the interpretation, calling her the *Errettung aus dem Jammerthal*, rather than the valley of sorrows per se. A broader phrase analysis discloses the uvular *r* base of the second phonological layer in E*RR*+ettung coupling with the bilabial base of the final word Ja+*MM*+erthal suspended in a vowelless atmosphere. Through reversal within a left to right orthography, the MM + RR reduces to M+R. A right to left orthography, or a right to left semantic movement within layers disjointed from the first layer, would reveal the first-layer equations of meaning *Maria* =

The Code Expands

Errettung aus dem Jammerthal in harmony within the system. Whatever the case, the deliverance from the valley of anguish takes place not in the name *Maria*, but rather in the name *Jesus*, a statement of linguistic fact derived from the confrontation with vowels. We shall soon see how the vocalic confrontation alters the functionality of the obstruents within an unprecedented linguistic analysis of the motion of the divine covenant through Maria. But first, a new look at the heavens.

Himmel describes (on the first layer) that place from which angels, prophets, and an array of saints and lesser messengers travel to bless the earth with their divine presence. Heaven connotes the origin of all Biblical truth, the place from which everything is controlled, and whatever anyone else projects into it. As early as 1612 Böhme rejects this notion as well as all attempts to measure the distance between heaven and earth:

> Es haben die Menschen je und allwege gemeinet, der Himmel sey viel hundert oder tausend Meilen von diesem Erdboden, und GOtt wohne allein in demselben Himmel; es haben auch wol etliche Physici sich unterstanden, dieselbe Höhe zu messen und gar seltsame Dinge herfürbracht (*Aurora* xix, 3).[13]

Created skies reflect the heavens that generate them; all space everywhere originates from heaven: truths apparent to the selected few Böhme identifies as belonging to the *Lilien*:[14]

> Wie dann das Wort Himmel in der Natur=Sprache seinen eigentlichen scharfen Verstand hat vom Durchdringen und Eingehen, und dann mit der Wurzel bleiben im Stocke der Ewigkeit sitzen, darinnen recht die Allmacht verstanden wird, welches uns Meister Fritz wol nicht gläubet, denn er hat nicht die Erkentniss darinnen, es gehört in die Lilien (*Drey Principien* xxi, 22).

What is the further knowledge? By dividing the word into *Him*+*mel*, Böhme highlights the divisionary aspect of the bilabial closure. He takes the etymology one degree further by subdividing the final syllable *-mel* into *-m+el*, then approaching the *-el* from the perspective of derivation from both the German *Engel* 'angel' and the Hebrew *el* 'angel'. Böhme overtly justifies the German derivation:

> Die Sylbe Him fähret aus dem Hertzen, als aus des Vaters Kraft, oder aus der Seelen Essentien, und stösset über sich in Ternarium Sanctum, da fasset sichs mit beyden Lippen und führt den Engels=Namen unter sich, als die Sylbe Mel bedeutet der Engel Demüthigkeit (*Drey Principien* xxii, 85).

We see the EL more clearly in the word *Immanuel* (Immanu+el). Böhme credits the word with meaning 'God in us' in agreement with the first-layer semantic interpretation of this non-Germanic loanword. Dissatisfied with the simplicity of the first layer, Böhme subjects the word to the rigorous analysis of the code:

> In der Natur=Sprache lautets recht, aber unsere Zungen von dieser Welt stammlen nur daran, und könnens nicht nennen nach unserem Verstande. Denn Im ist das Hertze GOttes in Ternario Sancto, denn es ist gefasset, wie du es in des Wortes Fassung verstehest (*Drey Principien* xxii, 84).

The *Wortes Fassung* 'the cohesion of the word' begins with the vocalic onset (*I*+mannuel) running into the bilabial closure *m*: the spirit halts at the astringent barrier. He continues:

> Ma ist sein Eingang in die Menschheit in die Seele; denn das Wort oder Sylbe dringt ausm Hertzen; und verstehen, dass Er hat das Hertze, als des Vaters Kraft in

The Code Expands 65

> der Seelen gefasset, und fähret mit dem Worte Nu in die
> Höhe, bedeutet seine Himmelfahrt nach der Seelen
> (*Drey Principien* xxii, 84).

Through the second syllable -*ma*- Spirit presses into manifestation, a manifestation which is not yet crude matter, but rather the refined realm of created man's soul. Once in his soul, the word *Immanuel* (+God in us) remains within. It is not expelled outward. Böhme explains this in the following syllable -*nu*-: the obstruent *n* remains behind within the soul as a *Schatten*, while the vocalic *u* takes on importance designating an upward glide toward (into) heaven. As it approaches the ethereal realms of the matrix transfer, it enters the realm of the angels; there the angel EL rejoices with the soul:

> El ist der Name des grossen Engels, der mit der Seelen
> über die Himmel triumphiret; nicht allein im Himmel
> sondern in der Trinität (*Drey Principien* xxii, 84).

As seen from the first chapter, Böhme's analysis of *Immanuel* (*Drey Principien*, 1619) is the prototype structure for the explication of the *Vater Unser* (*Dreyfach*, 1620). The idea, though, is the same: spirit>matter>spirit.

Much in the same manner as *Immanuel* and the *Vater Unser*, Böhme reexamines his explication of the word *Barmhertzigkeit*, rejecting the notion of semantic onset within recognizable, orthodox syllabic divisions. He begins in the same manner showing astringent compaction instigating the process of word formation:

> So ist das reine Element das Barm in den Essentien des
> Anziehens zum Worte; die Essentien sind Paradeis, und
> das Barm ist Element (*Drey Principien* xxii, 25).

The principle of centripetality, the *Anziehen* 'pulling together', takes place within a supernatural realm. The units within the

Anziehen, here *Essentien* 'essences', agglutinate into a compacted mass, into a *Barm*. Previously undesignated, the *Barm* now expresses the onset of material form (from the strong matter-bound astringent *r*). The entire process turns out to be a mirror which the Father uses to watch himself descend more completely into matter:

> So nun der Vater das ewige Wort immer spricht so gehet aus dem Sprechen der H. Geist: und das Ausgesprochene ist die Ewige Weisheit, und ist eine Jungfrau und das reine Element, als das Barm, ist ihr Leib: darinnen erblicket sich der H. Geist durch die ausgesprochene Weisheit (*Drey Principien* xxii, 25).

Böhme concludes the etymology showing that the Holy Spirit looks at itself through the light created by the Father within manifestation, positing this into the syllable *-hertz-*. The next syllable *-ig* contains the light generated in the previous syllable (*-ig*<*L* + *ich-Laut* + *t*) and deposits it in the final syllable *-keit*:

> Und des Vaters starcke und grosse Feuers=Macht gehet als ein Blitz in den Essentien, das heist Keit, gleich einer Macht, die durchdringet und das Wesen nicht zertrennet, gleich einem Schalle: und heisset dieses zusammen Barmhertzigkeit (*Drey Principien* xxii, 25).

The evenness of spiritual infusion, its *durchdringen* 'thronging through' matter without fractionating it into irreconcilable units (here, verbally expressed through *zertrennen* 'to splinter into pieces'), amazes Böhme, leading him to conclude that spirit exists within voice under exactly the same conditions.

More of God lowering himself into manifestation lies beneath the word *Jesus*. Böhme explains that:

> Sein Name Jesus zeiget das in der Natur=Sprache viel

The Code Expands

> eigentlicher an: denn die Sylbe JE ist seine Erniedrigung aus seinem Vater in die Menschheit, und die Sylbe Sus ist der Seelen Einführung über die Himmel in die Trinität, wie dann die Sylbe Sus in die Höhe durch alles dringet (*Drey Principien* xxii, 87).

The vocalic onset *I+e* (*Iesus*) represents the first inclinations of spirit toward matter. Through nonobstruency, the Father moves into the vocalic essences, entering the arena of matter in the sibilant *s*. Once through the sibilant matrix, the Spirit ascends into the *Höhe* 'heights' far from matter: the vocalic *u* (Ies+u+s) functions as the elevator. The relation of spirit to matter is temporarily brief in *Jesus*. Böhme ignores the final *s*.

Christus exhibits the same linguistic features as *Jesus*. The first syllable shows the Father penetrating into matter (Chris-) overcoming his astringent limitations in the second (-tus):

> Vielmehr wird in dem Namen Christus verstanden: der fasset nicht seine Menschwerdung, sondern gehet als ein geborner Mensch durch den Tod, denn die Sylbe Chris dringet durch den Tod, und bedeut seinen Eingang in den Tod, und den mächtigen Streit (*Drey Principien* xxii, 88).

For Böhme, death is human life. Spirit dies once it encapsulates within the sphere of human existence; it is reborn and lives after it enters that stage of the spectrum called death. Christ dies in becoming man and lives by reassuming his spiritual identity. The final syllable -*tus*:

> Bedeut seine starcke Macht, dass Er aus dem Tode ausgehet und durchdringet. Und verstehet man im Worte gar eigentlich wie Er das Reich dieser Welt und den englischen Menschen von einander trennet, und im englischen Menschen in GOtt bleibet; denn die Sylbe

Tus ist rein ohne Tod (*Drey Principien* xxii, 88).

That *-tus* (dental stop + vowel + hissing sibilant) is God's strong might (*starcke Macht*) is not accidental. Böhme selects the initial *st* cluster from the adjective *starck-*, breaks the obstruents apart S+T, then reverses their order (T+S). The vocalic *u* (+upward ascendency) modifies the obstruent construction into T+u+S. He marks *Chris-* as the *Eingang in den Tod* 'entrance into death', with a velar stop *k* functioning as the matrix marker. Once within the duality of the material cosmos, the Father encounters *Streit* 'altercation' (*Drey Principien* xxii, 88). The root **st* (< T-S) expands into the root **str* (< STR+eit), with the addition of an astringent component (*r*) denoting battle, confrontation and altercation: the forces Jesus encounters walking through the *Jammerthal*.

The phonological intensity which characterizes the *Beschreibung der Drey Principien Göttliches Wesens* develops into an abstract discussion of language in the next work *Hoch und tiefe Gründung von dem Dreyfachen Leben des Menschen*, a work started during the later portion of 1619. As seen in the *Vater Unser* (Chapter I), Böhme realizes that further refinements are necessary if the reading audience is going to understand the minute shades of differentiation between Word and word. *Vom Dreyfachen Leben* (1619/1620) continues the linguistic discussion:

> So aber GOtt das Wort ist, das alle Dinge hat gemacht so muss er in allen Dingen seyn gewesen, dann ein Geist ist nicht ein gemacht Wesen, sondern ein geboren Wesen in sich selber, welches das Centrum der Geburt in sich selber hat, sonst wäre er zerbrechlich (*Dreyfach* i, 41).

As seen earlier, God resides within all things as spirit, a spirit that is not created (*gemacht*), but rather is born within itself: the creator and the created are identical. Underlying language production is the same operative mechanism:

The Code Expands 69

> Dann wo ein Wort ist, da ist auch ein Sprecher, der es spricht. So nun das sein Vater ist, der es spricht und das Wort ist sein Sohn, welches aus dem Centro des Vaters gesprochen wird, und der Vater in seinem Centro sich ein verzehrend Feuer nennet; der Sohn, als das Wort aber, ein Licht der Liebe, Demuth, Sanftmuth, Reinigkeit (*Dreyfach* i, 42).

The Word, organized around the speaker (Father), is matterless since at this developmental stage "es war alles ein nichts" (*Dreyfach* i, 43). Although the subtle progressions from the speaker (Father) willfully externalizing himself through the agency of the Word are not yet delineated, Böhme hints at the direction of his thinking in this regard:

> Denn das ewige Wort ist der ewige Wille, und eine Ursache der ewigen Natur, und die ewige Natur ist der ewige Vater, in deme alle Dinge durchs Wort sind geschaffen (verstehe in der ewigen Natur) (*Dreyfach* i, 53).

The second chapter clarifies the above statement by introducing the notion of *Essentien* as the component parts of *Wesen*. The essences are evoked into manifestation by the will (Word), in turn connecting themselves to the speaker (Father). Böhme wonders at this point how physical duality can be reconciled with a unified divine *Wesen*, a God that manifests, but not within manifestation.

This results from the effects of two wills, each controlling either the negative or positive aspect of manifestation. Existing behind or before the tangible externalized features of love and misery are *Willen* which Böhme calls *Natura* and *A und O, Anfang und Ende* 'nature, a and o, beginning and end' (*Dreyfach* ii, 10). *Natura*, Böhme warns, cannot be equated with God, but with the eternal potential for manifested nature *to* exist. Transitoriness (*A und O*) lends the temporary guise of existence to *Natura*

(*Dreyfach* ii, 10). The astringent matrix is still present:

> Dann in der herben Matrix, als im Fiat, wird alles gefasset, und der Geist des Worts formts in dem Centro derselben Essentz in welcher sich der Vater beweget, und durchs Wort spricht, also dass es im Wesen ist und bleibet. Dann was aus dem Ewigen formiret wird, das ist Geist und ist ewig, als die Engel und die Seelen der Menschen (*Dreyfach* ii, 64).

Angels and the souls of men, while residing in the realms of spirit, are not completely out of man's reach. Böhme hints that two types of words exist, two languages. Angelic words cannot reduce to human language. The reduction leaves nothing, since spirit does not reduce to matter, but willfully descends into it. All attempts at angelic phonation fail, producing nothing more than human language: "dann wir können nicht englische Worte führen: und ob wir die führeten, so erscheints doch in dieser Welt alles creatürlich, darzu vor dem irdischen Gemüthe irdisch" (*Dreyfach* ii, 66). Böhme reminds the reader that man originates in the unity of God, the *Gantze*, even though frozen within multiplicity, nothing more than a *Particular* (*Dreyfach* ii, 66) capable at best of piecemeal linear communication: "Das soll der Leser betrachten" (*Dreyfach* ii, 66).

Böhme brings the Father closer to manifestation through positing into the features of the Word, astral configurational patterns, prototypes for the seven qualities. The Word also contains the possibilities of creating a *Bild* 'picture, image' much in the same way that people are endowed with the ability to visually interiorize. Their interiorizations, while not real in the sense of manifestation within matter, represent potential configurations, astral ideas, or a *Bild*. Closely related to *Bild* is *Imagination* (*Dreyfach* iii, 49) which is prerequisite for man's salvation from matter. Through exercising this power, Böhme sees man reentering the Word, here identified as Christ:

The Code Expands

> GOtt der Vater hat uns in Christo wieder=erboren, dass wir sollen mit unser Imagination wieder ins Wort, als in seines Licht=flammenden Hertzens Centrum, eingehen, dass der H. Geist wieder aus uns ausginge, mit Kräften, Wundern und Thaten wie bey Christi Aposteln zu sehen (*Dreyfach* iii, 48).

The Son/Christ/Word, spoken out of the depths of the Father Speaker, forms the basis for the question "into what essence is this word spoken?" (*Dreyfach* v, 40). Böhme resorts to past statements to answer this: once spoken out, the Word becomes the *Ausgesprochene* and is an image of the action of the Trinity (*Dreyfach* v, 41).

Once in manifestation, Böhme asks a question concerning the nature of that which has arisen: "Was ist GOttes schaffen gewesen?" (*Dreyfach* v, 85). Böhme selects the preterite *schuf*, following its manipulations in the mouth, reminding the reader that the physiological mechanism underlying words is a key to a deeper understanding of language:

> Wann du dis begreiffest, da verstehest du alles in seinem Namen, warum ein iedes Ding also heisset (aber den Begriff der drey Principien must du haben zur Natur=Sprache) dann ihrer sind drey die das Wort bilden, als Seele, Geist und Leib (*Dreyfach* v, 85).

Not only *schuf* but all words of all languages are doorways to spiritual contemplation. Transcendence occurs "mit allen Worten und Namen der Völcker Sprachen, ein iedes in seinem Verstande" (*Dreyfach* v, 87).

Phur (*Dreyfach* ii, 21, 40, 41), *Mercurius* (*Dreyfach* ii, 42),[15] *Barmhertzigkeit* (*Dreyfach* iii, 23), *Immanuel* (*Dreyfach* iii, 50) and *Meer* (*Dreyfach* ix, 50) overburden much of the third work with repetitive linguistic analyses encountered in the earlier writings. Böhme nonetheless breaks new ground, and through a reevaluation of the word *schuf* draws the reader closer to his methodology.

Schuf 'created' seems to have fallen from the workbench during 1612, is ignored in the *Drey Principien*, yet comes to light again in *Vom Dreyfachen Leben*. Böhme utilizes it speaking directly to man's reason:

> So saget die Vernunft: Was ist GOttes Schaffen gewesen? Das Wort Schuf hats in seinem eigenen Verstande nach der Natur=Sprache; so du dieselbe Sprache verstehen wilt, so mercke im Sinne, wie sich ein iedes Wort vom Hertzen im Mund fasset, was der Mund und die Zunge damit thut, ehe es der Geist wegstösset (*Dreyfach* v, 85).

Passive resignation to untested principles leads the seeker further into delusion. Böhme strongly advocates physically creating, then paying attention to vocalized words. In this way, more than the few Böhmian words in his writings will be meaningful. The student will have a tool:

> Siehe, mercke, ob es war sey, was ich dir von der Natur= Sprache sage; versuche es und dencke ihm nach, nicht allein mit diesem Worte Schuf, sondern mit allen Worten und Namen aller Völcker Sprachen, ein iedes in seinem Verstande (*Dreyfach* v, 87).

Underlying this forceful and direct challenge is the belief that "das Innere spricht aus das Äussere" (*Dreyfach* v, 90). Conceptually clear, Böhme feels that the process may be detrimental to man, his thirst for knowledge standing in the way of his transcendence:

> Es ist dem Menschen wol nicht gut, dass er es wissen muss: weil er aber ist aus dem Innern ins Äussere gangen, und stehet nun im Suchen, so muss er wieder ins Innere

eingehen, alda in diesem Geheimniss schauet er die Geheimnisse der Schöpfung (*Dreyfach* v, 87).

In *schuf*, the dental closure *sch* followed by the labial vocalic opening *u* allows the *Druck vom Hertzen* to expand outward, while the labiodental closure *f* terminates the word (*Dreyfach* v, 88). Böhme concentrates on dorsal height; at word onset, he notices the high dorsal position, and at word termination, the low. The lowness occurs after the final labiodental *f* where "die Zunge verkreucht sich und schmeuget sich im hintern Gaumen" (*Dreyfach* v, 88). Since the back vowel *u* precedes the final *f*, Böhme understands that the low dorsal position established by the vowel carries forward to the obstruent. In the *Aurora*, the astringent uvular *r* does the same thing: it "schmäuget sich im untern Gaumen, und fleucht sich als vor einem Feinde" (*Aurora* xviii, 71). Böhme is not absentmindedly reiterating linguistic terminology, nor is he equating the uvular *r* with the partially astringent *f*. Instead he is concerned with examining the commonality of both sounds:

> Es [the *f*] weckt die herbe Mutter in der strengen Macht nicht auf, dass sich kein Feuer entzündet. Das R ist der Character des Feuer=Quells, dann ein ieder Buchstabe ist ein Geist... noch hat ein ieder Buchstabe einen Urstand am Centro: aber es ist wunderlich, und wird doch im Sinn ergriffen, so das Licht im Centro scheinend ist (*Dreyfach* v, 88).

Böhme directs the threefold compass of man's *Wesen*—his *Seele* 'soul' (first principle), *Geist* 'spirit' (second principle) and *Leib* 'body' (third principle)—toward the spiritual nucleus sounds of language. He notes that the body must be aware of the first two principles (soul and spirit) in order for language to have depth. This realization strengthens the acoustical vibrations as they leave the mouth, molding them into perfect vehicles of expression.

He asks the reader to equate every word with its inner content:

> Also verstehet der Sinn das Wort, und die Formung des Worts. Mercke: Wann der dreyfache Geist des Menschen spricht Schuf, so mercket der Sinn auf die Form des Worts (*Dreyfach* v, 96).

Content originates in the domain of *Geist*; form and structure, in the domain of *Leib*. *Geist,* a common denominator in all words, never surfaces directly within the outer shell of the word as it is expressed (*ausgedrückt*) from the heart; rather it controls and manipulates the articulators, its hands. Together with the lips, tongue, and teeth, the gums and the breath stream articulate shape around the *Geist*. Embedded within the *Sinn* 'sense' > *Wort* > *Formung des Worts* 'structure of the word' Böhme notices that the sibilants (the *sch*) are associated with the fire image posited within a first-layer understanding of Lucifer. They pave the way for Lucifer to exist within a domain. Since he has to exist somewhere, Böhme explains him as:

> In GOtt ist die Welt gewesen vor der Zeit, aber ohne Wesen. Nun hat Lucifer, der Gross=Fürst ausm Centro der Natur den Grimm und das Feuer erweckt und entzündet, welcher in der Ewigkeit nie erkant ward: dann er wolte in Feuers=Macht über GOtt herrschen, darum ward der Feuer=Quell seine Wohnung (*Dreyfach* v, 98).

Concurrent with Lucifer's megalomaniac desires, the world of matter, under the auspices of astringent compaction, takes shape:

> Es ist alles materialisch worden; was vor den Zeiten in der Natur der finstern grimmigen Wesenheit nur ein Gestiebe war, das ward alles in dem Anziehen grob und derb und harte: und das wolte GOtt also particular vor der Majestät (auf creatürlich also geredt) nicht haben (*Dreyfach* v, 100).

The Code Expands

Lucifer's attraction to the sibilant hissing and the magnitude of the force of *Anziehen* 'centripetality' lead Böhme through a hasty analysis of the terminal syllable *-uf*. He visualizes flames leaping from the mouth as the word is articulated:

> Dann die Lippen thun sich auf, und der Obergaumen mit den Zähnen fasset sich mit der untern Lippe, und zischet der Geist durch die Zähne; das ist also: wie sich die Lippen, als der äussere Umfang, aufthun, also hat sich aufgethan die Matrix der Gebärerin, verstehe in der Entzündung: Das Zischen ist das Feuer, und aus dem Feuer die Luft, als ein Geist der Matrix, welcher ietzt erwecket, und zuvor im Centro nicht erkant ward, sondern alleine in der Weisheit vor der Dreyzahl (*Dreyfach* v, 102).

Since it is impossible to omit words containing the *sch* and the *f* sounds, Böhme devises a countermeasure which he calls *Imagination*. Every speaker of every language calls forth mental images before the mind's eye. These mental images, under the control of man as matter, can be directed toward a goal, or simply allowed to evaporate as nonproductive daydreams. Böhme chooses the former. By casting mental images, *Imaginationen*, into the linear sequence of words (into the sounds as they are being articulated), the speaker protects the words from Luciferian intrusion, in effect, creating a wall of thought which Lucifer cannot penetrate. An awareness of matrices, for example, transforms the common word *Himmel* into a powerful image of a blocking wall, a barrier elicted by the articulatory features of the *m*. By introducing this image into the linear phonetic sequence, the first-layer value of the word is greatly altered. Knowledge of *Imagination* coupled with the awareness of how to redirect it into word shells elevates the student of letters to a disciple of truth. Böhme feels that *Imagination* and the three principles unite common people with the apostles: higher knowledge is impossible without this awareness. He says:

> GOtt der Vater hat uns in Christo wieder=erboren, dass wir sollen mit unser Imagination wieder ins Wort, als in seines Licht=flammenden Hertzens Centrum eingehen, dass der H. Geist wieder aus uns ausginge, mit Kräften, Wundern und Thaten wieder bey Christi Aposteln zu sehen (*Dreyfach* iii, 49).

Undisciplined, unbridled, self-constructed and justified imagination leads nowhere. *Geist* must be within the seeker before the letters of the scriptures speak. Böhme advocates *Imagination* working closely with a sense of inner *Geist* as a methodology whereby the student can extract the crucial root sounds from words in order to reconstruct the passage through the Word back to divine union. The *Buchstabengelehrte* are hopelessly lost:

> Wir haben GOttes Willen in der H. Schrift klar, aber ohne GOttes Geist haben wir eine Hülse und ein todtes Wort; GOttes Geist erwecket erst das lebendige Wort in uns, dass wir den Buchstaben und das aufgeschriebene Wort verstehen. Das weiset sich gnug aus, dass die Kunst=Gelehrte nur Buchstaben=Gelehrte, und nicht von GOtt Gelehrte sind, sonst zancketen sie nicht um Christi Ehre und Lehre, und würden sonst nicht also um den Kelch Christi tantzen (*Dreyfach* xvi, 23).

A refinement of the notion of *Imagination* leads Böhme directly into borrowing the shell *Signatur* 'signature' to express the next phase of his linguistic anchor.

CHAPTER III

THE PLATEAU: *DE SIGNATURA RERUM ODER VON DER GEBURT UND BEZEICHNUNG ALLER WESEN* (1622) AND *VON DER WAHREN GELASSENHEIT* (1622)

As seen, Böhme's mystically arranged world is a world through which the invisible actively expresses itself to the visible through, at best, an indistinctly understood network of self-contained and semantically interrelated feature specifications. The question as to whether Böhme actually perceives the world within the framework of a mystical school, a theological movement, or even the widely spread Paracelsian underground conventicles, must for the moment be set aside. Speculation within the Böhmian world, a source of information continually evolving with respect to itself, reveals the beginning reliance on the term *Signatur*, a term which liberates Böhme from the astringent grasp of the obstruents, paving the way for vocalic acceptability.

When the reader encounters the term *Signatur* in *De Signatura Rerum oder von der Geburt und Bezeichnung aller Wesen* (1622), Böhme is well aware that a definition of the term must be forthcoming. From the title alone, the reader wonders if Böhme is going to borrow the acoustical framework of the non-Germanic *Signatur* to somehow express the birth and designation of all *Wesen*. Will the word become another *Hülse* 'shell' into which he posits new and unusual significations? How can the code, which has reached the peak of communicative capacity, express more with the same words?

Uninterested in repeating himself (at this point!), Böhme concentrates, instead, on incorporating the word *Signatur* into the linguistic argument. He reveals much important information in the first lines of this work:

> Alles was von GOtt geredet, geschrieben oder gelehret wird, ohne die Erkentniss der Signatur, das ist stumm und ohne Verstand, denn es kommt nur aus einem historischen Wahn, von einem andern Mund, und daran der Geist ohne Erkentniss stumm ist: So ihm aber der Geist die Signatur eröffnet, so verstehet er des andern Mund, und ferner wie sich der Geist aus der Essentz durchs Principium im Hall der Stimme hat offenbaret (*De Signatura Rerum* i, 1).

The unseen *Geist*, moving through the invisible potentials within the essences, makes itself visual within the realm of the third principle (matter). Böhme teases the reader by purposefully breaking off the sentence "So ihm der Geist die Signatur eröffnet . . . (*De Signatura Rerum* i, 1). What then? A comment to the close followers and intimate friends reveals self-imposed injunctions placed over the arcanum: *verstehet er des andern Mund* 'understand the other language'. In order to look into the other *Mund* 'mouth', the source of articulatory possibility, Böhme returns the reader to the concept of resonance, *Hall*, which takes on the feature of +*Stimme* 'voice'. *Hall* becomes language: "dann mit dem Hall oder Sprache zeichnet sich die Gestalt in eines andern Gestaltniss ein" (*DSR* i, 4). In the above, the *Gestalt* 'form' is the actively manipulating subject. Böhme allows this word to employ the agent *Hall* (+voice, +language) as a catalyst in his self-conversion into *Gestaltniss* 'form'. *Gestalt>Gestaltniss*, the active subject adding the dessonential *-niss* signals that manifestation exists and that ideational forms are evolving into physical structures. The sibilant *s*, the fiery signal on the outer side of the teeth, accompanies the *Gestalt* every time it expands into another self. Only the outer vehicle of expression changes; the inner message is always the same. Language functions in the same manner. A person wishing to communicate his intent to another person extends the idea from within himself toward the other person. The idea is originally subtle, nonmatter, and incapable of structurally containing linguistic (here, vibrational) content. These mental features create around themselves a *Gestaltniss*, a vehicular form which appeals to the demands of the materially oriented senses. The recipient of the *Gestaltniss* plunges through the externality of the word, returning to the ideational origin of the word shell. The invisible, through the garb of visibility, returns to itself, liberating its producer (articulator), man, from astringent bondage. Resonance (here the *-ss*) is the linguistic matrix. Astringency predominates within the phonetic range of obstruent resonants, forming a language, which although subtly refined by mental interactions, nonetheless draws its communicative strength, its veracity, from the eternally reverberating and gently fluctuating natural sound. It is here that *Geist* meets itself:

> Ein gleicher Klang fänget und beweget den andern, und im Hall zeichnet der Geist seine eigene Gestaltniss welche er in der Essentz geschöpfet hat, und hat sie im Principio zur Form gebracht (*DSR* i, 4).

As strings tuned the same will vibrate together if only one string is plucked, *Geist* existing in perfect harmony with *Hall* will descend into language under optimal conditions: knowledge of the *Signatur*. *Hall* (outbreath of vocalic H + vowel + lateral *l*) is the first alignment of spirit with matter. Böhme selects *Hall*, a word with low astringency and high nonobstruency, to indicate the universal validity of *Signatur*, a principle easily available to all who will contemplate language. He says:

> Eins, dass man im Worte verstehen kann, worinnen sich der Geist geschöpfet hat, im Bösem oder Gutem; und mit derselben Bezeichnung gehet er in eines andern Menschen Gestaltniss und wecket in einem andern auch eine solche Forme in der Signatur auf, dass also bey der Gestaltniss in einer Form miteinander inqualiren, alsdann ists Ein Begriff, ein Wille und Ein Geist auch ein Verstand (*DSR* i, 4).

Through the manipulative aspect of the signature (a point which Böhme does not discuss in public), dissimilar people may obtain direct access to the one concept, one will, the one spirit, and the one understanding behind all multiplicity. Never believing that people are nothing more than varying, fluctuating arrangements of the spirit becoming matter through the vehicle of matrices and the qualities, Böhme exhorts all readers to search for the signatures, the *Hülse* of their divinity:

> Und dann zum andern verstehen wir, dass die Signatur oder Gestaltniss kein Geist ist, sondern der Behalter oder Kasten des Geistes, darinnen er lieget (*DSR* i, 5).

Böhme's universe is filled with creations alive with power emanating from and coursing throughout their manifested shells. Nature, a symphony of interrelated vibratory structures, hides from the casual observer, unless, like Böhme, the observer forces nature to resound according to its innate laws. Through aware manipulations of these laws, the signatures, man can control more of the process of becoming, more of his own involvement with a matter randomly interpreted as out of control. Through signatures man can shape and direct nature. The *Klang* (as an expression of *Hall* in matter), the sounds of the world (physical and astral), is the signature of nature, the *Natur-Sprache*:

> Dann die Signatur stehet in der Essentz, und ist gleichwie eine Laute die da stille stehet, die ist ja stumm und unverstanden: so man aber darauf schläget so verstehet man die Gestaltniss, in was Form und Zubereitung sie steht, und nach welcher Stimme sie gezogen ist: Auch ist die Bezeichnung der Natur in ihrer Gestaltniss ein stumm Wesen, sie ist wie ein zugericht Lauten=Spiel, auf welchem der Willen Geist schläget; welche Seiten er trifft, die klinget nach ihrer Eigenschaft (*DSR* i, 5).

Man, the most integral part of the speaking cosmos, possesses a series of understandable, legible signatures, structures embedded within the texture of his external physiology. Signatures attract continuing spiritual involvement with matter as well as serve as maps back to the divine source. Signatures exist not only on man's face (metoscopy), head (physiognomy) and hands (chiromancy), but most importantly in his *Gemüt*. As seen earlier, this ordering principle of premanifested forces evolves into the vehicle of the senses. Man's physical actions group together into natural fields of similar effect on the manifested plane, expressing through action (verbally) the energetic state of the *Signatur*. The semantic field of action and effect is unified under the aegis of a signature, the variant grades of which reveal themselves through the modifications found within *Gemüt*. These differing aspects of *Gemüt* and their realizations within manifestation are accessible realities for the master of the inward journey, the paragon man-saint. Böhme sees all humanity in need of the "künstliche Meister der sein Instrument schlagen kann, das ist der rechte Geist, der hohe Macher der Ewigkeit" (*DSR* i, 6). Man must not only be an open, willing conduit, he must find someone to actively play upon his passive instrument. This relationship occurs when the inner mechanism of realization is brought to life by the *Meister* or through close study and practical application of his writings. Regardless of the internal or external methodology, should a state of deep internalization occur (should man be able to penetrate the astringent layer of personality back to the center of *Gemüt*), then all that remains is to understand the mechanics of reintegration of consciousness back into matter, back into astringent form. Böhme expresses this type of projection transcendence within the linguistic structure of speech as a contemplative object:

> So aber derselbe im Menschen erwecket wird, dass er im Centro des Gemüthes räge wird, so schläget er das Instrument der menschlichen Gestaltniss: Alsdann so gehet die Gestaltniss mit dem Hall im Wort vom Munde

aus; Wie sein Instrument in der Zeit seiner Menschwerdung gezogen ist also lautet es, und also ist seine Erkentniss: Das Innere offenbaret sich im Halle des Wortes, dann das ist des Gemüthes natürliche Erkentniss seiner selbst (*DSR* i, 6).

Man is not cosmically protected, that is to say, invulnerable, while undergoing the contemplations of language. *Gegenhall* enters the process. Böhme derives this word from the first and third layers of the code: *gegen* 'toward' (layer 1) and *Hall* 'resonance' (layer 3): resonance without *Klang* (material vibration). *Gegenhall* is a powerful force:

... mancher Mensch auch manches Thier, ob es sehr bös oder gut geneigt ist, doch von einem Gegenhall zum Bösen oder Guten beweget wird, und oft seine ingeborne Gestaltniss sinken läst wann ihm der Gegenhall auf seiner verborgenen Lauten oder Gestaltniss schläget (*DSR* i, 9).

Gegenhall is the reverberation of ideational potential in (rather than toward) the physical matter of language. It is the idea within the word reuniting with its point of departure, *Geist*. The linguistic chain is endless: spirit>matter (word)>spirit (effect of the word as it is cognized, apprehended and recognized)>matter (physical communication elicited by the recipient as a reaction to the word). Animals, Böhme notes, react to the same linguistic stimuli emanating from the Word (i.e. the desire to manifest within *Begreiffligkeit*), although their reaction is not one of understanding (*Verstand*) but of cruder categories of semanticity. With a more unrefined operative semantic system, the animal is easily swayed by the basic articulatory message within the sounds of the language used. Whereas tone and pitch suprasegmentally mark subtle semantic distinction for humans, for animals they are the entire semantic system through which man's intent is clarified within their *Gemüte*. Pitch and tone communicate to the animal, the shape of the *Hülse* being only a vibratory channel. Böhme notices that animals are ruled by basic units of behavior:

> Auch so ein Thier, so das böse ist, und ist aber mit Gewalt gebändiget, und zu anderer Eigenschaft gezogen worden, läst seine erste instehende Gestalt nicht leichtlich mercken, dieselbe werde dann erräget, so gehet sie vor allen andern Gestalten hervor (*DSR* i, 13).

Gegenhall, identical with, yet removed from, *Geist*, is powerful enough to cause a *Gestaltniss* to come into being. With this *Gestaltniss* (articulated phonological shell), the *Gemüt* may direct ideational plans of misery, anger, wrath and hopelessness through the linguistic matrix into matter. The problem at this point is how to separate the *Gegenhall*>*Gestaltniss* which reflect positivity from those which are channels for negative *Gemüt*. Böhme avoids the issue, demanding comprehension of *Signatur*, the linguistic code, and the points of articulation as prerequisites to deeper contemplations.

That good is adversely modified by evil, and that the pious become corrupt through association with evil, are Aurorean notions still in Böhme's mind:

> ... man siehet dass ein böser Mensch doch von einem guten zur Reue seiner Bosheit beweget wird, wann ihme der Fromme mit seinem liebreichen Geiste sein verborgen Instrument schläget: Desgleichen geschieht es auch mit den Frommen; so ihn der Böse mit dem Geist seines Grimmes sein verborgen Instrument schläget, so wird im Frommen auch die Zorn-Gestaltniss erwecket und ist je eines wieder das ander gesetzet, dass eines des andern Artzt sein soll (*DSR* i, 9).

The game of relativity begins. Man, animals, and plants react

(*DSR* i, 12-14) within the restrictions of their own *Gemüt* to the loudest surge of the Word through them. The similarities, or chord, control the possibilities within a general behavioremic class of signals. Böhme needs more time to describe in detail the linguistic signals he finds overtly operative within similar expressions of anger/fear and pleasure/security, signals which the semanticized phonology can express in combination. What is important at this point is that "ein iedes Ding hat seinen Mund zur Offenbarung" (*DSR* i, 16).

The semantic nucleus is still important since "ein iedes Ding (redet) aus seiner Eigenschaft, worzu es gut und nütz sey, dann ein iedes Ding offenbaret seine Mutter, die die Essentz und den Willen zur Gestaltniss also gibt" (*DSR* i, 17). What is it that Böhme hears? Are they sounds or visual images called forth from the linguistic code? Does nature speak randomly and in an uncontrolled, intermingled and semantically undefined network of vibrations? Can nature reduce itself—even for a moment—into the paradigmatic extent of the Böhmian code? Böhme gives the reader a clue to the answer in his reexamination of the word *Sulphur*:

> Sul ist im ersten Principio der freye Wille oder die Lust in dem Nichts zu Etwas, es ist in der Freyheit ausser der Natur; phur ist die Begierde der freyen Lust und machet in sich dem phur als in der Begierde ein Wesen; und dasselbe Wesen ist strenge wegen des Anziehens, und führet sich in drey Gestälte ein ... und fort in die vierte Gestalt, als ans Feuer: Im phur wird der ewigen und auch der äussern Natur Urstand verstanden, dann die Härtigkeit ist eine Mutter der Schärfe aller Wesen und ein Behalter alles Wesens; aus dem Sul, aus der Freyheit Lust, wird die finstere Angst ein scheinend Licht, und im dritten Principio, als im äussern Reich, ist das Sul das Oele der Natur, darinnen das Leben brennet und alles wächset (*DSR* ii, 12).

The Plateau   85

The etymological path is complicated: the first syllable *sul-* (S + vowel + L) aligns the divine will towards manifestation, in effect designating that the *Nichts* shall become an *Etwas*. The phonology, though, tells another story. Böhme notes that *sul-* is *in der Freyheit ausser der Natur* 'free outside of nature', a condition which would be adumbrated by the strong astringency within the first principle into which it is posited. Reducing the *sul-* to its root **sl* (s + [V] + l) and generating *Seele* explains the correlation of the first syllable *sul-* with two closed systems of expression. The soul, enjoying its absence of matter, is free beyond nature. Böhme notes also that since matter cannot exist without light, the first syllable *sul-* generates the light which enables the astringency of *-phur* to appear: the *Sul* is the *Oele der Natur* 'oil of nature' feeding the *phur*. That *Sul-* is closer to *Seele* than to *Oel* appears to be the main concern with the etymology: *sul-* < **sl* not from **l* (Oel), although the secondary connection is with the root **l*, thereby justifying the selection of *Hülse* 'shells'.

Böhme bifurcates the semantic field within the syllable *-phur*, creating a centripetal/centrifugal distinction within all matter. Phonologically analyzed, Böhme's consistency is predictable: the initial *-ph* (f) is −astringent, since in *schuf* (*Dreyfach* v, 88) it does not awaken the astringent mother of power. The final *r* is pure astringent potential. Böhme expands the issue by allowing each segment to develop in its own direction, owing no allegiance to the point of its origin *-phur*, in a larger sense *sulphur*:

> ... es ist Ein Wort, und ist auch im Urstand Ein Wesen, und scheidet sich aber selber in zwo Eigenschaften, als in Freud und Leid, in Licht und Finsterniss, dann es macht zwo Welten, als eine finstere Feuer=Welt in der Strengheit, und eine lichte Feuer=Welt in der Lust der Freyheit, dann die Lust der Freyheit ist die einige Ursache, dass das Feuer scheinet, dann das urständliche Feuer ist finster und schwartz, dann im Feuer=

> Schein wird im Urstand die GOttheit verstanden, und im Finstern als in der Angst=Qual, wird der Urstand der Natur verstanden (*DSR* ii, 13).

The split culminates with the creation of two worlds "eine finstere Feuer=Welt und eine lichte Feuer=Welt" (*DSR* ii, 13), both riddled with the fire. Böhme mentions the world of *Strengheit* 'severity' as the first world, that of *Freyheit* 'freedom', the second. This arrangement is the mirror opposite of the semantic direction of the entire word: *sul-* (freedom from manifestation) + *-phur* (astringent bondage), but a severity which begins with the astringent *r* and works back to the less obstruent, hence free, *f* (ph-). This freedom, though, is delusion within multiplicity, reflecting a lack of awareness as to its material bondage.

Böhme tirelessly reiterates the notion that the inner contains the outer outside of itself as a mirror (*DSR* ix, 3). Since *Geist* controls *Begreiffligkeit*, the root or path back can be extracted from information gleaned from *das Äussere* 'the outer, the external':

> Also hat ein iedes Ding, das aus dem Innern ist geboren worden, seine Signatur. Die oberste Gestaltniss, so im Geiste des Wirckens in der Kraft die oberste ist, die bezeichnet das Corpus am meisten, dieser hangen die anderen Gestaltnissen an, wie man das an allen lebendigen Creaturen an Gestalt des Leibes, an Sitten und Gebärden siehet. (*DSR* ix, 4).

Böhme carefully distinguishes between undefined externality and that aspect of manifestation "Die oberste Gestaltniss" (the prime material form), which characterizes a spiritual genesis underlying existence. From this category (*Die oberste Gestaltniss*) Böhme employs a domino effect to describe the evolution of physical shapes, customs, gestures and language. He continues:

> ... am Halle, Stimmen und Sprachen, sowol an Bäu-

men, Kräutern Steinen und Metallen; alles was das Ringen in der Kraft des Geistes ist, so stehet auch die Figur des Leibes dar und also ist auch sein Wille (*DSR* ix, 4).

The physicality of form does not result from within the center of the seven manifested qualities, far removed from the interactions within a moving, created world, but rather from the combinatory arrangements of the manifested qualities within the world. Once spirit becomes matter, it loses an awareness of itself as spirit, that it was once "gleich wie GOtt selber in seiner innersten Geburt" (*Aurora* xviii, 20). Only now and then does the physical vehicle, the *thirischer Leib* 'animal body' catch a vague reflection of this truth "gleich als wenn es wetterleuchtet" (*Aurora* xix, 18). Armed with the knowledge of signatures, Böhme's later image of man involves probing behind the astral blueprint which directs physical formation. He reasons that all forms must possess one highlight, one characteristic signature which differentiates it from all others. There are problems, since nature is not always legible:

Denn die Natur lässet nicht alle Stunden mit sich gauckeln, wie die Geister wollen; sondern es muss alles nach dem Geiste geschehen, welcher dazumalen Primus ist (*Aurora* xvi, 52).

How does this insight materialize as the notion of a *Signatur*? The qualities are signatures.

Fat creatures are generally jollier than thin ones, Böhme reasons, since the sweet quality predominates within them. Qualifying with the outward centrifugality of bitterness, sweetness is able to extricate itself from the vicious in/out cycle, surfacing more abundantly within the area of fat creatures. He warns, though, that excessive fatness results in excessive sweetness, a condition leading to too much light, which through its alliance with

Verstand creates melancholy. Within the fatty condition there is too much water, which leads to disease and pestilence. Lean creatures, on the other hand, are generally unhappy, for their bodies are not under the control of sweetness. Their only hope is to somehow generate inner heat, which through its alliance with light will generate a body capable of assuming the role of the pious. They come into being "mit ihrem Gegensatz" (*Aurora* xv, 23), as a polar antidote to the forces of negativity. Without these saints, sages, prophets and seers, the world would consume itself in its primary astringent urge. Bodies created under the predominance of love (*Aurora* xv, 19), even though oppressed by the kindled wrath fire, have love as their consolation and "Trost und starcker Helm wieder die Grimmigkeit und das angezündete Feuer" (*Aurora* xv, 21).

Language, though, triumphs over physiology, offering man a controllable corpus of potentially transcendent signals, seen above as signatures. Now, the *sprechendes Wort* 'speaking word' is pre-manifested (astral) arrangement and the inner aspect of the *ausgesprochenes Wort* 'articulated word' (*DSR* ix, 22, 23; x, 17). Böhme values the articulated word as highly as his knowledge of its signature (the inner speaking word):

> Das Ausgesprochene ist ein Model des Sprechenden, und hat wieder das Sprechen in sich; dasselbe Sprechen ist ein Same zu einer andern Bildniss nach der ersten: dann beyde wircken, als das Sprechende und das Ausgesprochene (*DSR* xiii, 2).

Time juxtaposes alongside of eternity as Böhme probes deeper:

> Das Sprechende in sich selber als in der Ewigkeit, und das Ausgesprochene auch in sich selber, als in der Zeit: das Sprechende ist der Meister und das Ausgesprochene ist der Werckzeug (*DSR* xiii, 3).

The unity of the *Sprechende*, the master controlling his apprentices, splinters into distinct units as it passes through the matrix of matter:

> Das Sprechende macht die Natur der Ewigkeit und das Ausgesprochene macht die Natur der Zeit, ein iedes macht in seiner Fassung zwo Eigenschaften, als Licht und Finsterniss; darinnen stehet das Element aller Wesen, welches sich in dem Ausgesprochenem in vier Elementa scheidet, aber im Sprechendem nur Eines ist (*DSR* xiii, 3).

Into the articulated, the *Sprechende* posits the feature of reason, assuring that once material individuation occurs, complete astringent obfuscation will not take place. The articulated side of the matrix further subdivides into seven characteristic unities (*Qualitäten*)(*DSR* xiii, 21) which Böhme revives from the *Aurora*, calling them *Gestirne* 'constellations'. As the pinpoint specks of light on a dark night reveal structural patterns to the observant sky watcher, all of nature reveals pinpoints of semantic interrelationship, which when brought together and analyzed as a corpus, form recurring patterns. Böhme calls the first constellar arrangement of spirit *Chaos*, not since everything is helplessly misaligned and intermingled, but precisely since the pattern within the confusion is difficult to discern. *Chaos* is where "darinnen alles lieget, aber verborgen ... aber geistlich" (*DSR* xiii, 22). With the aid of the *Siebenfache Rad* 'sevenfold wheel', the positivity of *Vernunft* reveals the original state of chaos: spirit. By calling the elements into interaction, Böhme sees God using them to form containers, *Wesen*, for the rationally ordered aspect of chaos. This forms "das elementische ... und ist ein sichtbarer greifflicher Leib" (*DSR* xiii, 22). Chaos becomes the articulated:

> Der erste Leib, als das Chaos, oder erste Gestirne, welches geistlich ist, das ist das ausgesprochene Wort aus

der ewigen Fassung, dasselbe hat wiederum sein Sprechen in sich (*DSR* xiii, 23).

In order to describe the internalization process necessary for transcendence, Böhme presses into service the terms *Gelassenheit* 'letting things go, resignation' and *Selbheit* 'selfness, egocentricity'. It is the addition of *Gelassenheit* (centrifugality) and *Selbheit* (centripetality) to the human *Wesen* that lends man his superiority over the animals:

> Alles eigenes Suchen und Forschen in der Selbheit ist ein vergeben Ding; Der eigene Wille ergreift nichts von GOtt, dann er ist nicht in GOtt, sondern ausser GOtt in seiner Selbheit, aber der gelassene Wille ergreifts, dann nicht er thuts, sondern der Geist in dem er stille stehet, dessen Werckzeug er ist, der offenbaret sich in Göttlichem Halle in ihm, so viel Er will (*DSR* xv, 22).

Selbheit, the awareness of the self as an object, exists outside of God in vain. Prerequisite to the revelation of *Geist* within is "stille stehen," a contemplative silence calling for peace and nonmotion within. This stillness anticipates the origin of *Selbheit*, knowledge without which man is hopelessly lost within the unpolished world of matter. Man egocentrically remains under layers of various astringent interqualifications, unable to recognize the *Signatur*, the abbreviation of truth:

> Und ob er in der Selbheit durch Forschen oder Lernen viel begreiffen mag, welches nicht ohne ist, so ist aber doch sein Begriff nur aussen im ausgesprochenen Wort, als in einer Form des Buchstabens, und verstehet nichts von der Form des ausgesprochenen Worts, wie das in seinem Grunde stehet, dann er ist nur in der Form von aussen geboren, und nicht in der Kraft der Allgebärerin welcher Grund weder Anfang, Infassung noch Ende hat (*DSR* xv, 23).

The Plateau 91

Unimpressed with realizations obtained from research and scholarship (*Buchstaben*), Böhme's concept of comprehension *Begriff/ begreiffen* (*DSR* xv, 23) is bound within matter: grabbing (*greiffen*) demands corporeality. He suspends a detailed discussion of the steps between *Selbheit* (the subject as object) and *Gelassenheit* (the reabsorption of the object as acting subject back into the original generative subject), concluding the *De Signatura Rerum* with optimistic counsel:

> Die Stimme GOttes führet ihre Freude durch die Creatur, als durch ein Instrument, immer und ewig aus: Die Creatur ist die Offenbarung der Stimme GOttes; was GOtt in der ewigen Gebärung seines ewigen Worts, aus dem grossen Mysterio des Vaters Eigenschaft ist, das ist die Creatur in einem Bilde, als ein Freuden=Spiel, damit der ewige Geist spielet (*DSR* xvi, 17).

It is now late winter (February 1622), and Böhme pauses until the arrival of spring before contemplating another massive writing project.

Böhme postpones the linguistic coup de théâtre until early fall, concentrating instead on clarifying *Selbheit* and *Gelassenheit* to a reading audience pressing him for further information concerning "becoming still within." The tract, *Von der wahren Gelassenheit, Wie der Mensch mit seinem eigenen Willen in seiner Selbheit müste täglich sterben, und wie er seine Begierde in GOtt einführen, was er von GOtt bitten soll, und wie er aus dem Sterben des sündlichen Menschen mit einem neuen Gemüthe und Willen, in GOtt ausgrünen soll* (1622), employs Adam and Lucifer as examples of "was die Selbheit thut, wenn sie das äussere Licht zum Eigenthum bekommt" (*Gelassenheit* i, 1).

Böhme shows their attempts to transcend physical limitation through the powers of *Imagination*. This, though, is delusion, since they aim for the wrong *Centrum*: Lucifer desires the "Feuers=Mutter" while Adam searches for "die Mutter daraus Böse und

Gut quillet" (*Gelassenheit* i, 4). Neither succeeds since a divinely appointed illumination must aid *Selbheit*, through the vehicle of reason (*Vernunft*), back to the source of all existence. Böhme describes the functionality of this knowledge:

> Aber höre wie du es brauchen solst: Das Licht GOttes eröffnet sich zum ersten in der Seelen, es scheinet aus, wie ein Licht aus einer Kertzen, und zündet zur Hand das äussere Licht der Vernunft an, nicht dass es sich der Vernunft, als dem äusseren Menschen gantz einergebe in sein Regiment: Nein, der äussere Mensch besiehet sich in dem durchdringenden Scheine als wie ein Bild vor einem Spiegel, er lernet sich alsbald in der Selbheit kennen, welches an ihme selber gut und nützlich ist (*Gelassenheit* i, 21).

Divinity, reflected through (deflected around) matter, and apprehended by the faculty of human reason, is the positive, hopeful method whereby the process of *Selbheit* realizing itself as subject having become object can occur. There is a problem, though, when the faculty of reason looks into the external arrangements within matter, rather than toward the internal nondifferentiated and semantically complete divine light. Rather than waste precious time delving into molecular arrangements and rearrangements, charting the motion of inanimate bodies through time and space, Böhme charts the path to *Gelassenheit* by comparing inner with outer space. *Erscheinung* 'reflection within matter, appearance' illuminates all space; inner space, though, with its characteristic absence of gross matter, hence lack of reflection, leads into *Gelassenheit*. External light, which many hold for a sign of spiritual illumination, is another delusion:

> Wann nun dies geschieht, so mag die Vernunft, als die creatürliche Selbheit, nichts bessers thun, als dass sie sich ja nicht in der Selbheit der Creatur beschaue, und ja

The Plateau 93

> mit dem Willen der Begierde nicht in das Centrum eingehe, und sich selber suche, sie bricht sich sonst von GOttes Wesen ab, und isset vom äusseren Licht und Wesen, dadurch sie die Gift wieder in sich ziehet (*Gelassenheit* i, 22).

Böhme notices that in order to sidestep the ambivalent (helper/destroyer) reason, thereby freeing oneself from the clutches of *Selbheit*, a transcendence through the *Gemüt* is necessary. The acceptance of the mental attitude of *Demuth* 'humility, servile attitude toward the Creator' leads man away from the possibility of egocentric attraction to rational modes of attachment, away from *Selbheit*. By understanding the divine descent (*Geist>Begreiffligkeit>Geist*), then yielding completely into it (abandoning all matter attachments), the power of human consciousness withdraws from the astringent gravity of *Selbheit* into a more subtle unmanifested (astral) vehicle. This new state, being motionless since it is matterless, is the *stille stehen* seen earlier. *Vernunft*, that portion of consciousness in matter which interprets molecular structures (beings as well as actions and effects), providing comfortable, convenient justifications, is for Böhme nothing less than Lucifer in action within. Man "muss in der gelassenen Demuth bleiben, gleichwie ein Quell an seinem Ursprung, und muss ohne Unterlass aus GOttes Brünnlein schöpfen und trincken, und aus GOttes Wege gar nicht begehren auszugehen" (*Gelassenheit* i, 30).

Who is this Lucifer? We meet the intriguing scapegoat character in the *Aurora*, where he personifies all that Böhme cannot answer. Originally, Böhme tells us, Lucifer was the most beautiful of the angelic kings (*Aurora* xii, 100; xiii, 90). He was a little son of God, an heir to the divine throne: "Du solst wissen, dass es zwischen GOtt und Lucifer kein ander Unterschied ist gewesen, als wie mit den Eltern und ihren Kindern, und noch viel näher" (*Aurora* xiv, 87). For this reason "Er [God] hat ihn auch zum Erben seiner Güter gemacht, und ihm den gantzen Locum, darinnen er ihn schuf, zum Besitz eingeräumet" (*Aurora* xiv, 87). He wore a beautiful crown, ruling with all of his angels as a powerful God (*Aurora* xii, 106). The light from Christ, the Son of God, reached into and penetrated his heart (*Aurora* xii, 104). He was enjoined to Michael, another angelic king, and Christ, through the vehicle of a matterless light (*Aurora* xii, 101, 104). As he enters the realm of *Begreiffligkeit*, he loses his original matter, taking the name Lucifer ("expelled from the light"):

> Dieser hochmächtige, herrliche und schöne König hat seinen rechten Namen verloren in seinem Falle; denn er heist ietzunder Lucifer, das ist, ein Verstossener aus dem Lichte GOttes. Sein Name ist anfänglich nicht also gewesen; denn er ist ein creatürlicher Fürste oder König des Hertzens GOttes gewesen in dem hellen Lichte, der allerschönste unter den 3 Königen der Engel (*Aurora* xii, 100).

Lucifer's fall is problematic for the young Böhme. On the one hand, he sees Lucifer falling into manifestation: an astral form becoming a physically oriented entity. On the other hand, he is at a loss to pinpoint one location within *Begreiffligkeit* where Lucifer can be found. Instead, Böhme suspends him somewhere between the purity of *Geist* and the corporeal aspects of *Begreiffligkeit*, just on this side of the matrix within the force of field alignments preceding manifestation in matter. The negative, harsh features associated with the qualities reflect Lucifer's banishment from the realm of spirit: "Die Natur aber hat GOtt darum also hart angezündet und sich darinnen erzörnet, dass Er den Teufeln damit ein Wohnhaus bauete, und sie darinnen gefangen hielte, auf das sie wären Kinder seines Zorns, in denen Er mit seinem grimmen Eifer herrschete, und sie in dem Zorne" (*Aurora* xxiii, 98). Böhme hints that the process of *Geist* becoming *Begreiffligkeit* evolves solely because God has nowhere else to place the wayward angel:

> Er hat den Salitter zusammen gezogen, und dem Teufel hiemit eine ewige Herberge zugerichtet. Denn ausser GOtt kan er nicht gestossen werden in ein ander Königreich der Engel; sondern es muss ihm ein Locus zur Behausung bleiben (*Aurora* xvi, 74, 75).

The highest apostles and prophets fall into the snares of Lucifer once they abandon their realms of *Gelassenheit* for the materiality of *Selbheit*. By listening to their sense of reason, people enter the arena in which Lucifer operates. Böhme advises the reader not to mentally contemplate (nor to rationally attempt to describe) the indescribable *Wunder GOttes* 'miracles of God' since this contemplation demands that reason classify and decode the incoming physical message. Instead, Böhme advises the reader that through combining the external manifested rational core of matter with the internal willing desire to silently observe (without comment) the spring from which matter rushes into being (God), man will be able to employ the *Vernunft-Licht* 'light of reason' to penetrate astringency back to *GOttes-Licht* 'light of God' (*Gelassenheit* i, 35). There is a mysterious note of caution to those who understand: once the state of contemplation begins "so soll sie sich des noch nicht annehmen, als eines Eigenthums, sondern GOtt die Ehre geben, welchem alleine ist die Erkentniss und Weisheit" (*Gelassenheit* i, 35). Only when the descent into *Selbheit* is reversed, then man "ist der Sünden frey" (*Gelassenheit* i, 39). Then man becomes the willing instrument and eagerly awaits divine power to pass over its linguistic apparatus:

> Er begehret nur das zu thun, dazu ihn GOtt geschaffen hat, das GOtt durch ihn thun will. Und ob er wol das Thun ist, und seyn muss, so ist er doch nur als ein Werckzeug des Thuns, mit deme GOtt thut was er will (*Gelassenheit* i, 39).

Above all, man must be unencumbered, mentally uncluttered, and awake:

Wer aber in Sünden schläffet, und in seinen fetten Tagen des Bauchs, der spricht: Es ist alles Friede und stille, wir hören keinen Schall vom HErrn. Aber des HErrn Stimme ist an den Enden der Erden erschollen und gehet auf ein Rauch, und mitten im Rauche eine grosse Helle eines Glantzes, Amen! Hallelujah, Amen! (*Gelassenheit* ii, 55).

CHAPTER IV

THE WORK: *MYSTERIUM MAGNUM ODER ERKLÄRUNG ÜBER DAS ERSTE BUCH MOSIS* (1622)

By early fall 1622, Böhme begins writing his linguistic masterpiece, the *Mysterium Magnum, oder Erklärung über Das Erste Buch Mosis... Eine Erklärung des Wesens aller Wesen: Dem Liebhaber in Göttlicher Gabe weiter nachzusinnen.* By redefining both sides of the linguistic matrix, Böhme delves deeper into the mysterious interrelationship between language potential (possibilities for matter to exist) and language production (words and matter in manifestation). He draws the distinction:

> Alle Kräfte, Farben und Tugenden liegen in Einer, und ist eine unterschiedliche in einander wolgestimmete gebärende Harmoney; oder wie ichs setzen möchte ein sprechendes Wort, da in dem Wort oder Sprechen alle Sprachen, Kräfte, Farben und Tugenden inne liegen, und mit dem Hallen oder Sprechen sich auswickeln, und in ein Gesicht oder Sehen einführen (*Mysterium* i, 7).

Protolanguage, the *sprechendes Wort*, contains the blueprint of the articulated language, *ausgesprochenes Wort,* power to transmit ideational messages through external channels (*Kräfte*), or through colors (if referring to angelic speech), or through virtues (employing language as an antidote against evil). These features, unfolding out of the speaking word, become some sort of apprehensible reality (*in ein Gesicht oder Sehen*). The seen (*Gesicht*<ge [+past] + s + Vowel+cht) surpasses the speaking word only within matter. In like manner, the speaking word is surpassed by its ideational divine origin, an origin which Böhme closely investigates within the *Mysterium Magnum*. What is the great mystery? He

opens the work with linguistic observation:

> Das Centrum der ewigen Natur... da sich das ewig=
> sprechende Wort in eine Gebärung einführet, und auch
> eine solche geistliche Welt in sich macht, wie wir im
> ausgesprochenen Wort eine materialische sind (*Mysterium* ii, 7).

Rather than address the significant nature of the *Centrum der ewigen Natur* 'center of eternal nature', Böhme deflects his thinking into the nature of the generative device which perpetuates the great mystery.

Böhme's inner world, the mental screen upon which he projects his linguistic observation, emerges as an externally unified, although somewhat jumbled, array of human language observations. He notes that in order for the speaking word to be eternal (which it is), it must be free from motion and time. Where else but *within* can this be possible? And if there is unity within eternity, then unity (+eternity) needs only to experience the mystery of divine will toward object (accusative) manifestation. In this motion toward compaction within matter, the divine will assumes a temporal and spatial aspect. *Speaking* in the inner world is the eternal divine command for the Word to become words. Man's speech mirrors this process:

> In der innern geistlichen Welt fasset sich das Wort in ein geistlich Wesen als in ein einiges Element, da ihr 4 darinnen verborgen liegen. Als aber GOtt, als das Wort, hat dasselbige einige Element beweget, so haben sich die verborgene Eigenschaft offenbaret, als da sind 4 Elementa (*Mysterium* ii, 11).

Speaking is the verbal command which exists within itself, undifferentiated within divinity. It is the *ewiges Gute* 'the eternal good' (*Mysterium* iii, 3). Through this vehicle Böhme sees divinity

The Work 99

expressing itself in manifestation. He compares the process to the vibrational interaction found in musical instruments:

> Sie [the manifested characteristics] sind seine Saiten in dem allwesenden sprechenden Worte, und sind allesampt in die grosse Harmoney seines ewig=sprechenden Worts gerichtet. Also dass in allen Gradibus und Eigenschaften die Stimme des unerforschlichen GOttes offenbar und erkant werde, sie sind alle ins Lob GOttes erschaffen (*Mysterium* viii, 31).

Recognizing the grades and degrees of refinement possible within the *Geist-Begreiffligkeit* spectrum, Böhme moves the angels into this range. Those closest to either side of the matrix serve functions and have names which reflect their degree (or grade) of distance. If they reside on the other side of the matrix, Böhme calls them *Engeln* 'angels'; on this side of the matrix they are *Zeit-Geister* 'time ghosts'. Once through the matrix, these creatures are no longer angels:

> Denn alles was lebet, das lebet in dem sprechenden Worte: Die Engel in dem ewigen Sprechen, und der Zeit=Geister in dem Wieder=Aussprechen aus der Zeit Formungen, aus dem Halle der Zeit, und die Engel aus dem Halle der Ewigkeit als aus der Stimme des geoffenbarten Worts GOttes (*Mysterium* viii, 32).

The closer they are to the divine mystery, the more holy they become: "Darum sind auch die Engel in ihren Chören in der Kraft der Göttlichen Macht unterschieden, und hat einer viel ein heiliger Amt zu verrichten als der ander" (*Mysterium* viii, 33).

Angels as *Zeit-Geister* 'time ghosts' being closer to man than *Engeln* develop out of the concept of the *Signatur*. Angels (and signatures) are on Böhme's mind during the *Aurora* period. He sees them as indestructible since they lack flesh and blood (*Aurora* v, 5). They have no teeth, intestines or reproductive organs (*Aurora* vi, 12, 17). Since classified as *Geist* (-time), they do not eat within the space of *Begreiffligkeit*, as man does. There are no material objects for them to digest, since for them matter does not exist. Man must pull apart the essences in order to derive nourishment from his food objects; angels only need to absorb subtle premanifested energies which Böhme calls heavenly (astral) fruits:

> Die himmlische Früchte aber, die er isset, die sind nicht irdisch: und ob sie gleich in Form und Gestalt sind wie die irdischen, so sind sie doch nur Göttliche Kraft, und haben also einen lieblichen Schmack und Ruch, dass ich das mit nichts in dieser Welt vergleichen kan, denn sie schmecken und riechen nach der H. Dreyfaltigkeit (*Aurora* vi, 14).

Since the angels have not fallen through the matrix into manifestation, they do not have to reproduce in order to project their spirit into other dimensional shapes:

> Er [the angel] ist von Göttlichen Kraft zusammen= gefüget auf Form und Art gleich einem Menschen, auch mit allen Gliedern wie ein Mensch; aber die Geburts= glieder und auch keinen Ausgang von unten hat er nicht, er bedarf es auch nicht. Denn der Mensch hat seine Geburts=Gleider darzu auch seinen Ausgang erst in dem kläglichen Fall bekommen (*Aurora* vi, 12, 13).[1]

In addition to "singen, klingen, posaunen und schallen" (*Aurora* xi, 61), the angels walk with each other within the divine realm, observing wonderful shapes of astral energy surrounding them (*Aurora* xii, 29). They do not have wings. Böhme calls anyone who thinks they do outdated and old-fashioned: "Es haben die Alten den Menschen die Engel mit Flügeln vorgemahlet, aber sie dürffen keine, sondern die haben Hände und Füsse wie die

Menschen, aber auf himmlische Art" (*Aurora* xii, 83). As *Geist* they are not only able to change their shapes at will, but also have multidirectional extension faster than human thought can comprehend (*Aurora* xii, 48, 81).

Böhme differentiates them according to their predominant quality, a classification he has not abandoned by the time of the great mystery: "es ist in iedem etwan eine Qualität die stärckeste; nach derselben Qualität ist er auch glorificiret" (*Aurora* xii, 8). That the Aurorean angels have material qualities predominating within, highlights the mystical distance Böhme brings them by 1622. The material qualities fix them at the subtle, invisible vanishing point of the *Begreifflichkeit* spectrum. They are the *Zeit-Geister* of the *Mysterium Magnum*. What, then, are the *Mysterium Magnum* angels? Before answering this question, we need to bring to light Böhme's earliest statements of angelic possibility. If the feature of water predominates, they are "lichte gleich dem heiligen Himmel" (*Aurora* xii, 10). If astringency predominates, they are brown (*Aurora* xii, 9). If bitterness predominates, they are:

> Gleich einem köstlichen grünen Steine, der da siehet wie ein Blitz, und wenn sie das Licht anscheinet, so scheinets gleichwie rothgrünlicht, als ob ein Carfunckel daraus leuchtete, oder als ob das Leben da Ursprung hätte (*Aurora* xii, 11).

Although they appear invisible to man (*Aurora* xix, 32), the reverse is not true. They willfully help man in his struggle against manifestation incarnate, Lucifer:

> ... in der innersten (Geburt) aber wohnen sie bey uns. Und so wir mit dem Teufel kämpfen, so halten sie seine Schläge in der inresten Geburt auf und sind der H. Seelen Schutz (*Aurora* xix, 32).

Only as *Zeit-Geister* can the angels help man, since within time and space manifestation is their common denominator. Though at opposite ends of the spectrum of *Creatur* (+*ausgesprochen*), they can and do interact within their common *Signatur*. Watery angels and fat people interact within their common water-signature, as do astringent people with brown angels.

The angelic source within the *ewiges Gute*, being beyond the realm of molecular interaction, is enough for Böhme at the present time. Rather than explore the mystery of their geniture, he employs their spectral range to highlight further linguistic comment. A syntactical awareness, a linear progression within language, develops as Böhme returns to the apostle John:

> Unsere Seele war vorm Anfange der menschlichen, seelischen Creatur ein Ens des Worts GOttes im Worte, Joh. I:1 und ward aber vom sprechenden Worte GOttes dem Menschen=Bilde in ein natürlich und creatürlich Leben eingesprochen... Dieses creatürliche Seelen= Leben wandte sich in Adam von dem Göttlichen Sprechen ab, in eigen Wollen und Sprechen, und war deshalben vom gantzen ungründlichen Wesen abgebrochen und von GOtt geschieden (*Mysterium* lvi, 23).

The soul before the onset of temporality is the syntactic subject, a force which in expanding through a semantic verbal channel, directs its self-contained energy toward a goal, here the *creatürlich Leben*. Should the descent continue further, additional verbal amplification may deflect off the first object onto another of similar qualitative composition, or it may be absorbed completely by the object, which, in turn, produces another independent object. Viewed from the platform of linear syntax, the protolanguage is the unmanifested divine subject: the mystical nominative.[2] As it expresses (*aus-drücken*) itself through the matrix into matter, the action of expression reaches a boundary: the end of the mystical verb and the beginning of the manifested accusative.

Verbally reaching through the matrix defines the action of *Einsprechen* 'speaking out into and through' and sets the standard for the *sprechendes Wort* becoming the *ausgesprochenes Wort*. Once spoken out (*eingesprochen*), the mystical nominative descends into a manifested object, an *Ausgesprochenes*. Böhme cautions the reader not to accept the manifested accusative for a divine nominative, since through the addition of time and space, the manifested object creates objects of its own desire. Through the agency of human articulation and mental involvement, each word of every object becomes a temporal subject causing its own series of verbal actions within three dimensions. Since man forgets that matter is accusative rather than an original nominative, only the act of contemplating the *Einsprechen* can open the doorway back to spirit. Human language mirrors the divine: "Es ist keines GOtt, sondern GOttes geformtes und ausgesprochenes Wesen, ein Spiegel des Geistes" (*Mysterium* viii, 25). Human language is externalized divinity:

> Die äussere Eigenschaften wohnen in sich selber im äussern als im ausgesprochenen Worte, und sind gantz äusserlich, sie können in ihrem einigen Vermögen nicht die Kräfte der heiligen Welt erreichen: allein die heilige Welt durchdringet sie, sie wohnet auch in sich selber (*Mysterium* xi, 34).

Böhme includes the process of planetary creation into the linguistic descent of the holy world into the banal.

The beginning of externality, corporeality, palpability—matter—is the first day. From within the *ewiges Gute*, God projects an *Impression* which generates the day:

> Er hat ihn [the first day] aus der Impression ausgeführet, und sich mit seinem Worte beweget: das ist die allerinnerlichste Bewegung gewesen nach dem sprechenden Worte der Kraft (*Mysterium* xii, 6).

Astringency characterizes the first day as it emerges from the *sprechendes Wort* into object form: "Sontag, das ist der wahre Paradeisische Tag, da die Kräfte in grosser Herrligkeit in einander gewircket haben" (*Mysterium* xii, 7). The compaction leads to a clump which is the planet: "... denn am Sontage ist der entzündete Sulphur und Salnitter der Irdischen Eigenschaft aus der grossen Tieffe der gantzen Heirarchien aus den geistlichen Welten in einen Klumpf geschaffen worden, das ist die Erdkugel" (*Mysterium* xii, 7). The remaining six days of creation are reflected off of this clump. Creation, *Geschöpfe*, and nature's manifold array of feature specifications are the transparent rays of the divine descent, seen here as the *Sprechende* (subject) > *einsprechen* (verb) > *Ausgesprochene* (object which diminishes into a time subject). *Einsprechen* assumes the position of the bilabial closure within the process. He explains:

> ... die erste Bewegung des Worts, da sich das Licht der Natur hat in der Essentz angezündet, ist die Freude der Creation oder Geschöpfes, die hat sich mit den andern Tagen durch alle Eigenschaften der Natur eröffnet, da man iede Eigenschaft mag einen Himmel nennen (*Mysterium* xii, 18).

To account for the multiplicity of manifested forms within creation, Böhme explains that as *Himmel* leads its unique feature bundle through the matrix, these features as units of semanticity intermingle with similar semantic features of other *Wesen*. In this manner, strings—or chains—of individual units conglomerate together lending manifestation the illusion of multiple form. One ideational pattern does not produce one material object; rather, at the moment of matter onset, all possibilities occur simultaneously: the sky interacts with the earth, the earth with water, water with fire, together in harmony. That water quenches a fire is of less importance than the knowledge that the ideational pattern responsible for the generation of water is an exact signature that can nullify (within matter) the physical effects of ideational fire. One aspect of matter can cause a physical imbalance in the state of another; it can never nullify an ideational pattern.

Böhme continues opposing cause and effect:

> Denn er (der Himmel) hat und bringt seine sonderliche Wirckung in sich mit in die andern; und hat sich ieden Tag eine Eigenschaft beweget und offenbaret, darinnen ist ein sonderliches Gewircke offenbar worden (*Mysterium* xii, 18).

More at ease with linguistic derivation, Böhme casually allows the words *sonderliche Wirckung* to evolve into the preterite-based (hence material) *sonderliches Gewircke*. In *sonderlich* 'peculiar, particular, amazing' Böhme relies on the first-layer semantic field, deriving it from *sonder-* 'without anything else, for itself alone, separated from all else' and *-lich* 'like, -ly'. *Wirckung* 'effect' and its extension *Gewircke* 'effect' share the verbal *wir(c)ken* 'doing, effecting, bringing into the state of being able to do, working'. With *Wirckung* the verbal action is (+present) operative, whereas in *Gewircke* (+past) it is completed.[3] The *sonderliche Wirckung*, then, is "the state of activity which in itself is a separating, sundering motion causing an effect" and is distinguished from the *sonderliches Gewircke* 'the state of having been brought into effect through the agency of a separating and sundering motion'. Because of this distinction, Böhme sees all grasses, herbs, and trees (all +*Gewirck*) reflecting a divine origin. This is:

> Anders nichts als Er hat das ausgesprochene Wort der Kräfte in den Eigenschaften beweget; so haben die Eigenschaften das Licht der Natur in sich empfunden, davon sind sie hungrig worden, und haben sich impresset, das ist gefasset und compactiert oder coaguliert (*Mysterium* xii, 38).

In addition to the terms derived from *sprechen (sprechendes Wort, einsprechen, ausgesprochenes Wort)* Böhme exploits new compounds, utilizing the distinctions he understands within the word *Aushauchung* 'exhalation'. As the compound suggests on the first layer, *hauchen* (< *Hauch* 'breath, voiceless expiration from the mouth') coupled with the directional preposition *aus* 'away from' gains significance with respect to the act of *Einsprechen*. *Aushauchung* precedes *Einsprechen* as the first willful divine inclination (nonverbalized and nonphonologized) toward verbalization. *Aushauchen* leads the ideational blueprint of human languages from the mystical nominative, up to the matrix (verbal), and coupling with the act of *Einsprechen*, guides the entire process through the matrix of manifestation into the manifested accusative:

> Die Schöpfung der äussern Welt ist eine Offenbarung des innern Geistlichen Mysterii, als des Centri der ewigen Natur mit dem heiligen Elemente: Und ist durch die Bewegung des Innern als ein Aushauchen, erboren worden durch das ewig-sprechende Wort, welches aus der innern Geistlichen Welt das Wesen hat ausgesprochen; und da es im Sprechen doch kein solch Wesen gewesen ist, sondern als ein Brodem oder Rauch vor dem Innern (*Mysterium* x, 5).

Aushauchen is the first modification of divine will toward matter, the "Mund des Verstandes im geformten Willen der Weisheit" (*Mysterium* xxix, 3). It yields not only organized nominative configurations necessary for the Word>words, but also plans for the physical arrangement of elements which will produce the organs of perception (*Mysterium* xiii, 11, 13-16; xvi, 21; xxii, 24).

What about language? Has minute analysis of the *Geist-Begreiffligkeit* spectrum elevated Böhmian linguistics from the lower levels of phonology and morphology of the earlier period to a new mystical syntax of creation?

Böhme unexpectedly begins to take up the linguistic problems of phonology, formulating them into an exhaustive linguistic statement:

> Nun mercket uns gar eben alhier; Wie sich nun iedes Wort im Munde zur Substanz fasset, als zum Aussprechen, wie es der Werckmeister bildet, der in den Sensibus ist, als das Fiat, und wie die Zunge mit thut, wenn sie das fasset, und durch welchen Weg sie das ausführet, entweder durch die Zähne, oder über sich, oder mit offenem Munde; Item, wie sich die Zunge schmeuget im Fügen des Worts, welchen Sensum sie wieder zurücke= zeucht, und nicht will gantz ausstossen, wie denn mancher Sensut kaum halb ausgestossen wird, mancher aber gar, mancher aber wieder halb gegen dem Hertzen gezogen; und wie nun das Wort gebildet ward; also ist auch das Ding in seiner Form und Eigenschaft, das das Wort damit nennet ... Also ist es äusserlich bezeichnet, und innerlich in der Compaction der Sensum: einer solchen Tugend oder Untugend es ist (*Mysterium* xxxv, 56).

Aside from the generalized statements of dorsal position, Böhme introduces the reader to the term *Sensus*, a word clarified within the framework of a language he calls the *sensualische Sprache*. Behind the physical manipulations of the articulators, there is a force—a *Sensus*—which guides the tongue toward rendering the Word into the multitude of human languages. The *sensualische Sprache* is a language "der gantzen Creation, und verstehet woraus Adam hat allen Dingen Namen gegeben, und woraus der Geist GOttes hat gedeutet in den Alten" (*Mysterium* xxxv, 57).

In the thirty-fifth chapter of the *Mysterium Magnum* Böhme formulates his most concise linguistic statement under the chapter heading "Wie sich der menschliche Baum durch Noahs Kinder habe in seinen Eigenschaften ausgebreitet, und wie sich am Thurn zu Babel sind in den Eigenschaften, durch die Verwirrung der

Sprachen, in unterschiedene Völcker zertheilet worden." Böhme calls forth Adam from the Biblical past to exemplify in action the theory of the linguistic code. The code not only verifies the holy writ, but also explains Adam's puzzling relation to the world of matter.

Böhme's Adamic design contains a spiritual core growing in itself, expanding through all powers and dimensions associated with its source, God. Adam is a perfect divine reflection until the moment of the fall when his spiritual essence attracts to itself the astringent garb of elemental matter. His astringent body, divorced from the original mystical subject, develops under its own self-power and movement, until generations after the banishment from Eden all manifested accusatives come to an abrupt halt. The flood, engulfing the human population in astringency, establishes the underlying world *Signatur* for the following post-flood period: astringency. The period of *Einsprechen* (the flood) verbally sets the multitude of human languages into action, reducing human communication to fractionated articulations. With the loss of metalinguistic communication, Böhme wistfully yearns for the first language of created (*ausgesprochen*) people: "dann alle Menschen hatten nur einerley Sprache; die Sprachen aus den Eigenschaften waren vor der Sündfluth nicht offenbar" (*Mysterium* xxxv, 7).

With the arrival of the flood, the linguistic nucleus of an entire language network prepares itself for its passage through the matrix. Böhme notes that the multiplicity of leaves and branches rightfully drains power from the stem:

> Gleichwie ein junger Baum, der voller Kraft und Saft ist, sich in Aesten und Wachsen schöne erzeiget, wann er aber anhebet zu blühen, so gehet die gute Kraft in die Blüte und Frucht (*Mysterium* xxxv, 11).

Noah's mission cannot fail, since his offspring will draw power from the main stem. Before the flood, though, Böhme notices that this sensual (+*Begreifflich*) language contains the pattern for the post-flood languages "denn es lagen alle Sprachen darinnen" (*Mysterium* xxxv, 12). Post-flood languages reflect the divine power channeling itself in different directions, according to their various astringent *Hülse* 'containers'. Any awareness of the original language terminates abruptly as human languages fall prey to the powerful forces of dissolution operative within their phonological laws:

> Weil sich aber der Verstand in viel Zungen und Eigenschaften zertheilete, so ward die Natur schwächer, und fiel der hohe Verstand der Eigenschaften der Geister der Buchstaben denn das Innerliche führete sich in ein Aeusserliches (*Mysterium* xxxv, 13).

The diminishing power of *Verstand* 'understanding' increases as man moves through time and space, further from the original pre-flood languages:

> So ist ihnen der rechte Verstand erloschen, denn sie führeten die Geister der sensualischen Sprachen in eine äusserliche grobe Form, und fasseten den subtilen Geist des Verstandes in eine grobe Form, und lerneten aus der Form reden, wie denn heutiges Tages alle Völcker nur aus derselben Form ihrer gefasseten sensualischen Sprachen reden (*Mysterium* xxxv, 58).

Speaking through form leads man into argument and confrontation. While arguing among themselves as to the description of the most perfect language, Böhme reproaches *Magistros* and *Doctores* for overlooking the transcendence possible in their first native articulations of the breath stream, German:

> ... und keiner verstehet seiner Mutter Sprache: Sie verstehen nichts mehr vom Geiste als der Bauer von

> seinem Werckzeug zum Ackerwerk, sie brauchen blos allein der gefasseten Form der groben componierten Wörter und verstehen nicht was das Wort in seinem Sensu ist; daher entsteht Zanck und Streit, dass man um GOtt und seinen Willen streitet. Man will lehren was GOtt sey und verstehen nicht das Wenigste von GOtt (*Mysterium* xxxv, 61).

The cult of *Buchstaben* 'letter' worship, the elevation of the first layer of language to the role of perfect vehicle for divine expression, is an illusion with which Böhme discredits all *Magistros* and *Doctores*, high priests of the *Cainische Kirche* 'church of Cain' (*Mysterium* xxviii, 27). This church "will GOtt mit etwas Aeusserliches versöhnen" (*Mysterium* xxviii, 27), hoping through ceremonies (*Mysterium* xxviii, 28), holy orders (*Mysterium* xxviii, 29), and "Worten, Lesen, Singen, Predigen und Hören" (*Mysterium* xxviii, 30) to gain prestige and earthly honor. These theologically inspired linguistic analyses are failures, since their vehicle of expression derives its entire justification from the first layer of language, the *Buchstaben*, rather than from the third layer of signatures. A reality cannot be based upon any numerical possibility within form:

> Sie aber sagen, das aufgeschriebene Wort sey Christi Stimme, ja das Gehäuse ists wol, als eine Forme des Worts, aber die Stimme muss lebendig seyn, welche das Gehäuse als ein Uhrwerck treibet: Der Buchstabe ist ein Instrument darzu, als eine Posaune, aber es gehöret ein rechter Hall darein, dar mit dem Hall in Buchstaben concordirten (*Mysterium* xxviii, 56).

How does Böhme insure that the *Stimme* 'voice' is alive? Each letter (*Buchstabe*) contains an individual, unique and characteristic acoustical property, its *rechter Hall*, which when projected into speech, intermingles with the qualities present from other letters.

The balance between the letter, the point of articulation, and the person articulating, coupled with the visual addition of an image (*Bild*) through the agency of *Imagination*, constitutes the meaning of the word. Should the person articulating be unenlightened (unseeing), then his uttered words reflect only that characteristic. Should the speaker think of nothing but greed, then his words reflect "menschliche Wollust... und dasselbe nach dem fetten Bauche und weltlichen Wollüsten geformet und erkläret: also ist der Geist erloschen" (*Mysterium* xxviii, 58).

Concerning the practical extension of idea into deed, Böhme notes as early as 1620 that something called *Alphabeten* 'alphabets' are prerequisite to a deeper understanding of the mystery. In a short tract, *Gründlicher Bericht von dem Irdischen und Himmlischen Mysterio* (May 1620), Böhme discusses the role and origin of the *Alphabeten*:

> Auch finden wir hierinnen den Baum der Zungen, als der Sprachen, mit 4 Alphabeten: als eines mit den Characteren des Mysterii bezeichnet, darinnen die Natur=Sprache lieget, welche in allen Sprachen die Wurtzel ist: und wird doch in der Ausgeburt der Vielheit, (oder der vielen Sprachen,) nicht erkant, als von ihren eigenen Kindern welchen Verstand des Mysterium selber giebet, denn es ist ein Wunder GOttes (*Bericht* vii, 6).

The unknown arrangements within the *Natur=Sprache*—the first language—form what Böhme calls the first alphabet. Hebrew, "welches das Mysterium eröffnet, und den Baum mit den Aesten und Zweigen nennet" (*Bericht* vii, 7), is the second.[4] Greek, "welches den Baum mit der Frucht und aller Zierde nennet, welche erst recht die Witze ausspricht" (*Bericht* vii, 8), is the third. Latin, the language of "viel Völcker und Zungen" (*Bericht* vii, 9), is the fourth. An unclear fifth is "GOttes Geist, der aller Alphabethen Eröffner ist; und dasselbe Alphabet mag kein Mensch erlernen, er eröffne sich dann selber im Menschen=Geiste" (*Bericht* vii, 10). The alphabets interact and penetrate the seventy-two human languages in such a way that these human languages arrange themselves into five major categories, or *Hauptsprachen* (*Bericht* vii, 11).

No longer a *sensualische Sprache*, each human language falls from the unified spectrum as evolutionary offspring. In time they become individual realms of expression, which in being removed from the divine source, tend toward self-determination as independent subjects. They feel removed from contact with God:

> Dann sie hatten GOtt verlassen, und wurden Heiden und GOtt liess sie gehen in ihren Wundern, dann sie wolten Ihme nicht anhangen, sondern wolten ein eigen Gewächse seyn, und ihre eigene Vernunft (welche doch mit allen Farben vermischt war) solte sie regieren (*Bericht* vii, 13).

Alphabeten (+*sensualische Sprache*) are channels through which divinity descends, passing through the matrix, emerging as "die Viele der Sprachen" (*Bericht* vii, 15). *Alphabeten* generate not only acoustical vibration but also *Buchstaben* 'letters, written linguistic characters' (+*Begreiffligkeit*):

> Dann die 4 Alphabeten liegen in Einem Baum, und gehen aus einander, aber die Viele der Sprachen müssen sich mit ihren Characteren behelfen, als Hausgenossen, und wollen sich doch auch Eigene seyn, und spreussen sich alle wieder den Baum (*Bericht* vii, 15).

Three years later, Böhme returns to the linguistic thinking of the *Bericht*, deciding on five *Alphabeten* which yield the seventy-two manifested languages:

> Denn 77 ist die gantze Zahl Göttlicher Offenbarung durchs geformte Wort, 72 sind Babel, als die Zungen der

The Work 113

> Wunder; die andern 5 sind heilig und liegen unter den 72 verborgen, und urständen aus dem I oder Joth, und das JOTH stehet in dem I als in dem Einen, das ist das Auge der Ewigkeit ohne Grund und Zahl (*Mysterium* xxxv, 16, 17).[5]

It is through the vehicle of the five alphabets that God speaks directly to his holiest saints (*Mysterium* xxxv, 17). How is it that saints, who are *begreifflig* 'corporeal', can understand a language that is not *begreifflig*? What is the connection? Böhme draws the nonobstruency of the five manifested vowels closer to the vocalic origins of the five alphabets (*Mysterium* xxxv, 17), repeating tirelessly that the five (languages) originate within the vowel JOTH (*J=I*):

> Die fünf Sprachen stehen dem Geiste GOttes zu, welcher durch seine Kinder redet, wenn und wie Er will, aber die zwey und siebentzig stehen der menschliche Selbheit und Eigenheit zu, daraus der menschliche eigen Verstand Lügen und Wahrheit redet: Darum sollen die zwey und siebentzig Sprachen als Babel, durchs Gerichte GOttes, und das Reine vom Unreinen geschieden und im Feuer bewäret werden (*Mysterium* xxxv, 18).

Babel becomes even more confused as Böhme notes that dialects form within close proximity to each other:

> ... wie man das vor Augen siehet, dass man an keinem Orte der Welt unter allen Haupt=Sprachen auf 5 oder 6 Meilen einerley Sensus in einer Hauptsprache findet; sie verdrehen sich fast alle 5 oder 6 Meilen, alles nach den Eigenschaften derselben Poli oder Höhe (*Mysterium* xxxv, 75).[6]

It is not the consideration of dialect variants, complete with their inherent semantic shifts, obscured phonologies and variant syntactical structures that interest Böhme at this point, rather the exceptional role of the vowel within all dialects and languages. As a nonobstruent, the breath stream remains unarticulated and relatively free from astringency as it passes out of the mouth into manifestation. Underlying all languages, Böhme notes, is the *Aushauchen* 'exhalation' of vocalic sounds, and in this feature, rather than in astringency, all languages are unified. The spirit underlying all letters (*Buchstaben*) is "des Einigen Geistes in der Natur=Sprache" (*Mysterium* xxxv, 49), which as the five major vocalic sounds *A, E, I, O,* and *U,* descend into the articulated (*ausgesproches*) word *Jehovah*:

> Denn der Name JEHOVAH hat nichts in sich, als nur die 5 Vocales A, E, I, O, U. Die andere Buchstaben deuten an und sprechen aus die Natur, was der Name GOttes im geformten Worte in der Natur, in Liebe und Zorn, in Finsterniss und Licht zugleich sey; Die 5 Vocales aber deuten an einig allein was Er im Licht der Heiligkeit sey, denn mit den 5 Vocalibus wird die Natur tingiret, dass sie ein Freudenreich seyn mag (*Mysterium* xxxv, 49).

Why then if *Jehovah* is purely vocalic (nonobstruent), does Böhme choose to orthographically record the name with the letter *H*? Pure vowels cannot ground themselves within manifestation without the assistance of a matter-bound astringent obstruent, in this case the mildly fricative sound *H*. Böhme inspects the *H* more closely: it "zeiget an wie sich der heilige Name GOttes *in das Geschöpfe aushauche* und offenbare ... das *H* deutet an die Göttliche Lust oder Weisheit, wie sich die Göttliche Lust aus sich selber aushauche" (*Mysterium* xxxv, 50) (author's italics). More important are the vowels, reflections of the *sensualische Sprache* (*-Geschöpf*) within articulated manifestation (*+Geschöpf*). He understands them in the following progression: the *I* is the name

The Work 115

JESUS (<*I*) (*Mysterium* xxxv, 51). In this way *E* comes to represent the name *Engel* 'angel' (<*E*), while the *O* is the heart (<*H*?), "die geformte Weisheit oder Lust des I als des JESUS, und ist das Centrum oder Hertze GOttes" (*Mysterium* xxxv, 51). In a disjointed progression, Böhme's *O* depends on the presence of the *I* for its existence, but within a new word, JESUS, the *I* precedes the *E*: IEsus/IEhovah. Both Jesus and the *O* are the center or the heart of God. Being the heart, the point of manifestation, the matrix and its most linguistic extension, the bilabial wall, the *O* reflects initial points of matter onset through the mildly astringent exhaled *H*. The progression I + E + O generates I + E + (H)O. These lead into the expression of the *U*, where it assumes the role of *Geist*, the -s+U+s of Jesus (*Mysterium* xxxv, 51), a position agreeing with the +heavenly ascent feature seen earlier in *Immanuel*. Böhme sees the vocalic *A* with the features of temporality within three dimensions—the beginning (*Anfang*=A+nfang) and the end; the will of the entire idea of the divine; and the Father (*Vater* =V[U]ater). Even orthography is subservient to the mystical implications inherent in the vowel *a*. By diagramming this progression within a stylized triangle with a diagonal extension (△), the *A, O* and *U* continue to interrelate as a linear progression. The reader notices an angular V, a triangular O, and taken as a whole *Gestalt*, the diagram displays itself as a lower-case cursive *a*. Böhme notices that the characterized *a*:

> ... deutet an die Dreyheit der Eigenschaften der Personen und das V. am Triangel deutet an den Geist im H. als im Hauchen, da sich der gantze GOtt in Geistes= Weise mit seinem aus sich selber Ausgehen offenbaret (*Mysterium* xxxv, 52).

Fascinated with the *aus sich selber Ausgehen* 'going out of the self by one's own effort (*selber*)', Böhme sees the vocalic exhalation *H* containing *Geist* within. In this manner he elevates it to the status of nonobstruent vowel rather than consonant. What of the consonants? Böhme derives them from the shell of the word *Tetragrammaton*, interpreting the second-layer phonology rather than the first-layer cabalistic connotation:[7]

> Die andern Buchstaben ausser den 5 Vocalibus gehen aus dem Namen TETRAGRAMMATON, als aus dem Centro der ewigen Natur aus dem Principio, und deuten an, und sprechen aus die Unterschiede der geformten Weisheit, als des geformten Worts in den 3 Principien, darinnen die gantze Creation lieget, sie sind der Sensus der Creation, als die Eigenschaft der Kräfte, und der wahre geoffenbarte GOtt im Wort der Natur (*Mysterium* xxxv, 53).

Rich with the astringent obstruents (dental stop, uvular resonant, velar stop) as well as the bilabial stop, the *T, R, G,* and *M* ($<$ T + [T] R + G[R] + M + [T] + N[M?]) issue forth into manifestation as the array of obstruent *Buchstaben*. Within the inaudible universe of the *sensualische Sprache*, before the onset of *Buchstaben*, the force of God as JEOVA in attracting to itself the manifestation-ridden *H* prepares its descent into words. Resounding within matter, within the physical matrix of *Tetragrammaton, Jehovah* becomes the *Jesus*. The sibilant hissing characterizes his temporary association with corporeality. Böhme describes Jesus as:

> Das Wort ... ist der Unterschied, und deutet an die Stimme JESU aus JEHOVAH, die Stimme war TETRAGRAMMA: Aber der im Garten ging, war TON, als das Centrum der Licht=Welt; und die Stimme TETRAGRAMMA ist das Centrum zur Feuer=Welt, als das erste Principium, und das TON das zweyte Principium (*Mysterium* xxiii, 14).

Had divinity not desired to travel through the principles into matter, JESUS would not have evolved forth into manifestation (which also would not have been called into motion): "so stund der Name JESUS im Feuer=Schwert verborgen, und war nicht offenbar, bis auf die Zeit, dass sich GOtt wolte darein bewegen, und denselben offenbaren" (*Mysterium* xxvi, 13). Furthermore, the material anchor *H* appears in the name *JeHsus*, lending more of a physical surface to this unique divine extension (*Mysterium* xxxvi, 48). Which physical surfaces, *Hülsen*, attract Böhme's attention at this point? The symbology of the Genesis and the line of the Covenant.

He describes Eden:

> Das Wort Eden ist anders nichts, als wie Mosis von der Erden saget, sie sey öde und leer gewesen, das ist, sie solte ihre Macht nach dem Grimme der Eitelkeit nicht offenbaren, sie solte still halten als eine Mutter zum gebären. Dann das Innere wolte durchs Aeussere herrschen, als die geistliche Welt durch die Zeit, der Himmel durch die Erde; die Erde war leer ohne Frucht, aber der Himmel war ihr Mann, der sie fruchtbar machte, und durch sie gebar bis auf den Fluch, da verbarg sich der Himmel vor der Erden (*Mysterium* xvii, 6).

Aside from the overworked cliché "das Innere durchs Aeussere," Böhme notes that the onset of temporality (from the spiritual world) holds the reins of time, controlling manifestation. The heavens control the earth, impregnating it with material possibility. What of Eden? It is bleak and desolate, quiet within itself, and able to express itself as *Macht* 'power to effect ($<machen$)'. Adam, residing in Eden ($<$ E+ [-R] + DN) "muss Englisch gewesen seyn" (*Mysterium* xix, 23), that is, astringentless and nonelemental, invisible to the sensibilities of modern man. In this condition, Adam lives in harmony with what Böhme calls the *Liebes=Wort* 'word of love'. Falling through the matrix severs his contact with the all-loving divine being, and at the same time establishes him as the first speaker of the *sensualische Sprache*. With linguistic onset (sensual language) Adam reacts to his nakedness:

> Moses spricht: Sie höreten die Stimme GOttes des HErrn, der im Garten ging: Wer ist nun diese Stimme der im Garten ging? denn Adams Ohren waren am Göttlichen Geheiss und Gehöre erstorben, und waren im Grimme aufgewacht; Er vermochte in eigner Macht GOttes heilige Stimme nicht mehr zu hören, denn er war an GOttes Heiligkeit, am Himmelreich todt, wie ihm GOtt sagte: Welches Tages du von diesem Baum issest, solst du sterben (*Mysterium* xxiii, 12).

In calling to Adam, who has hidden himself from the voice, Böhme sees God clearing a path through the clouded mechanism of Adam's being. Can the divine entrap itself in astringency? Is there an escape?

In calling to Adam "Ich will Feindschaft setzen, des Weibes Same soll der Schlangen den Kopf zertreten" (*Mysterium* xxiii, 29), the divine *Stimme* (+*Begreifflig*) is gross matter, far from the subtle realms of the sensual language. Utilizing the alphabetic JEHOVA, the holy voice descends into manifestation, rhythmically incurring the existence of all *Geschöpfe*, projecting its will on the matrix. In this manner, Eve originates. The multiple astral configurations responsible for her shape within time and space attract to themselves a physicality which reflects spirit trapped in matter. Once any physical being hears the acoustical vibration JEHOVA, an inner motion ensues whereby the entire consciousness network realigns with its origin. Böhme describes this as "es einleibete sich aufs neue mit dem heiligen Worte, als ein Ziel eines ewigen Bundes" (*Mysterium* xxiii, 29). This divinely appointed rearrangement of matter allows God to reach into manifestation, through the spirituality of the line of the covenant, placing JeHsus on the throne of corporeality:

> Und dieses Wort, das sich in des Weibes Samen, einver-

> hiess und einleibete, war dasselbe Wort das sich in Marien Samen bewegete, und den Namen JEsus aus dem Centro der tiefsten Liebe im Worte eröffnete, und das verblichene himmlische Ens, mit Einführung des heiligen lebendigen Entis, in dem verblichenen Ente Mariae lebendig machete (*Mysterium* xxiii, 30).

No longer the deleted nonentity, the vowels, by virtue of their more divine reflection, begin to operate within the code. Through their proximity to less material realms, they assume the role of linguistic cement in later etymologies. *Himmel* and *Erden* (*Mysterium* x, 47) reflect this new change.

Rather than repeat the entire significance of the bilabial *m*, Böhme concentrates on the characteristics of the divine *Aushauchen*, the *H*: the sound is "aus der geistlichen heiligen Welt in eine Zeit oder Anfang geschaffen" (*Mysterium* x, 47). It is the point where the *Nichts* 'nothing' becomes an *Etwas* 'something':

> Denn mit dem Wort Himmel verstehet man das Aushauchen des Verbi Fiats, welches das Wesen (darinnen Lucifer sass) hat mit dem Schuf aus sich, das ist, aus der geistlichen, heiligen Welt in eine Zeit oder Anfang geschaffen (*Mysterium* x, 47).

Erde reveals the feature of astringent compaction:

> ... und mit dem Worte Erde verstehet man den Grimm im Wesen, dass das Wesen ist im Grimme gefasset worden. Und aus den Eigenschaften des finstern Sulphuriis, Mercurii und Saltzes, als aus den Kräften des Urstandes der Natur, in eine Compaction oder Coagulation eingeführet (*Mysterium* x, 47).

Compression within the first syllable *Er-* (vocalic emanation + astringent uvular compaction) allows matter to arise within the second -*den* (*Mysterium* x, 48). The state of becoming, the *Er-*, involves counterbalancing the state of having already become, the -*den*, a process controlled by the state of becoming breaking apart leaving behind *Schatten*. The earth as a whole, the *Erden*, is the meeting ground for elemental force fields: the state of becoming, being, death, *Zerbrechlichkeit* and *Begreiffligkeit*. Through the principle of astringency in opposition to bitterness, fragility and palpability form a sheath around the *Geist*. The divine will, from within materiality, projects itself through the death state (+*Begreiffligkeit*) as life:

> ... da aus dem Sterben ein lebendig Weben ausgehet; und aus dem Gestorbenen eine tödliche Materia, als Erde, und Ein tödtlich Wasser, und auch ein tödtlich Feuer und giftige Luft, welche in den Cörpern der Irdischen eine sterbende Qual machen (*Mysterium* x, 48).

Böhme allows an active *lebendig Weben* 'living container of being' to evolve from the verbal substantive *Sterben* 'the process of dying'. From the *Gestorbenen* (again a verbal substantive although marked with +past, therefore completed) Böhme derives substance, matter, and earth, water, fire and air (in negative aspects). Although the earth is nothing but a dead clump upon which verbal and substantive transactions bring meaning and distinction to the planet, Böhme finds solace in the knowledge that *Himmel* is a series of minor and major matrices in succession, and as a whole, *Himmel* is divided from *Erde* by a wall of water. On the one side of the watery matrix *heiliges crystallinisches Wasser* 'holy crystalline water' (+spiritual, -coagulated) (*Mysterium* x, 50) divides itself from *materialisches Wasser* (+vulgar, +death-ridden, +coagulated, +astringent) (*Mysterium* x, 50). This information allows Böhme to explain the hidden meaning in the description of the waters in Genesis:[8]

The Work 121

> Vnd Gott sprach/ Es werde eine Feste zwischen den Wassern/ vnd die sey ein Vnterschied zwischen den Wassern. Da machet Gott die Feste/ vnd scheidet das Wasser unter der Festen von dem Wasser vber der Festen/ Vnd es geschah also, Vnd Gott nennet die Festen/ Himmel (*Genesis* I, 6, 7).

The waters signify the elements, either manifested or unmanifested. The astral possibilities within the unmanifested elements allow Böhme to adjectivally modify them with semantic features marking clarity and transparency: *heilig* 'holy' and *crystallinisch* 'crystalline'. Material water is dense, dark and more astringent than the former. The *Feste* 'fortress' between them is the point within the aqueous spectrum of holy water becoming material water where molecules can no longer be discerned. Viewed upward from the earth, this is the *Himmel*; from the other positions, the air. The waters are differing speeds of motion, a gradation involving an ever denser integration of material elements. Since motion precedes all material interaction, subtle motion—thoughts, visual images, *Imaginationen*—powerfully directed through the vibrating gross material structure of an articulated (*ausgesprochenes*) word, can affect the matrix of the recipient. Calling a person a *Narr* 'fool' (+high astringency) is not only self-debasing, but also dangerous:

> Denn das Wort Narr ist in sich selber in der Essentz anders nichts als ein entzündet grimmig Feuer=Rad, eine Unsinnigkeit; und wer seinen Nächsten unbillig also heisset, der hat ein Wort im Feuer=Rade, und im Grimm GOttes geboren, und ist des schuldig; denn das geborne Wort urständet aus der Seelen und Leibes Ente (*Mysterium* xxii, 65).

Böhme claims that with respect to the line of the covenant, there is "klaren Verstand in den Namen derer, welcher der Geist

GOttes hat durch Mosen in die Linien der Fortpflantzung gesetzet" (*Mysterium* xxix, 17). Böhme engages in a detailed etymological exegesis of the names of Cain through Zilla's daughter Naamad, and from Seth to Noah and his offspring, satisfied that the linguistic code is clear (*crystallinisch*) enough for divinity to reveal itself, and for Böhme (as well as the reader) to see the revelation. Since Böhme's Christ (JeHsus) cannot be ushered into manifestation through a lineage completely ruled by the astringent *Signatur*, he opposes sound against sound, and person against person, in an attempt to justify the established path from Adam through Jesus.

Böhme begins with the name *Cain*, a name that signifies the divine will engrossing itself within its desire to become matter. Once matter, Cain's *Gemüt* falsely identifies with the "äussern Welt Regiment . . . darein auch der Teufel im Grimm der Natur mit seiner Begierde schloss, und die Herrschaft dieser Welt in der Selbheit begehrte" (*Mysterium* xxix, 19). His brother Abel reflects the redemptive qualities of being *ausgehaucht* (H+Ab+el) as well as angelically derived (the postclitic designator -*el*) (*Mysterium* xxix, 20). Abel, an "ausgehauchter Engel" (*Mysterium* xxix, 20), perishes without leaving a trail of *Schatten* (offspring) behind. Böhme justifies Abel's childlessness with the fact that the asexuality of angels is a feature of the -*el*. Since the angels do not have "Geburts=Glieder und auch keinen Ausgang von unten . . . er bedarf es auch nicht" (*Aurora* vi, 12), and since Abel is more angelic than Cain, Böhme sees Abel as the prototype of the coming Christ:

> Weil aber Habel ein Vorbilde Christi war, welcher solte ohne Mann empfangen werden, nur blos aus dem einverleibten Worte im Weibes=Samen, welcher solte den Tod leiden für die Menschen, so muste Habel ohne Frucht und Aeste durch den Tod [i.e. through manifestation] gehen (*Mysterium* xxix, 23).

Habel, as Böhme points out, is ill suited as the matrix upon which

The Work 123

the divine Word could project itself. A woman must appear.

Cain's son Hanoch (H+ano+H) is "ein Aushauchen des Lebens" (*Mysterium* xxix, 28), revealing a double *Aushauchung*—a semantic framework—around the central obstruent nasal n. We see the exhaled H + nonobstruent A + nasal stop N + nonobstruent O + exhaled ach-Laut orthographically rendered as H (cH), or from the third layer, exhalation into matter > the beginning and end (temporality)> the *Geist* remains half in and half out > the heart, the Son of God > the *Geist* escapes the heart thundering outward as exhalation (see p. 7). The double H frame serves as a wall around the name, a wall which Böhme associates with the meaning of the name Hanoch. He is "ein Kind der Selbheit, das sich in der Natur in ein eigen Regiment und Willen einführet das ihme ein Regiment oder Region, oder Land oder Stadt ins Gemüte einmodelt" (*Mysterium* xxix, 28). *Selbheit*, egocentricity, and the boundaries of a region, country or city, circumscribe divinity within HanocH.

Hanoch's son Irad($*n$ [< Hanoch]>$*r$[Irad])reflects the inherited propensity towards astringency from the center of his father. The astringent r and the forceful dental stop d carry the semanticity of Hanoch (+egocentricity, +cities) one step further: Irad becomes the ruler, the "Richter (R+ichte+r = R+icht+R) und Herrn (H+e+RR+N), als ein Gewaltiger (Gewaltig+R) und Tyran (Ty+R+an)" (*Mysterium* xxix, 30, 31). The paternal tendency towards *Selbheit* controls the son's main ambition as he manipulates all things within his realm. Irad's son, Mahujael, unlike Abel, is not granted the angelic postclitic, instead carries on the tradition of his father. He desires to attract (+astringent) to himself "den Reichthum der äussern Welt ... in seiner Herrschaft, als allerley Creaturen und Frucht" (*Mysterium* xxix, 34). Rather than analyze Mahujael, Böhme moves on to explain the name of his son, Methusael. Intrigued with the structure of this name, Böhme praises it as "der rechte Wunder-Name, da ihme das Leben Göttliche Macht zumisset" (*Mysterium* xxix, 35). What aspect of divine power does Böhme understand in this strange non-Germanic name? Is it a linguistic expansion of *H+ano+H*? Instead of exhibiting the *Aushauchung* fence, Methusael reflects a semanticity more firmly grounded in obstruent materiality. Böhme derives the first syllable *Me-* (bilabial matrix + vocalic nonobstruent) from the possessive adjective *mein* 'my': "mein ist die Göttliche Macht: ich bin ein Engel von Gott . . . " (*Mysterium* xxix, 35). He strengthens the argument:

> Aber dieser Engels=Name in Göttlicher Macht fasset sich erstlich in der fleischlichen Selbheit: denn die Sylbe Me, welche das Wort des Namens anfähet, fasset sich in der äussern Welt Geburt in der Meinheit (*Mysterium* xxix, 36).

The birth within *Meinheit* 'myness, sense of myself' closely links him with his great-grandfather, Irad. The divine descent into individuality (*Me-*) terminates with the transcendent reintegration with spirit, seen in the final *-el*, a process whose beginning and end, rather than the medial *thu* and *sa*, intrigue Böhme.

Methusael's son, Lamech, fascinates Böhme with regard to the initial lateral. As seen in the *Aurora*, the *Geist* passes over and around both sides of the dorsum during the creation of the *l* sound. Böhme sees this in Lamech: the postclitic angel *-el* from his father Methusa+el descends into the beginning of his son (e)L+ ame+H. Lamech means:

> . . . nun die Verborgenheit Göttlicher Ordnung nach dem Englischen Rath, und heisset in der Natur=Sprache an diesem Orte alsoviel, als eine Sendung des Engels über die Herrschaft der Menschheit, als über die Regionen der Welt, über das fleischliche Leben, das würde dem Fürsten der Obern in der Natur untergeben seyn (*Mysterium* xxix, 37).

His two wives, Ada and Zilla, function as a bifurcated channel through which two aspects of spirit pass. Whereas Lamech has both angelic and *ausgehauchte* features, the wives reflect *Geist* within two substances: physical and astral. Lamech's dual nature allows him to take two wives:

> Das menschliche Leben erkante den Schaden der ihme war in seinem Stamme entstanden, und nahm hinfort zwey Weiber, das sind zweyerley Essentz und Willen: Als Ada heisset, die Seele gehet mit dem Willen durchs Gemüthe ... Aber die Zilla hatte ihm das Leben auch zum Weibe der Gebärerin genommen, das ist fleischliche Freude und Wollust (*Mysterium* xxix, 39).

The divine expression through Lamech and Ada produces the brothers Jabal and Jubal. The strong Ablaut relationship between these names leads Böhme to conclude that "Jabal deutet an den einfältigen Menschen, als da sind Bauern und dergleichen" (*Mysterium* xxix, 40), whereas Jubal (through association with the first-layer *Jubel* 'joy') expresses himself through music as "Wollust und Freude" (*Mysterium* xxix, 41). The simpleton and the musician—Böhmian opposites—appear again, only on a higher level, within the children of Lamech and the lusty Zilla. Their son Tubalkain reflects the mother's *fleischlich* 'fleshy, material' quality, ruling supreme over the highly compacted realm of the metals:

> Und die Zilla gebar auch, saget Moses, als den Tubalkain, den Meister in allerley Ertz und Eisenwerck; das ist, die feurische Begierde ist Zilla, die fasset in sich eine Substanz des Sulphuris und Mercurii in menschlicher Eigenschaft, und führt sich mit ihrem Geiste aus der Substanz aus, in eine Beschaulichkeit, in welchem Verstande der Mensch hat die Künste der Metallen erfunden (*Mysterium* xxix, 42).

Naema, on the other hand, is more spiritually advanced than her brother. She is "in ihrer Eigenschaft himmlisch" (N+ae+M+a <H+i+MM+el), that is, essentially astral, and as such, prefigures the qualities of Mary. Naema becomes:

> Eine Jungfrau, unter ihrem Bruder verborgen; Und wird alhie die zweyfache Erde verstanden, als in zweyerley Eigenschaften, eine himmlische, und eine grobe irdische als ein Wesen aus der finstern Welt Eigenschaft, und ein Wesen aus der Licht=Welt Eigenschaft (*Mysterium* xxix, 44).

Her fate, though, is similar to Abel's: she vanishes from manifestation without leaving a lineage. Moses "saget doch nichts von ihr, dass sie auch geboren habe oder sich befreyet" (*Mysterium* xxix, 45). Böhme speculates that her inability to serve as a divine channel may be more closely related to the seventy-sevenfold curse placed upon Lamech by Cain (*Genesis* iv, 24), than to any inherent inner character flaw. *Geist* chooses not to fully express itself within this branch of the Adamic tree.

Böhme continues the lineage of the covenant through Seth, a late child of Adam and Eve. Seth (sibilant hissing *s*, possibly also *th*) signifies rapid motion, since "sein Name heisset in der Natur-Sprache ein aushauchender Sprung aus dem Leben durchs Feuers= Centrum der Seelen" (*Mysterium* xxx, 10). His son Enos demarcates the first appearance of divinity self-consciously aware within manifestation. The name (vocalic nonobstruent + nasal blockage + vocalic nonobstruent + hissing sibilant) allows *Geist* mild astringency (*n*) and a wide channel (*o* 'the heart') in its outward extension into creation. In this manner, Enos more fittingly approaches Böhme's idea of a divine model than his cousin Hanoch, a fact which Böhme highlights in the following:

> Denn der Name Enos deutet an in der Natur=Sprache eine Göttliche Lust durchs Leben, da sich das geformte

The Work

> Wort wolte im Halle und Schalle des Lebens schauen: Darum fing der Geist GOttes aus dem Bunde durchs Leben der Menschen an zu lehren von GOtt und seinem Wesen und Willen . . . (*Mysterium* xxx, 11).

His son Kenan (*Mysterium* xxx, 17) is an identical extension of the father, an "ausgehende wiedergefassete Lust Göttlicher Beschauligkeit in welcher sich das gelehrte Wort formete" (*Mysterium* xxx, 17). Mahalaleel (Ma + H + alale + EL), the son of Kenan, "heisset in der Natur=Sprache eine englische Form eines englischen Reiches, da der Geist das Reich Christi in diesem Namen vorbildete" (*Mysterium* xxx, 18). His son Jared (Iared), only a minor derivation removed from Hanoch's son Irad (both from the root *rd, I+[a]+R+[e]+D = I+[∅]+R+[a]+D) is a leader, like Irad, but unlike Irad is a leader in spiritual realms. He becomes the "Priester oder Fürsten des geistlichen Reiches" (*Mysterium* xxx, 19). Böhme includes a cherub in the etymology:

> Es zeigets aber die Natur=Sprache klar an, dass Jared nur ein Vorbilde eines geistlichen Reiches sey, denn der Name führt den Cherub mit sich durchs Wort aus; denn das geistliche Reich war auf Erden im Grimme GOttes mit gefangen bis auf Christum, welcher den Zorn zerbrach (*Mysterium* xxx, 20).

His son Henoch (H+eno+H) is a divine temporalization in the essences, an "ausgehauchter Odem Göttlicher Lust" (*Mysterium* xxx, 27), and again, one etymological step removed from Hanoch. The shift from *A* (beginning and end, +temporal) to *E* (angel, -materiality) explains Henoch's unusual death. No mere physical passing, Henoch's physical form dissolves in ecstacy, into the state of *verzücken* 'rapturous magnetism within the state of ecstacy or trance' (*Mysterium* xxx, 47, 48) as *Geist* rejoins itself. He leaves behind not only many *Schatten*, but also a son, Methuselah.

Methuselah intensifies the *Geist* as it passes through him. It "gehet in starcker Macht durchs Wort aus; und wenn das gefassete Wort ausgegangen ist, so beschaucts sichs" (*Mysterium* xxxi, 1). Other than a brief comment on the fiery quality of the medial syllable *-sa-*, Böhme has little to say about the aged man. Lamech, Methuselah's son, rather than channelling divine energy through two wives, concentrates himself into his son, Noah. On a cosmically extended scale, Noah within the line of the covenant marks the boundary between time periods. Like the bilabial *m*, Noah demarcates a matrix. Böhme gives the reader a clue within the code: the name Noah = *N* (nasal blockage, half within and half outside the mouth) + *O* (the Son within manifestation, the heart) + *A* (the beginning, the Father) and *H* (the exhalation into matter). Why does the Son precede the beginning, if he is the beginning? Why the *O* before the *A*? Böhme explains:

> In diesem Namen Noah siehet der Geist in Lamech vor sich ins Ende [in front of it is the Son in matter] und hinter sich in Anfang [behind it is the Father in eternity], und fasset sich im Anfang und Ende in eine Form, und heisset dieselbe Noah, das ist, ein Kasten der Wunder was im Anfang und Ende, und in der gantzen Zeit wäre (*Mysterium* xxxi, 5).

Lamech's *Geist*, operative within Noah, once around the nasal detour, contemplates the future Jesus emanating forth from the Father. In addition to being a *Kasten der Wunder* 'chest of miracles', Noah is the shell wherein *Geist* is dreaming of itself.

Noah's sons, Sem, Ham, and Japeth (*Mysterium* xxxi, 5), are the "Vorbilde der drey Principien" (*Mysterium* xxxi, 11). Sem "ist ein Bilde der Licht Welt, und Japeth ein Bild der Feuer=Welt, da das Licht durchscheinet ... aber Ham ist ein Bild der äussern Welt" (*Mysterium* xxxi, 10).[9] The flood which follows is spiritually significant, Böhme warning the reader not to take this too lightly "und soll das niemend lächerlich ansehen, denn der das thut, hat unsern Geist und Sinn noch nicht verstanden ... sondern er hat nur einen äusserlichen Natur=Verstand gleich einem Vogel der in der Luft flieget und nicht weiss was das Wesen ist" (*Mysterium* xxxii, 22). Rather than view the flood from the perspective of the *äusserlichen Natur=Verstand* 'external understanding of nature', Böhme enjoins the reader to remember that the essence of water necessary for a physical flood is *himmlisch* (*-Begreifflig*) 'heaven-like, astral'. The flood which surrounds Noah and his family is not a flood of water, rather a *turba*, a withdrawal of manifestation from its state of eternally becoming, a cessation of motion, an end of matter (*Mysterium* xxxii, 23). By sealing himself within the arc, Noah presses through a matrix into a new world, a world created on the blueprint pattern of the first. The arc, from the perspective of three dimensions, is necessary: it affords Noah and his family the beginning of a new manifestation in three dimensions (again):

> Und der HErr schloss hinter ihm zu; Das deutet der Geist, Er schloss zu die ander Zeit der Welt, welche am Ende war ... so schloss der HErr mit Wasser zu, und auch hiemit die Thür seines Einganges, da er solte in der dritten Zeit ausgehen (*Mysterium* xxxii, 30).

Böhme is fascinated with Noah's reintegration into matter. When the arc comes to rest on Ararat, the *turba* rearranges itself into a world: first the peak appears, then the slopes, then surrounding valleys, and finally the entire planet. The word Ararat ($A + r + A + r + A + t$) embodies the entire process: the vocalic A (+Anfang) three times in succession abbreviates the three beginnings of the three periods of time. The first r is the matrix through which Adam falls into matter. The second is the matrix through which Noah travels in the arc. The dental stop T seals off the Word at its present state of development, leading Böhme to conclude:

> Dieser Name (Ararath) deutet uns in der Natur=Sprache an einen Berg oder Zusammenfassung eines Wesens aus

> dem Centro der Natur, aus der Grimmigkeit, als da sich GOttes Zorn hingelegt hat, so stund der Kasten auf dem hingelegten Zorne: die letzte Syllaba in diesem Worte Ararath deutet an, dass der Grimm der Ewigen Natur aus dem Centro sich habe in ein webend Regiment gefasset, und werde hinfort durch die Natur reiten, als ein Kriegsmann (*Mysterium* xxxii, 33).

Selbheit leaves the arc, unfortunately bringing with it the wrath from the eternally-becoming nature. It evolves through nature (matter) as a warrior, bent on infusing dualities into matter.

The linguistic argument resumes with a descriptive investigation of the names Esau and Iacob (<Shem). In the name E+sau, Böhme watches *Geist* cloak itself with the mantle of materiality, smothering out the vocalic (+astral) nonobstruent E. The *-sau* appears as "pig" within the etymology, while the angelic *E* takes on a more generalized meaning. Böhme says that the *E* "ist der Urstand aus dem Uno, als aus Einem (E+inem), ist die wahre in Adam geschaffene Engels=Eigenschaft" (*Mysterium* lii, 36). The second syllable, the *-sau* (+pig), is "das gefassete Thier der Eigen-Lust" (*Mysterium* lii, 36), which obfuscates the original spiritual descent, so that as matter, only the external animal, man, is visible:

> ... so stund noch die Sau dar, als der äussere Thierische Mensch, welcher das E als das Engels=Bilde hatte in ein Thier verwandelt ... da zwar das E noch innen war, aber mit der Sau umschlossen (*Mysterium* lii, 36).

Furthermore, Jacob holds Esau by the heel (*Mysterium* lii, 38) in order to check his extension into matter. Iacob holds "ihn von hinten ... und wieder zurücke aus dem Lauffe seines eigenen Willens ziehe in die erste Mutter, daraus die Natur entstanden ist, als zu einer anderen neuen Geburt" (*Mysterium* lii, 37). In this manner, Böhme understands that the state of complete and independent *Selbheit* demands disconnection from *Geist*. Iacob,

The Work 131

though, guides the masses of disconnected Esaus back to divinity, back to *Geist*:

> ... und deutet ferner an, wie der Geist Christi in Jacobs Linea werde den Esau in dieser Zeit bey seiner Fersen fassen, halten und straffen, und ihme seinen bösen Wandel seiner Füsse wehren durch seine Kinder (*Mysterium* lii, 40).

How does Jacob hold the masses closer to divinity?

In the name Jacob (Iacob), the vocalic onset *I* followed by the *A* signifies the first motion towards descent into manifestation, the corruption of the *Alphabeten* into *Buchstaben*: "das I das A fasset, und sich im A empor schwinget, und die sensualische Zunge in die mentalische einfasset, als in das COB" (*Mysterium* lii, 41). The obstruent velar stop *k (C)* is the matrix, the dividing line between alphabetic vowels and letters, the line between more and less *Geist* or less and more *Begreifflichkeit*. The new A.B.C. which Böhme promises the reader, the code through which they can read through matter, is his name: $I + A + C + O + B = A + B + C + Sensualisches\ Alphabeth\ I + O$. In the second syllable the unmanifested swings into direct interaction with the manifested. The letters are meaningful only in relation to their divine points of reference:

> Das O zum Centro des Worts wird gesetzt, da sich der Schwere Name GOttes ins O fasset; und wird recht darinnen verstanden, wie sich des Vaters Natur, als der sensualische Geist im A C und B ins I und O fasset ... (*Mysterium* lii, 41).

Böhme elevates the obstruency of the *C* and the *B* towards the nonobstruency of the vowels through consonantal interaction with the *Centrum der höchsten Liebe* 'center of highest love' (*Mysterium* lii, 41), the *I* (<Iesus) and with the *Centrum des fasslichen*

Wortes in der GOttheit 'center of the corporeal word in the divine', the *O* (<center of the heart).

Böhme allows the *I* (the *Iesus*) to remain powerful and dominant within the word Iacob (I+acob), otherwise the *Geist* would slide away into smothering Esau-like materiality. The *I* is a catalyst for the astringent *C* and *B*, enabling them to open from within themselves passages back to divine presence. In a bold move, Böhme equates the name Iacob with Jesus, unifying them through alphabetic specifications:

> ... so hiess der Name Jacob JESUS, denn das I führete sich in Adams Natur in seine verschlossene Engels= Eigenschaften wieder ein, so ward aus dem A ein E: denn der Vater gab seine Natur in der Menschheit dem Sohne, als dem I, und der Sohn machete wieder durch das I einen Engel daraus (*Mysterium* lii, 42).

Through splitting the right diagonal of the *A* (the \ ) at the crossbar into two separate staves, then placing these at the top and the bottom of the left diagonal of the *A*, Böhme orthographically reproduces the *E*. Moreover, the *I* (+Son) moves into the *E* (+Engel), rather than towards the *A* (+temporal nature), in order to stress the timeless and indestructible quality of the JESUS. Böhme continues:

> Denn das I ging in die tieffeste Demuth und Niedrigkeit, so stund die Figur also, JE daraus der feurische Liebe-Geist ausging, und sich in die Höhe schwang, und seinen Character vor sich setzete mit dem S und V: denn S ist des heiligen Feuers Character, und das V des Ausganges aus dem Feuer sein Character (*Mysterium* lii, 42).

The quality of holy fire emanating from the syllabic barrier -*S+u+S* (IEsus) elevates him above Jacob. Iacob is only a spiritual

The Work 133

indicator of the divine will towards manifestation as Jesus: divine will > alphabetic arrangement > Adam and Eve > the fall > Seth through Noah > the flood (-astringency) > Iacob > Maria directly into JESUS.

But what about the derivation Maria > Jesus? Returning for a moment to 1620, to the *Von der Menschwerdung Jesu Christi... Wie das Ewige Wort sey worden; und von Maria der Jungfrauen, wer sie von ihrem Urstand gewesen, und was sie sey in der Empfängnis ihres Sohnes JEsu Christi für eine Mutter worden...,* Böhme sees Maria as the "gebenedeyete unter alle Weibern dieser Welt" (*Menschwerdung* I, viii, 5). In order to appreciate this appellation as the prototype for IESUS, the earlier comments need to be brought forth.

Maria, according to Böhme's *Menschwerdung*, is the most perfect of Eve's children. This perfection qualifies her for the role as divine channel, although this austere and holy appointment does not elevate her to the position of a saint:

> Nicht dass sie eine Göttin sey, die man für GOtt ehren soll, denn sie ist nicht das Ziel, und sie sprach auch: Wie soll das zugehen, sintemal ich von keinem Manne weiss: sondern das Wort des Lebens ins Vaters Centro, das sich mit der Bewegung der Gottheit in die Menschheit eingab und in menschlicher Essentz eröffnete, ist das Ziel: das ist der Zweck, da wir hinlauffen sollen, in die Wiedergeburt (*Menschwerdung* I, viii, 5).

As the obedient, uncomprehending servant, Maria acquiesces to the will of the angel (*Menschwerdung* I, ix, 16). Through a realignment of Maria's dormant *Gemüt* toward the stream of divine energy descending into matter, its passage through her physicality causes impregnation. *Geist,* already having imprinted into her astral features the potential toward regeneration, creates an infant through the flesh and blood astringency of her body. In this way, *Geist* becomes matter, substance and the perfect reflection of itself within matter: the Son. Böhme fears that the readers may misunderstand:

> Dieselbe Wesenheit, ob sie gleich in Maria eröffnet ward in ihrem Fleisch und Blute, und menschliche Essentz in sich nahm, war gleichwol dieselbe Zeit, weil Christus in Marien Leibe lag, im Himmel, im Element, an allen Orten: Sie fuhr nicht über viel Meilen irgend von einem Orte in Mariam, nein; sondern das eingeschlossene Centrum, das Adam hatte im Zorn GOttes in Tod geschlossen, das schloss das Wort der Gottheit auf, und führete Göttliche Wesenheit in das Jungfräuliche in Tod geschlossene Centrum ein (*Menschwerdung* II, ix, 3).

The newly developed perspective of vocalic semanticity as seen in the *Mysterium Magnum* aids the bewildered reader in understanding the more gradual degrees between the *Wort* and *Wesen*, between Maria and Jesus, between *Geist* and *Begreiffligkeit*.

As we have seen with Iacob and Iesus, divinity deflects in two directions from the consonantal astringent obstruents: into and away from a long lasting association with matter. In the word *Maria*, Böhme selects the verb *einleiben* 'to become as a body with', in describing the nature of the divine relationship. She is the final matrix, the final barrier through which IEHOVAH must pass in order to extend itself into the purest state of manifestation. The bilabial M (M+aria) is the first wall which the *Geist* as A penetrates, encountering then the high astringency of the R. The final vowels I and A show spirit in matter reverting to nonobstruent alphabetic *Geist*. Maria is the matrix (M+a+R+ia = M+a+[T]+R+i+[x]) although less astringent without the dental and velar stops. In Maria, the descent into words concludes:

> So ging die heilige Stimme GOttes aus Jehovah, in des Weibes Matricem in das verblichene himmlische Ens ein,

und einleibete sich aufs neue mit dem heiligen Worte, als in ein Ziel eines ewigen Bundes ... und diese eingeleibte Wort in Evä Samen stund in der Matrice, als ein Ziel eines gewissen Bundes; und ward in Evä Samen von Mensch zu Mensch in dem himmlischen Theil mit fortgepflanzet ... (als ein glimmend Moder mit fortgepflanzet ward) bis auf die Zeit der Erweckung in Maria, da der Bund am Ende stund ... (*Mysterium* xxiii, 29, 31).

CHAPTER V

A NEW DAWN IN THE FINAL YEAR: *TAFELN* (1624), *CLAVIS* (1624) AND *BETRACHTUNG GÖTTLICHER OFFENBARUNG . . . 177 FRAGEN* (1624)

With the linguistic realization that Jesus evolves into matter through the materiality of a partly astringent but mostly *himmlisch* Maria, Böhme, in reflecting on his life's work, realizes that he is coming close to formulating his ultimate statement. Pausing briefly after the *Mysterium Magnum* (1623), Böhme yearns for an overview, a focal point of clarity over the dominion of his thinking and writing. Out of this organizational effort, he produces the visually designed *Tafeln von den Dreyen Principien Göttlicher Offenbarung, Wie GOtt ausser der Natur in sich selber, und dann in der Natur, nach den dreyen Principien, betrachtet wird; Auch Was Himmel und Hölle, Welt, Zeit und Ewigkeit, samt allen Creaturen sey, woraus alles entsprungen; was das Sichtbare und Unsichtbare sey?* (February 1624) and the word dictionary *Clavis oder Schlüssel, das ist Eine Erklärung der vornehmsten Puncten und Wörter, welche in diesen Schriften gebrauchet werden* (March and April 1624). Both show an organizational clarity only beginning to reveal a refinement of the earlier linguistic principles, a refinement which is clarified and described in the last unfinished treatise *Betrachtung Göttlicher Offenbarung was GOTT, Natur und Creatur, sowol Himmel, Hölle und Welt, samt allen Creaturen sind; Woher alle Dinge in der Natur ihren Ursprung haben genommen, und wozu GOtt dieselbe habe geschaffen; was sie nütze sind; sonderlich dem Menschen Was Adam und Christus sey; durch den gantzen Process und Lauff der Welt bis ans Ende, und in die Ewigkeit geführet und in 177 Fragen gestellt Von einem Liebhaber Christi und seiner Kinder, zu mehrem Nachdencken, was der Mensch sey.*

A New Dawn in the Final Year

The first organizational manifesto, the *Tafeln*, aside from reviewing the basic Böhmian theosophy (as mentioned in the title), reveals the aging mystical linguist still entranced with the manipulations and modifications of language. Now, though, the visual gains much strength as Böhme observes the letters (*Buchstaben*) separating and rearranging themselves into other letters, passing through movement sequences between each frozen moment, the letter. In the word *Adonai*, Böhme begins the linguistic descent:

> Das Wort ADONAI deutet an das Aufthun oder Selbst= Bewegniss der ungründlichen ewigen Einheit, was die ewige Gebärung, Aufthun und Ausgang der Dreyheit GOttes in sich selber sey (*Tafel* 9).

The *A* breaks apart into three staves, the "dreyfaches I" (*Tafel* 9), then rearranges itself into a cross, summarizing the descent "als in einen Anfang, Ein und Ausgang" (*Tafel* 9). The second letter, the *D* (A+D+onai), is the motion within the cross, that necessary prerequisite for matter to interqualify. This motion allows matter to appear, revealing itself within *Begreiffligkeit*. It is "das Aufthuende" (*Tafel* 9). Motion and matter extend through all space, a space which Böhme circumscribes with the next letter, the *O*. The *O* is the boundary of the realm of *Begreiffligkeit*, the "Geburt der Stätte GOttes in sich selber" (*Tafel* 9). Within the realm of created matter, the triune spirit rearranges itself as the three staves (seen in the *A*) and groups together forming the fourth letter, the *N* (Ado+N+ai) (*Tafel* 9). The *N* is astral, manifesting itself only within the *A*: again a simple rearrangement of the starting point. He says:

> Das untere (A) ist der Gegenwurf oder das Wircken des dreyfachen I oder Geistes, davon ewiglich Bewegniss Kraft, Farben und Tugenden entstehen oder urständen (*Tafel* 9).

The three staves rejoin in the final letter *I*, where Böhme sees trinity flowing out of, yet still remaining within, unity. He diagrams the etymology as follows:[1]

```
AD........Vater..........Wille............JE
O...........Sohn...........Lust............HO
N..........Geist..........Scientz........VAH
A..........Kraft..........Wort..........Leben
I...........Farben.........Weisheit......Tugend
```

Böhme directs the reader's attention to the second column beginning with *Vater*: "Das Wort Vater ist der ewige Anfang des Wirckens und Wollens in dem dreyfachen I der Einheit" (*Tafel* 10). Etymologically related, the first word in the third column reflects the *Wollen>Willen* (both from *wl*), a plural attested in the text, but not in the diagram: "Das Wort Willen deutet an das Wollen oder Bewegen in der aufthuenden Einheit" (*Tafel* 15). From this *Einheit* 'unity' Böhme derives the following syllable *JE* positing it with the feature of *Aushauchung*: vocalic nonobstruents *I* and *E* are mildly aspirated as *(h)IE*. Together they are "ein Hauchen der Einheit" (*Tafel* 21). The birth of the place of God in himself, seen above in the *O*, circumscribes the products of *Kraft*—matter—within its corresponding second-column semantic relative, the word *Sohn*:

> Das Wort Sohn ist das Gewirckete[2] der Kraft, als die Einfasslichkeit des Willens, darinnen sich der dreyfache Geist schleust, als eine Stätte der Göttlichen Ichheit (*Tafel* 11).

The reader is pleasantly awakened with the new and unusual compounds *Gewirckete, Einfasslichkeit*,[3] and *Ichheit*.[4] Before utilizing these constructions, Böhme calls the *Sohn* the place of divine I-ness, temporalizing and localizing the descent. This awakening of spirit within the selfness of matter followed by the subsequent attraction to *Wesen* is the corresponding word *Lust*: "Das Wort Lust deutet an die wirckliche Empfindlichkeit des Willens oder Wollens" (*Tafel* 16). The last column reflex, the *HO*, shows little horizontal contact with *Lust*, rather is "ein Hauchen des JE" (*Tafel* 21). The astral *N* becomes the *Geist* in the second column, the feature of *-begreifflich* uniting them. Böhme describes *Geist* in terms of a massive energy which is checked by the film of matter it attracts to itself. Each stage of the descent corresponds to a differing aspect of the life cycle. He selects the Aurorean *Blume* 'flower' as the point of reference:[5]

> Das Aufthun oder wirckende Wachsen ist der Anfang: Die Kraft des Wirckens ist der Umschluss und cörperliche Einfassung des Wachsens; Und der Geruch welcher aus der Kraft ausgehet, ist die Bewegniss oder das wachsende, ausgehende Freuden=Leben der Kraft, daraus die Blume entspringet (*Tafel* 12).

There is no relationship between the word *Geist* and its third-column correlate *Scientz*. Böhme evolves this word from the preceding vertical *Lust*. Whereas in *Lust*, the "wirckliche Empfindlichkeit des Willens" (connection to the first vertical) is intended, the word *Scientz* 'science' invades the evolving *Lust*, becoming the "wirckliche empfindliche Wissendschaft" (*Tafel* 17). With this knowledge, Böhme describes the *Wort* depending upon the *Wissendschaft* 'manner of knowing' as an eternal divine projection. There will always be knowledge: "Das Wort Wort deutet an, wie sich die ewige Liebe der empfindlichen Einheit mit der Wissenschaft ewig ausspricht in einen Gegenwurf" (*Tafel* 18). As seen, *VAH* has nothing in common with *Scientz*, rather depends on the *HO*: "VA ist ein Hauchen des O" (*Tafel* 21). *Leben* derives from *HO* becoming "dieses dreyfache Hauchen" (*Tafel* 22) rather than from *Wort*. Once the word is projected into matter, Böhme calls it *Weisheit* a wisdom hidden within every word awaiting its reintegration within the all-encompassing divine *Geist*. Trailing on the end of the derivation, *Tugend* is in apposition to itself: "Tugend, das deutet an die unmessliche Tugend solches hauchenden Lebens" (*Tafel* 22). *Kraft* in the second column derives directly from the *A* (p. 137), where the interactions of the three-staved *I* generate not only *Kraft* 'power', but also the word beneath it *Farben* 'colors' and also the straggler *Tugend* 'virtues' (*Tafel* 9). *Kraft* is also related to the composite JEHOVA + *Leben*, since it carries the feature +*Hauch*: "Das Wort Kraft deutet an das hauchende, ausgehende, verständliche, empfindliche Leben" (*Tafel* 13).

Toward the middle of the work, Böhme takes a moment to clarify the mystical etymology of the word *Tinctur*: "Das Wort Tinctur ist das schiedliche Wort, daraus die sieben Eigenschaften fliessen" (*Tafel* 29). The first letter *T* is the opening of unity, the *Aufthun der Einheit* (*Tafel* 29), the reason for breathing into manifestation. The *i* is the flowing out of unity as the cross (+temporal), with vocal onset in the nasal *n* summarizing the resonant aspect of the triune spirit. The velar stop -*k* (here *c*) breaks the resonance, dividing the word into sounds (*Tafel* 29). The following *t* opens glory into matter, a glory which leads to love in the symbolic shape of the *u* (here *V*):

> V ist nun des H. Geistes Character mit dreyen Spitzen; Zwey in die Höhe bedeuten das Feuer und Licht, und der dritte unter sich bedeutet die Einheit in der Liebe, als die Demuth (*Tafel* 29).

The final *r* generates the visible world (*Tafel* 29).

Böhme analyzes *Tinctur* again in the following citation, although this time he concentrates on the position of the staves with respect to the letter they form. The *T* is the Father, since it is composed of the "dreyfaches I" (*Tafel* 30), which when agglutinated forms the *T*. The next letter, the *i*, is born within matter as Jesus (I+esus) (*Tafel* 30). The staves join together to form the following letter, the *n*, concerning which Böhme casually remarks that "N ist das dreyfache I im Geiste" (*Tafel* 30). The curved *i*, the

A New Dawn in the Final Year

following letter *c*, is Christ (C+hristus) (*Tafel* 30), whereas the *t* is the "Vater in Christo" derived from the initial *T*. The vocalic *u* is the spirit (*Geist*) of Christ (-obstruent) in the Word. As the entire brief explication rests within the astringent *r*, Böhme delivers a testimonial to its strength:

> R ist der Königliche Thron, um welchen Licht und Finsterniss streitet, da Satan und Christus gegen einander stehen, da man Liebe und Zorn in Einem Grunde, aber in zweyerley Offenbarung verstehet, den Unsern alhier verstanden, welche GOtt angehören, aber den andern an diesem Ort ein Schloss davor (*Tafel* 30).

To those readers Böhme includes among the ranks of *den Unsern* 'those of us', the significance of the astringent *r* is overtly clear. To the others who cannot penetrate matter, finding *Geist* underneath its delusive sheath, Böhme says that these writings will be a lock rather than a key. In order to open the arcanum, Böhme prepares a key, a *Clavis*, which will aid the reader in his ascent toward the *königliche Thron* 'divine throne'.

In the next organizational writing, the *Clavis, oder Schlüssel, das ist Eine Erklärung der vornehmsten Puncten und Wörter, welche in diesen Schriften gebrauchet werden,* Böhme credits the old rabbis with accurately comprehending the complexities underlying the name Jehovah (!):

> Die alten Rabinnen bey den Juden haben etlicher massen dieses verstanden, denn sie haben gesagt, dieser Name sey der Allerhöchste und Heiligste Name GOttes, damit man die wirckliche Gottheit im Sensu verstehet; und es ist wahr (*Clavis* 15).

So as to avoid later misunderstanding, Böhme abbreviates the entire descent of spirit into matter in still another analysis of the letters IEHOVA: the initial *I* is the "Ausfluss der ewigen, unzertrennlichen Einheit" (*Clavis* 16) and the basis of the *Göttlicher Ichheit* 'divine self-ness'. As the basis of the word *Iehovah*, the initial nonobstruent triples itself as the new arrangement *E* (only the horizontal staves extend, the vertical staff is the original *I*). The *E* is unity (*Einheit*) (*Clavis* 16), although together the IE represents "ein Aushauchen der Einheit in sich selber" (*Clavis* 16). The *Ichheit (I)* and the *Einheit (E)*, the egocentric selfness and the ever expansive unity, express themselves within the *Hauchen* of the following *H*. This extension is circumscribed by the *O*, agreeing with the Iehovah derivation offered in the *Tafel*: the *O* is the extent to which the Father breathes the Son (through the action of the *IE*) into matter. The divine *I*-ness rejoices in the following *V* (U) becoming the "freudenreiche Ausfluss vom Hauchen" (*Clavis* 16), the final *A* reflecting the "Ausgegangene von der Kraft" (*Clavis* 16).[6]

The *177 Fragen* (see complete title p. 136) represents a depth of perception unprecedented in the earlier writings (through *Mysterium Magnum*). Earlier, though, Böhme writes to a new acquaintance, an Abraham von Franckenberg und Ludwigsdorff (1593-1652), indicating that he is unable to converse in the Latin tongue, but that the lowest in station (himself intended) have delivered the greatest spiritual truths (*Sendbrief* xli). Since the *Aurora*, Böhme has been justifying the letter sequence of his name, a sequence he feels outlines his role as mystical extrovert:

> Wer war Habel? Ein Schäfer: Wer war Henoch und Noa[7] [notice the absence of the *Aushauchung H*]? Einfältige Leute: Wer war Abraham, Isaac und Jacob. Viehehirten waren sie: Wer war Moses, der theure Mann GOttes? ein Viehehirte: Wer war David, als ihn des HErrn Mund berief? ein Schäfer. Wer waren die Propheten gross und klein? gemeine und geringe Leutlein; ein Theil nur Bauern und Hirten, die nur der Welt Fusshadern waren; man hielt sie nur für Narren. Und ob sie gleich Wunder und Zeichen thaten, noch sahe die Welt nur auf das

> Höhe, und der H. Geiste muste ihrer Füsse Schemel seyn: denn der stolzte Teufel hat je und allewege wollen ein König in dieser Welt seyn (*Aurora* ix, 3).

The prophet meets his student sometime during the year 1622, writing to him on February 20, 1623, that he has already finished a treatise on how the mystery speaks through matter:[8]

> Auch wie sich dasselbe Mysterium Magnum durch das Aussprechen der Göttlichen Scientz durch das Wort GOttes, im Loco dieser Welt in eine Schiedlichkeit und Fasslichkeit zur Creation eingeführet habe (*Sendbrief* xli, 6).

He concludes the letter with fifteen symbolic postscripts, two of which deal directly with linguistic speculation:

> Der Thurn zu Babel ist grundlos worden, man meinet mit den Stützen zu erhalten, aber ein Wind vom HErrn stösset ihn um (*Sendbrief* xli, 6; *Postscript* 5).

> Das Orientalische Thier kreiget ein menschlich Hertz und Angesichte; und ehe das geschiehet so hilft es den Thurn zu Babel mit seinen Klauen umreissen (*Sendbrief* xli, 6; *Postscript* 8).

Rejecting the validity of the Tower of Babel argument,[9] Böhme indicates to Franckenberg that the fractionated languages (matter) can be restored through "ein Wind vom Herrn," precisely the nonobstruent alphabetic vowels seen earlier. Not only vocalic in nature, the *Wind* affects the matter of the Tower of Babel—the astringency of its stone construction—pushing it over. The same idea controls the eighth postscript: the oriental animal evolves more easily within the realm of a Babel-free environment. Not only granted freedom to become, the oriental animal accepts the gifts of a human heart and a human face.[10] Böhme comments further in the *177 Fragen* on questions Franckenberg feels will elicit precise responses from the aging mystic.

Before answering the questions directly, Böhme reminds the reader (Franckenberg), that the writings that follow represent only a small part of his more exhaustive works. The answers in the compendium serve solely to lead the reader into the state of "Offenbarung unseres Herrn Jesu Christi" (*Fragen*, Vorrede 4). After a general introduction Böhme answers the first question "Was ist GOtt ausser Natur und Creatur in sich selber?"

He maps the semantic flow within the word *Gott*, adding some new information. We learn that *GOtt* (*Fragen* 1, 1-3):

- \+ is the eternal unity (1).
- \+ is immeasurable goodness (1).
- \- has things before or after (1).
- \- moves (1).
- \- has features (1).
- \+ is external to and within the world (1).
- \+ is deeper than thought (1).
- \+ is beyond the magic of numbers (1).
- \+ as a unity cannot be spoken out (1).
- \+ is the good (2).
- \+ flows out of itself into desire and motion which perceives the soft transparency of the unity (2).
- \+ is understood as living behind the stars by the *Vernunft* (3).
- \+ has a residence only within matter (3).
- \+ manifests through love within humanity (3).
- \+ throws an eternal idea (*Gegenwurf*) into love, which when in association with the physical body emanates divinity (3).

Beyond the magic of numbers, *Gematria*,[11] God's unity can never be disturbed or apportioned into number mysticism:

A New Dawn in the Final Year

> Ja wann man hundert tausend Jahren aneinander Zahlen ausspreche von seiner Grösse und Tieffe, so hätte man doch noch nicht angefangen seine Tieffe auszusprechen, dann er ist die Unendlichkeit (*Fragen* 1, 1).

The *unendlich* 'eternal' aspect of God can willfully enter a relationship marked by the feature +*endlich* 'end-able, temporal', once it creates what Böhme calls the *Abgrund*. This is the second question: "Was ist der Abgrund aller Dinge, da kein Geschöpf ist, als das ungründliche Nichts?" The *Abgrund* (*Fragen* 2, 1, 6):

+ is a residence of the unity of God (1).
+ is the *Ichts des Nichts* (1).
+ is God himself (1).
+ expresses itself through a threefold *Hauchen*, each containing three aspects, all which lead back to *einem Eigenen* 'an own' (6).
+ is JEHOVAH (6).

The word pair *Ichts des Nichts* 'the I-ness of the No-ness, the I-thing of the No-thing' to the modern mind seems a shrewd wordplay on the old Germanic word *icht* 'thing'. To Böhme, though, the negative particle *N* added to the *icht* (seen also in *Bösewicht* 'evil doer') negates both the first- and the third-layer meaning.[12] Rather than select *etwas* to oppose *nichts*, Böhme skillfully employs the homonymic shell *Ichts* to express God as the self, the I, and God as matter, the something. Its negative, the *Nichts*, is the impersonal original God, the state of "nonegocentripetality" (as opposed to egocentripetality or self-awareness within astringency). Since God "flows out of itself into desire and motion which perceive the soft transparency of the unity" (*Fragen* 1, 2), Böhme describes God as eternal goodness. Under the vehicular influence of its *Wollen und Wallen*[13] 'desire and motion', God perceives God as unity, as oneness, *Einheit*. From this unity, vocalic emanations ensue:

> In diesem aufthuenden Leben Göttlicher Einheit, werden fünf lautbare Sensus in der Empfindlichkeit der Liebe des Lebens verstanden, als A. E. I. O. U. darinnen das Göttliche Wollen und Wircken stehet; die führen sich in ein Aushauchen zur Schiedlichkeit (*Fragen* 2, 5).

The nonobstruents explain the hidden meaning of the word JEHOVAH, a meaning which once exhaled into manifestation reveals itself as differentiation and multiplicity (*Schiedlichkeit*). Böhme reetymologizes: the initial *I* "gehet in sich selber in ein dreyfaches Wesen" (*Fragen* 2, 7) producing the three-staved *E*. Together the *JE* signals the presence of the Father (p. 138), willfully breathing himself into the receptacle *HO*, which awaits it as "eine Fassung der Liebe" (*Fragen* 2, 7). Böhme controls the paradigmatic extent of the many powers which issue forth from the next syllable *HO* with the circumferential *O*. In this moment of the descent, God becomes the "ewige Etwas, oder Ichts" (*Fragen* 2, 7). As the *Ichts, Geist* continues the descent toward matter, by taking shape within the syllable *VA*: "Dann das V ist der Geist, als der Ausgang, und A ist die Weisheit darinnen sich der Geist fasset zu einem wirckenden Leben" (*Fragen* 2, 7). The next linguistic comment paraphrases the descent, placing it on the manifested side of the matrix:

> So heisset alsdann dieses dreyfache hauchende Leben in sich selber O. JAH. Dann die eingefassete Lust ist das O, als ein Auge des einigen Sehens, ein lauterlich Sehen; und das JAH ist der dreyfache Eingang seiner selber, als zur Empfindlichkeit des Wollens, welcher sich selber aufthut durch das ewige Hauchen (*Fragen* 2, 8).[14]

The circumferential *O* limits the *Begreiffligkeit* features of the world, allowing the triune JAH evolutionary space. The Son (I) assumes the finiteness of matter (A) as he breathes himself into creation (H). Now capable of realizing his desires (*Wollen*) within

A New Dawn in the Final Year 147

sensation (*Empfindlichkeit*), the descent concludes. Böhme moves on to discuss the inner meaning of the word *Adonai*. This Hebrew shell:

- is the emanation of the characteristics of the six powers (*Fragen* 2, 9).
- gives rise to the Mysterium Magnum as the name Tetragrammaton, this giving rise to all visible and invisible *Wesen* (2, 9).
- contains the six powers of eternal nature (2, 9).
- represents the six days of creation, bounded by the O (2, 10).
- has the six powers within (2, 11).
- is the *Stätte GOttes* 'place of God' (2, 11).

In addition to representing the six days of creation encircled by the material O, Böhme sees the word *Adonai* composed of six independent letters, each signifying a physical potential recorded in the astral pattern of the world: *Begierlichkeit* 'externalization of inner want', *Beweglichkeit* 'motion', *Empfindlichkeit* 'sense receptivity', *Feuer oder Leben* 'fire or life', *Licht oder Liebe* 'light or love' and *Schall Unterschiedlichkeit und Verständniss* 'vibration, differentiation within vibration, and understanding of the vibration'. These distinctions are penetrated by their source, the *Nichts*:

> Denn alle Dinge sehen darinnen als ein Nichts, dieweil das Etwas ist von diesem Sehen entsprungen, so siehet das Nichts, als die Ewige Einheit, durch alles ungehindert (*Fragen* 2, 12).

The third question "Was ist GOttes Liebe und Zorn? Wie ist er ein zorniger und eifriger GOtt, weil Er selber die unveränderliche Liebe ist? Wie mag Liebe und Zorn ein Ding seyn?" delves deeper into the etymology of the vocalic sequence *IAH*. The affirmative

JAH evolves from the third-layer *IAH* (Son + time + matter), surfacing as the *Ja* 'yes' to which Böhme opposes the *NEIN* 'no'.

Emanating from the *IAH* is the feature of reception; something or some potential force must accept the subject moving towards itself. This something, this *icht*, is what Böhme terms the *Gegenwurf* 'the thrown-against, object', which subarranges itself under the *NEIN* (<*JAH*). Since the positive and negative poles are the same subject, except at different points within itself, Böhme calmly asserts that they are both "neben einander . . . sondern nur ein Ding, scheiden sich aber in 2 Anfänge und machen zwey Centra, da ein iedes in sich selber wircket" (*Fragen* 3, 3). Within the original expression of the *JAH*, there seems to be a directional thrust towards the *NEIN*, an adverbial directive *Nein-wärts* (*Fragen* 3, 10). Final objectification occurs as the *JAH* becomes the *NEIN*, a *Wesen* whose origin within the third layer of the *JAH* precedes all things:

> Denn es [the JAH] hat kein Nein vor ihme, sondern das Nein urständet erst in dem ausgeflossenen Willen der Annehmlichkeit[15] (*Fragen* 3, 10).

What about the *NEIN*? What are its reflexes within the code? Böhme posits six qualities arising from within the eternal propensity toward *Ziehen* 'pulling': *Zorn* 'wrath', *Schärfe* 'sharpness', *Härte* 'hardness', *peinliche Empfindnis* 'painful sense reception', *Feuer-Quall* 'fire anguish' and *Hall, Schall Rede oder Unterscheiden* (*Fragen* 3, 31) 'vibration, speech or linguistic distinctional ability'. These qualities easily pattern with those posited under *JAH*, with language potential and linguistic realization being a common denominator. Why is the union of opposites preserved within the speaking reflex?

Böhme notes that within the sixth principle, the *Schall*, the Holy Names preserve themselves (*Fragen* 3, 32). In the *Schall*, the central fire (the generative principle) creates favorable conditions for elemental construction to take place, as well as for love to come into being. In the nonresistance of love, the gentle surrender of form into content, Böhme sees a receptive network filtering *Geist* through the name *IEHOVAH*, through the matrix of astringency into containers awaiting it. As such, all manifestation reflects the presence of resident powers (*Fragen* 3, 35), powers which assume the form of subjects over the objects of their creation. The world is a massive vibration of the Holy Name, and is "durch die Bewegniss des Wunderthuenden Namens ausgeflossen, und in Schiedlichkeit und Förmlichkeit gegangen" (*Fragen* 3, 35).

The fourth question "Was ist gewesen, ehe dann die Engel und Schöpfung war?" is directly answered with the word God. God, Böhme notes, contains within himself an idea, or a "geistliche Inmodelung,"[16] by means of which he views creation. The idea becomes visual (*bildlich*) once the divine centrality desiringly moves toward the *Jah/Nein*, leading eventually to matter (*Fragen* 4, 4). Franckenberg moves Böhme to a different topic, asking in the fifth question "Was war der Grund und das Wesen, davon die Engel sind geschaffen worden; was war dieselbe Kraft im Worte GOttes, welche ausfloss und Creatürlich ward?"

The power flowing outward begins with the *Idea (Geistige Inmodelung)* arranging itself under the *JAH* aspect (*Fragen* 5, 4). The *Idea* (+Jah) has no distinction; it is pure with respect to itself, unadulterated by duality. From itself, thrones of angelic offices and legions of angels spring forth (*Fragen* 5, 12), each controlled by a *Fürsten-Engel* 'Prince Angel'. Böhme mentions their names as Jachiel and Eliel (*Fragen* 5, 15), although does not comment on their duties or their origins. Their domain is the outer chaos of manifestation, the rim of matter nearest the matrix. Böhme avoids further comment, fearing general misunderstanding on account of the possibly heretical nature of the comment. Misuse of these ideas could bring about another Aurorean furor; misunderstanding could induce weakened minds to become superstitious as a result of miscomprehension: "Dann sie haben ein ander Chaos äusserlicher Art, davon alhier nicht weiter zu melden, wegen des Missbrauchs und Aberglaubens" (*Fragen* 5, 17). The public writings can divulge only certain censored spiritual information.

Böhme returns to the spiritual contemplation of the letters, mentioning that each letter is important on three layers as well as with respect to its position in individual words.[17] In this way, the code generates meaning:

> Wenn wir wollen der Engel Kräfte und Tugenden betrachten, und gantz recht verstehen, und nicht an Bildern hangen, wie die thörichte Vernunft allezeit thut, so betrachten wir nur die Geister der Buchstaben, in was Sensu und Kraft ein ieder stehet; und betrachten hernach die Zusammenfügung derselben buchstabischen Geister, davon das Wort oder Verstand entstehet, so haben wir den gantzen Grund mit Ja und Nein, ihr gantzes Fundament (*Fragen* 5, 18).

The angels (mentioned in the first part of the question) are accessible through the contemplation of the spirits of letters (*Geister der Buchstaben*), rather than through iconoclastic diagrams. With the power of angelic communication, the full control of the Word, Böhme remarks that man would know everything:

> Er führet die Macht aller Dinge in seinem Munde schwebend; hätte er den Glauben, dass er diese Kraft möchte bilden so hätte er den Grund aller Heimlichkeiten, und möchte Wunder thun wie die Engel; welches auch die Schrift bezeuget: So ihr glauben habet, als ein Senf= Körnlein, so möget ihr zum Berge sagen: Stürtze dich ins Meer (Matth. 21:21) Item: Das Wort ist dir nahe, nemlich in deinem Munde und Hertzen (Rom. 10:8) (*Fragen* 5, 24).

Franckenberg wants more information concerning the angelic

extent, asking in the sixth question "Was ist der Engel Amt und Thun, und warum führet sich GOttes=Kraft in Bildung ein?" This, Böhme answers, is guided by the projected controlled spectrum of descent, the "H. Cabala der Veränderung" (*Fragen* 6, 11). Rather than remark on the nature of this secret (Cabala), Böhme avoids negative suspicion,[18] concluding though, with a disguised message to the audience (Franckenberg), that he is involved in the circles of the enlightened few:

> Die weisen Heiden haben das Subjectum, als das Gegenbild solcher Thronen verstanden, und haben diese für Götter geehret, aber des wahren Grundes der Inwendigkeit haben sie noch gemangelt: bey den Christen aber ists gar stumm worden, ausser etlichen wenigen, denen es GOtt hat offenbaret, welche es haben in parabolischer Weise geheim gehalten (*Fragen* 6, 18).

Böhme comments on both Lucifer and the *Nein* aspect of divine descent answering the question "Was hat denn Lucifer beweget, dass er hat wieder GOtt gelüstert, und sich vom Guten abgewandt?" Lucifer:

+ is moved by the Nein (*Fragen* 7, 1).
+ has the will toward form, shape and construction (1).
+ desires to rule with the Nein over the Jah (6).
+ rules through the power of division within the Nein (6).
+ has features which are inimical to those of angels (7).

Lucifer, in receiving power from the *NEIN*, absorbs the features of the negative pole as well as *Herbe* 'astringency', *Stachlicht* 'prickling, stickling (light)', *Feindig* 'adversity' and *Aengstlichkeit* 'fear' (*Fragen* 7, 7) features. As the divine motion toward the *NEIN* (*Nein-wärts*) separates itself from the *JAH*, it impresses into the *Nein*, those features which oppose its *Jah*-construction:

the poisonous darkness in worms and animals reflects this within matter (*Fragen* 8, 10).

The eighth question "Wie hat aus einem Engel mögen ein Teufel werden, oder was ist ein Teufel? In was Essentz und Wesen steht er nach dem Fall?" although unanswered, gives Böhme latitude in which he can moralize. Just as the angel becomes a devil, "so ists schon geschehen: geschichts doch beym Menschen auch, dass ein guter Mensch verdirbet" (*Fragen* 8, 14). The ninth question "Weil GOtt Allmächtig ist, warum hat Er dem Lucifer nicht widerstanden, und solches geschehen lassen" and the tenth question "Was hat der Teufel begehret, darum er ist von GOttes Lehre abgewichen?" bring Böhme back to commentary concerning the validity of the *etliche wenige* 'certain few'. Too many people live in their fantasy, creating for themselves images of transcendence, *Bildlichkeit* (picture-li-ness), which are under the domain of Lucifer:

> Er [Lucifer] begehrete ein Künstler zu seyn, er sahe die Schöpfung und verstand den Grund, darinnen wolte er ein eigner GOtt seyn, und mit der Centralischen Feuers= Macht in allen Dingen herrschen, und sich mit allen Dingen bilden, auch sich selber wollen in alle Formen bilden, dass er wäre was er wolte, und nicht was der Schöpfer wolte; wie denn solches noch heute ihre gröste Freude ist, dass sie sich können verwandeln, und in mancherley Bildnisse bringen, und also Phantasie treiben (*Fragen* 10, 1).

Since contact with the JEHOVAH vocalism has not reached Lucifer, Böhme imposes a forced exile upon him, labelling this exile *Monstrum* 'monster' (*Fragen* 10, 6).

The Luciferian retreat into the *NEIN* does not signal the end of the battle of cosmic forces. By extending himself into manifestation in the physical form of a dragon (+Monster), Lucifer prepares to battle with Michael. In the eleventh question, "Was ist der

Streit zwischen Michael und den Drachen gewesen? Was ist Michael und der Drache, und wie ist der Sieg und die Ausstossung geschehen?" Böhme describes the *Drache*. It:

+ is a figure created in the aspect of the hellish fundament (4).
+ is *Hitze* 'heat', *Kälte* 'cold', *Härte* 'hardness', *Schärfe* 'sharpness', *Stachel* 'stickling', *Bitter* 'bitter' and the *Angst und Wehe* 'anguish and pain' (7).
+ is cleansed out of the holy name by Michael (14).
+ is fought against by the word JESUS (14).
+ is fought against before manifestation occurs in the divine principles (15).

Sharing the same features as Lucifer, the dragon as manifestation[19] battles Michael, as the unmanifested Lucifer (the *Nein*) attacks the nonmanifested Iesus (the *Jah*). Böhme is careful to stress that the altercation happens before manifestation; in manifestation, though, the temporalized and localized battle occurs between Jesus and the dragon in the desert of astringency (*Fragen* 11, 16):

> In diesem Streit muss der Göttliche Character der Idea siegen, weil er ein Engel seyn; in diesem Streite ist Adam gefallen: und in diesem Streite hat der Name JESUS, in unserer angenommenen Menschheit, in der Wüsten wieder diesen Drachen den Sieg erhalten, da Er 40 Tage versucht ward, und ihn endlich im Tode gantz überwunden (*Fragen* 11, 16).

Moses, likewise, experiences a similar confrontation. Coming down from Mount Sinai, he sees the people of Israel absorbed in matter (+astringent) identification:

> Deswegen ward die Gesetz=Tafel zerbrochen, anzudeuten, dass der Menschliche Wille der Eigenheit nicht

konte wieder des Zorns Fundament siegen, er muste nur zerbrochen und getödtet, und durch den Tod wieder in den heiligen Namen eingeführt werden (*Fragen* 11, 18).

Death (*Tod*), the shedding of the material shell, is prerequisite for *Geist* (now *Begreiffligkeit*) to reascend into *Geist* through the vocalic holy name.

With this in mind Böhme concentrates his argument on the thirteenth question, rather than answer the twelfth "Wie betrachtet man GOttes ewigen Rath in Göttlicher Anschauung . . . ?" The more important thirteenth question is:

> Wie ist die Ausstossung des Drachens und der Legionen Lucifers geschehen; wo ist er hingestossen worden, dass er kann ausser GOtt seyn, weil GOtt alle Dinge erfüllet? Oder was ist das Fundament der Höllen, darinnen er wohnet? (*Fragen* 13).

By the sixteenth sentence of this answer, Böhme directly addresses the puzzling dilemma of how God can be in the light and in hell at the same time, without manifesting as the light within hell. God lives within himself, within the *Gute-Wallen/Wollen-Einheit*, as the *Ichts* 'the I-ness'. Lucifer, living within the realm of the *NEIN*, within this realm is an *ichts* with regard to himself; God is the *nichts* 'no-thing'. Both realms exclude the other:

> GOtt ist im Lichte ein Ichts, und in der Höllen ein Nichts, dann die ewige Einheit ist allein im Lichte ein Wesen und Kraft, und die Lügen ist allein in eigener Annehmlichkeit ein Wesen und Kraft (*Fragen* 13, 18).

The linguistics underlying the *ichts* (< L+icht+e) and the *Nichts* (< Hölle+*N* + u+*N*+d + *N*+ichts) remain undeveloped as Böhme hurries to the next two questions: "Was ist der Teufel Amt in der Höllen" (*Fragen* 14) and "Hat das Fundament der Höllen zeitlichen Anfang genommen, oder ists von Ewigkeit gewesen; oder wie mag es bestehen oder nicht?" (*Fragen* 15). The fourteenth question is absorbed into the title of the fifteenth question, the final Böhmian commentary contained within four brief passages. Böhme adds no new information, the manuscript terminating with the words "Es muste . . . " (*Fragen* 15, 4). The reader (Franckenberg) is left with a list of unanswered questions, some of which address linguistic problems: "Was ist der Thurn zu Babel gewesen, und warum sind aldar die Sprachen verändert worden?" (*Fragen* 89); "Wie ist der Unterschied der Sprachen bey ihnen [the apostles] zu verstehen, dass sie haben zugleich auf einmal in Einem Sensu alle Sprachen geredet, dass sie alle Völcker verstunden?" (*Fragen* 146); and "Was ist das Buchstabische Wort, und das lebendige Wort Christus in solcher Ausgiessung beyeinander; wie werden sie unterschieden? sintemal sie nicht alle den H. Geist aus der Apostel Munde höreten lehren; denn sie sprachen ein Theil: Sie sind voll süsses Weins; Diese höreten wol Menschen= Worte, aber nicht Christum in seiner Auferstehung lehren?" (*Fragen* 148). At this point, Böhme's linguistic commentary comes to a close, rather than a conclusion.

Sixty years later, Edward Taylor (d. ca. 1684), an English gentleman in retirement in Dublin, occupied himself "in much Privacy and Retirement, where he made this [Böhme] his Work and Business" (Taylor 1691:a2). After his death, his manuscripts were preserved by a friend until their publication in London (1691). In addition to providing a highly abridged version of Böhme's writings,[20] Taylor answered the remaining *Theosophic Questions*. His understanding of the Böhmian linguistic system, while rudimentary, reveals an awareness of its deeper spiritual semantic core. In a parenthetical remark on the nature of the *Three Fold Life of Man (Dreyfach)* he states:

> The language of Nature is treated from the 84th v. to the end of this Chapter, which being also dispersed in several places of the blessed Authors excellent writings,

it is wished were all contracted in one distinct Treatise; not only to shew us the Monuments of our Ruins by the Fall, but also to stir us up to press inward out of the shadow and figure, into the substance, which is the inward Power-Worlds (Taylor 1691:314).

He answers the eighty-ninth question "What is the tower of Babel and wherefore were the Speeches altered?" with the Bōhmian plant image:

But when man had run into the multiplicity of the divided Properties, the Holy United Powers could no longer be imaged by him, and as a Branch cut off a tree retains a little of the worse part, but nothing like the vigor of the tree. He became a degenerate Plant, and was like a City infested with Intestine Fatal Broils, so that it can hold no commerce abroad, or like a man distracted, who cannot advise nor be advised, being a stranger to himself as well as to common Prudence (Taylor 1691: 115).

Taylor blames Lucifer for making a "harsh jarring Tone, and changing his golden letters into black and polysonous composition, raced himself and his whole Hierarchy out of that Fair Record" (Taylor 1691:162). Taylor then creates his own descent into material form:

Then did the creating Word speak or incert, and interline Man into that part of the Book which Lucifer and his Angels had been raced, which with the additional skill of Interliners, had the Out-principle as an adjunct to him, this was the second of the Intellectuals. And tho' the skill of the speaking Word were perfected, yet as usually it is in Interlinings, the obliterated Letters had left some flaws or scratches (tho' not in the holy Book,

A New Dawn in the Final Year

> yet) in the adjunct, shadower or cover the Out-birth, which now being new bound and lacerated pieces cemented; in the cover rested such stains and rents, that thereof came the perrilous, polysonous, stinging Animals, and Vegetables, the Beasts of prey bearing the impressions of the clauses of the dark world (Taylor 1691:162).

The stains and rents in the cover of the "Out-birth" develop into the consonantal system "as the vowels are the spirit of the whole Alphabet" (Taylor 1691:162), but he hastens to add that "the Living Word is the Eternal Creating Word" (Taylor 1691:164). In this manner, speaking in the Holy Spirit is to be in the divine presence; other speaking (via consonants and vowels) "is far below the life and power of that as the Consonants are below the vowels, which produce but Mute hissings" (Taylor 1691:164).

Taylor's wish to see Böhme's linguistic commentary collected together, the collection of that data in this study, and the application of the data within the linguistic argument, adds much insight to the confusion ascribed to the early Böhme. Böhme closes the *Aurora* with a puzzling statement of linguistic significance:

> Wenn aber diese Morgen=Röthe wird vom Anfang zum Niedergang scheinen, so ists vorbass mehr keine Zeit, sondern die Sonne des Hertzens GOttes gehet auf und wird RA. RA. RP. in die Kelter ausser der Stadt gestossen, und mit ihm AM. R.P. Diese sind verborgene Worte, und werden allein in der Sprache der Natur verstanden (*Aurora* xxvi, 120, 121).

Prophetically foreseeing his destiny as a writer of immortal words, Böhme's early linguistic platform overflows with a mild sense of frustration "nonetheless, the sun of God's heart ascends and is RA. RA. RP. forced into the wine presses outside of the city." The reader is quickly aware that RA. RA. RP. is code, which as Böhme says can be understood only within the language of nature.

Returning to the alphabetic significations encountered within the Böhmian corpus,[21] astringency within language is nowhere better mirrored than within the trembling, vibrating *r*. The vocalic *a*, not yet elevated to the functionality of the *Dreyfaches I* (*Tafel* 9), retains the role of being an opening between the gums which allows the *Geist* "Raum ... nach seinem Gefallen" (*Aurora* xix, 91). Since the character *Ra* is meaningless on the first layer of language, the reader must then focus on the second and third layers. On the phonological layer, the vibrating astringent *r* couples with the space wherein the Spirit is allowed to enter according to its pleasure. This is the world of manifestation, away from the vocal articulators, and from the point of view of the later linguistics, the manifested accusative. On the theosophic third layer, astringency exists alongside of *Geist*, containing it within the structure of the important obstruent *r*. *Begreiffligkeit* (R) eventually expresses itself as *Geist* (A), but the delineation of this process occurs seven years later in the *Drey Principien* (1619). The combination of *Begreiffligkeit+Geist* in sequence (RA.RA) followed by a double *Begreiffligkeit* astringency (RP.) appears together in the wine presses outside of the city, that is, in the secret conventicles discussing the early *Aurora* work. The importance of astringent matrices (RP. and the AM.) within the codified system, as well as the system itself, are the *verborgene Worte* 'hidden words'.

The nature of the signification *Ra Ra* caught the attention of Christian Steinberg, whom Böhme addresses in a letter of July 6, 1622:

> Auch ist darunter angedeutet, wie der Sectirische Streit in der Religion werde in solcher Offenbarung zu Grunde gehen, dann es werden alle Thüren aufgethan werden, und als dann werden die unnützen Schwätzer, welche ietzt als Riegel vor der Wahrheit liegen, weggethan

> werden, und sollen alle Christum erkennen, welche Offenbarung die letzte seyn wird: Da die Sonne des Lebens soll über alle Völcker scheinen; und alsdann gehet das böse Thier mit der Huren (welches unter den Charactern Ra Ra RPAM am RP angedeutet wird) ... Diese ausfürliche Deutung darf man anietzo noch nicht klärer machen, es wird sich alles selber zeigen, und dann wird man es sehen, was es gewesen ist, dann es ist gar eine andere Zeit. Wegen der Natur=Sprache berichte ich dem Herrn dass es sich also verhalte; aber das was ich darinnen weiss und verstehe, kann ich keinem andern geben oder lehren: Andeutung kann ich einem wohl geben, wie sie zu verstehen sey, aber es gehöret ein grösser Raum darzu, und müste eine mündliche Unterredung seyn, es lässet sich nicht schreiben (*Sendbrief* xxviii, 10-11).

Nearly ten years after the *Aurora*, Böhme fully equates the characters *Ra Ra RPAM* with the "böse Thier mit der Huren." The shift in the signification of the vocalic *A*, from passage into matter, to the temporal aspects of manifestation (*Dreyfach* ii, 10), severely reduces the earlier *RA* (which held a faint trace of *Geist*) to pure irreversible matter. All religious disputation collapses with the realization that the words of their altercations are at best astringent shells. Confusion engendered by the *Schwätzer* 'idle talkers, fanatics' is removed through recognition of Christ within. The astral *alphabetisch* revelation is the final experience, an experience which as the "Sun of Life" not only shines equally on all people, but also through linguistic contemplations can lead the awakened reader more quickly back to *Geist*.

The modern reader of Böhme now has the tool; however, the intricacies of using the tool, once imparted through "mündliche Unterredungen," are forever lost to modern times.

NOTES

CHAPTER I

1. The writings of Franckenberg (1639), Felgenhauer (1640, 1650), Kober (1624), Hegenicus (1669) and Weissner (1651) need close linguistic description before their semantic distance from Böhme can be ascertained. More problematic, from a linguistic point of investigation, are the following: Michael von Sercha (and his brother Karl), Dr. Balthasar Walther and Bartholomäus Scultetus, associates who left no attested commentary. Most intriguing insights may be found in Felgenhauer's *Büchlein Iehor, oder Morgenröte der Weiszheit* (1640) and Franckenberg's *Raphael oder Artzt-Engel* (1639). Both works were written as compendiums to Böhme's *Aurora* (1612) and are easily read in several hours. An analysis of their understanding of the consonantal code developed in the *Aurora*, while adding to our knowledge of Böhme the linguist, depends heavily on a misunderstood sense of Hebrew and of the *Qabala*, and must be postponed until a later time.

2. A reading through the verbally dense writings of Böhme precludes an active decision on the part of the commentator to diachronically arrange meaningful segments of textual information under mutually understood semantic rubrics. A reading through Böhme guides the reader around rough turns and unexpected bends, which even the most casual reader notices, and which the most impatient critic chastises. The earliest reading through Böhme is Taylor's *Jacob Behmen's Theosophic Philosophy Unfolded; in Divers Considerations and Demonstrations...* (1691), a curious work which includes translated portions of Böhme's major works as well as Taylor's own answers to Böhme's unfinished *Betrachtung Göttlicher Offenbarung... in 177 Fragen gestellt* (1624). See note 20, Chapter V.

The reading through Böhme's linguistic argument presented

in this study is based on the 1730 Gichtels edition *Alle Göttliche Schriften des Gottseligen und Hocherleuchteten Deutschen THEOSOPHI Jacob Böhmens*, recently edited and reprinted by Peuckert (1955). Roman numerals refer to chapter or heading, Arabic numbers refer to the segment. Although the 1730 edition presents a Böhmian German levelled out to meet the standard norm for the early eighteenth century, only the Silesian phonology has been tampered with. Buddecke (1963) offers transcriptions from the original manuscripts, but at best, they represent only a small portion of the collected writings.

3. Cf. Sparrow (1656). Erb (1978), the most recent Böhme translator, notices that Böhme "has pushed language beyond its limits" (Erb 1978:22). In his introduction to the modern translation *The Way to Christ*, Erb, like Sparrow, defines terms the reader will encounter, terms without which the reader would be hopelessly lost in his own semantically fabricated interpretation.

4. The discussion surrounding the label "mystical writer" leads the modern audience into incorrect semantic association with the overworked terms "occult," "parapsychological," and "secret." As shown by Bharati (1976), the linguistic signals contained in "mystical" writing must be carefully related to a more subtle source of inspiration: that of the prolific and published mystic as a linguist. He stresses close textual analysis, rejecting any attempt to classify mystical literature according to preconceived notions: "I object to all those mixed bags being called mysticism—overloading a term means watering it down, and eventually depriving it of any communicational operativeness" (Bharati 1976:37). This study does not attempt to place Böhme within the framework of modern consciousness movements, but hopes to reestablish the original Böhmian idiom through which a highly gifted writer spiritualized his world. Vetterling (1923) and Steiner (1942) offer non-European analyses of Böhme in radical attempts to tear Böhme from the stronghold of traditional theological interpretation.

5. The word *Natursprache* and its origins within European thought are first analyzed by Kaiser (1930). Böhme's use of the

word indicates that it functions as a metalanguage, a system of codified expression necessary to penetrate the linear description of nature possible in humanly articulated languages.

6. Cf. Böhme's *Sendbriefe* ii, 2; x, 2, 4, 5, 25, 35, 37, 38, 41, 42; xii, 5-8, 12, 13, 66.

7. Few scholars look seriously at Franckenberg's report since the expressions he employs are not semantically shared by critic and writer. Establishmentarian, ecclesiastical and nonmystical language automatically excludes the following passage as being in any way relevant:

> Unterdessen, und nachdem er sich als ein getreuer Arbeiter seiner eigenen Hand, in Schweiss seines Angesichts genehret, wird er mit des 17. Seculi Anfang, nemlich Anno 1600, als im 25. Jahre seines Alters zum andernmal vom Göttlichen Lichte ergriffen, durch einen jählichen Anblick eines Zinnern Gefässes (als des lieblich Jovialischen Scheins) zu dem innersten Grunde oder Centro der geheimen Natur eingeführet; Da er als in etwas zweifelhaft um solche vermeinte Phantasey aus dem Gemüthe zu schlagen zu Görlitz vor dem Neyssthore (alwo er an der Brücken seine Wohnung gehabt) ins Grüne gegangen, und doch nichts destoweniger solchen empfangenen Blick je länger je mehr klärer empfunden, also dass er vermittelst der angebildeten Signaturen oder Figuren Lineamenten und Farben, allen Geschöpfen gleichsam in das Hertz und in die innerste Natur hinein sehen können, (wie auch in seinem Büchlein de Signatura Rerum, dieser ihm eingedruckte Grund genugsam verkläret und enthalten,) wodurch er mit grossen Freuden überschüttet, stille geschwiegen, GOtt gelobet, seiner Haus=Geschäfte und Kinder=Zucht wahrgenommen, und mit iedermann fried=und freundlich umgegangen, und von solchem seinen empfangenen Lichte und innern Wandel mit GOtt und der Natur, wenig oder nichts gegen iemanden gedacht (Franckenberg 1651:11).

See also note 1, Chapter V.

8. Concerning the memorial Böhme says:

> Und fiel mir zu Hand also starck in mein Gemüthe, mir solches [Aurora] für ein Memorial aufzuschreiben: Wiewol ich es in meinem äussern Menschen gar schwer ergreiffen, und in die Feder bringen konte; ich muste gleich anfangen in dieser sehr grossen Geheimniss zu arbeiten, als ein Kind das zur Schule gehet: Im Innern sahe ich es wol, als in einer grossen Tieffe, dann ich sahe hindurch als in ein Chaos, da alles inne lieget, aber seine Auswickelung war mir unmöglich (*Sendbrief* xii, 9).

9. The most conservative interpretation of Böhme's inner *Erleuchtung* 'illumination' (Stoudt 1957) claims that Böhme's inner urge toward self-expression arose from his contact with the highly personable minister Martin Moller. "... He [Böhme] had attended Moller's conventicles where he met similarly-minded people: noblemen, physicians, peasants, burghers, fellow craftsmen. Surely it was this spirit which Martin Moller communicated rather than the pewter dish or fanciful objects, which brought the young Böhme a deep interest for the devotional life" (Stoudt 1957:51).

10. Cf. Peuckert (1961) for an accurate historical account of the period of silence.

11. The term *astringency* first appears in Sparrow (1656). Böhme posits a theory of molecular compaction around the centripetal aspect of *Herbigkeit* 'astringency'. This inward pulling aspect of all matter is prerequisite to all manifestation and underscores much of the Aurorean cosmology:

> Nun mercke, Die gantze GOttheit hat in ihrer innerlichsten oder anfänglichsten Geburt im Kern gar eine scharfe, erschreckliche Schärfe, indem die herbe Qualität gar ein

erschrecklich, herb, hart, finster und kalt Zusammenziehen ist, gleich dem Winter wenn es grimmig kalt ist, dass aus dem Wasser Eis wird, und darzu gantz unerträglich (*Aurora* xiii, 55).

By placing it first on the list of primary manifested forces, Böhme foreshadows its later importance as a *Signatur* (see Chapter III): "Der erste Geist ist die Herbe Qualität: Die ist in GOtt ein sehr lieblich Zusammenziehen, Vertrocknen und Kühlen, und wird zu der Bildung gebraucht." Cf. Konopacki (1977) and note 13, Chapter I for a full listing of textual citations.

12. The vowel is unimportant since it does not modify the breath stream. Passing freely from the depths of the throat into the mouth, then out into manifested nature, the vowel is only the vibration upon which *Geist* slides into *Begreiffligkeit*. The vocalic nonobstruent increases in importance, and is elevated into the code as the possibilities within the astringent obstruents are only able to express *Wesenheit* 'state of being'.

13. Cf. *Aurora* vii, 15-17, 19, 23, 24, 27, 31, 33, 41, 43, 47, 70; ix, 13, 14, 23-25; x, 19; xiii, 55, 69; xiv, 54, 70, 71, 80; xix, 92, 93; xxi, 73, 74; xxiii, 19.

14. Cf. *Aurora* i, 13, 19, 21; ii, 40; iv, 8; viii, 26-29, 31, 33, 70; ix, 13, 14, 20, 30; x, 16; xv, 6, 7; xxiii, 21.

15. Had Lucifer not fallen from the angelic (astral) realms, then there would be no need for a manifested world to exist. The Lucifer of the *Aurora* bears the burden since God "hat den Zalitter zusammen gezogen, und dem Teufel hiemit eine ewige Herberge zugerichtet. Denn ausser GOtt kann er nicht gestossen werden in ein ander Königsreich der Engel; sondern es muss ihm ein Locus zur Behausung bleiben" (*Aurora* xvi, 74, 75). Cf. *Aurora* iv, 3, 4; v, 35, 37, 38; vi, 16; vii, 7, 37; ix, 15, 33, 42, 44; x, 56; xii, 99-105; xiii, 2, 31, 32, 39, 90, 91, 102, 105, 116-20; xiv, 1, 3-5, 8, 28-33, 46, 47, 50, 56, 57, 72, 85, 96; xv, 10-14, 28, 31, 32, 48, 50, 52, 64-66, 72, 76, 77; xvi, 2, 27, 32, 59, 61, 63, 78, 79, 81-85, 87, 88, 91, 92-95, 101, 104, 106, 107; xvii, 31; xviii, 32,

34; xix, 46; xxiii, 91-94, 96, 97; xxiv, 20, 21; xxv, 59; xxvi, 21, 23, 123.

16. Cf. Borst (1957).

17. *Animalisch*, often mistranslated as "animal," misrepresents the original Böhmian term. *Animalisch* refers to a spiritual state wherein the forces of nature are unmanifested but nonetheless potential. It may best be rendered as "astral," or that combination of unmanifested possibilities which finally descends into matter as created nature. Cf. *Aurora* xv, 36, 39, 40, 41, 51, 63; xvi, 35, 36, 58; xviii, 20; ix, 18.

18. External manifestation is that aspect of *Begreiffligkeit* in which the linguistic system reflects the descent of *Geist* into the acoustically formed human languages.

19. The term *Salitter*, later modified (corrected) to *Salniter* (*De Signatura Rerum* iii, 19; xiii, 44; *Gnadenwahl* iii, 24; *Mysterium Magnum* x, 10, 21), signifies *Wesenheit* in the *Aurora* (Solms-Rödelheim 1960:63). The paradigmatic extent of the word is unclear within Böhme's mind. Cf. *Aurora* iv, 9, 10, 13, 15, 21; viii, 33; xi, 47; xiii, 90; xv, 38, 73; xviii, 10-15; xxi, 4, 13, 14; xxiv, 22-24.

20. The *Tieffe über der Erden* 'depths above the earth' is the unfathomable finite spatial extension of God within matter. This finite hugeness reflects divine presence within matter. Cf. *Aurora* xii, 2; *Vierzig Fragen* i, 234.

21. Buddecke (1963) records this sentence as "mit der geburt in ihrer Senligkeit" noting that every Böhme edition, with the exception of the 1730 edition, employs either *Sinnligkeit* or *Sehnlichkeit*. Both are denotatively in agreement with Böhme's early *Geist>Begreiffligkeit* argument. The trinitarian attitude (*Söhnlichkeit*) is unattestable in the *Aurora*.

22. Böhme's Aurorean anatomical system shows the senses as having their counsel chambers in the human brain. All information entering the body is processed by the five counsellors (*Rathe*) before a reaction on the physical surface of the body can occur. Cf. *Aurora* v, 22-35; vi, 6; x, 48, 49.

23. The following commentators base their analysis of Böhme's "mystical stance" on the first layer of Böhmian language, a language semantically equated with that of the commentator: Bartsch 1974; Bastian 1905; Borst 1957; Benz 1951, 1959; Bornkamm 1925; Brown 1977; Deussen 1922; Grunsky 1940; Hankamer 1927, 1960, 1964; Hartmann 1929; Heckel 1921; Jecht 1924; Kocher 1975; Koyré 1929; Martensen 1949; Monzo 1931; Peuckert 1961, 1967; Popp 1935; Stoudt 1957; Waldemar 1959; Wehr 1975; Wentzlaff-Eggebert 1944.

24. The following commentators recognize the existence of a phonological layer, although make no attempt to diachronically chart its extent: Benz 1936; Grunsky 1956; Heller 1964; Kayser 1930; Mendels 1953; Moulton 1952; Penny 1912; Schäublin 1963; Schulze 1959; Solms-Rödelheim 1960; Stewig 1953; Vetterling 1923. Excellent analyses of general problems in mystical phonology are Hoffstein (1975) and Melzer (1946).

25. This study is the first analysis of the linguistic code as a third-layer operative mechanism.

26. Böhme's growing awareness of *Wortbildung* from primitive roots begins in the *Aurora*. *Gib* 'give!' ($<$*gb*) extends itself into *Mitgebärung* 'that which is borne along with' ($<$*mt-gb-rng*) because of the commonality of the alphabetic root (obstruent) *gb*.

27. Cf. Prophet (1974) for a detailed account of the emergence of modern alchemy.

28. Böhme correctly reduces the full conjugation *gehet* to its minimal morphemic unit *ge-* ($<$ *g*). The modern reader must constantly bear in mind that each linguistic exegesis represents a unified analysis, complete within itself. Any attempt to collapse the roots *gb* and *g* into one common (from the orthographical view) *g* would misrepresent the intent of the obstruent code.

29. Vocalic clusters and diphthongs are individual (orthographic) representations.

30. Cf. *Aurora* viii, 41ff. and Schäublin (1963:79-84) for an account of the interrelationships between the forces of nature

and plant life (as an expression of the qualities within manifestation).

31. Böhme dislikes scholars:

> Vor diesen Spiegel will ich alle hoffärtige, geitzige, neidige und zornige Menschen geladen haben, da werden sie den Ursprung ihrer Hoffart, Geitzes, Neides und Zornes sehen, und auch den Ausgang und endliche Belohnung. Es haben die Gelehrten viel und mancherley Monstra herfürbracht von dem Anfang der Sünden und Ursprung des Teufels, und haben sich damit gekratzt; ein ieder hat gemeint er habe die Axt bey dem Stiele, und ist ihnen gleichwol sämtlich verborgen blieben bis auf dato (*Aurora* xiii, 1, 2).

Böhme directs sixteen questions to "unser Doctor" (*Aurora* xxiii, 34) doubting that they will be able to answer them: *Aurora* ii, 11; xiii, 2; xiv, 14, 27, 49, 74, 108; xxii, 26, 27, 41, 43, 44; xxvi, 41-44.

32. The seven powers in nature are the "forces" or "qualities" often mentioned in the *Aurora*. Since language is linear in its transmission, Böhme arranges these forces in the following order: astringency, bitterness, sweetness, heat, love, sound, and nature. Vetterling (1923:223ff.) offers the most compact description of these forces. Astringency (centripetality), bitterness (centrifugality) and sound (vibration within this interchange of forces) are the foundations of Böhme's linguistic system.

CHAPTER II

1. The 1682 and 1730 editions contain magnificently detailed copperplates which illustrate the texts they precede. The esoteric descriptions of the plates, as well as the plates themselves, are of unknown origin. Böhme's comments on the linear nature of thought as language would justify elaborate visual representations: "Ich muss in Stückwerk schreiben um des Lesers Verstand willen, damit er möchte was begreiffen und in den Sinn kommen" (*Aurora* xi, 66). Franckenberg, the most artistically visual of Böhme's first circle of students, undoubtedly influenced much of the diagrammatic representation. His *Raphael oder Artzt Engel* (1639) overflows with mystical doodling within a symbolic framework of Böhmian thought.

2. In this sense, 'that which can be apprehended by the senses and grabbed, material'.

3. Böhme notes that when any of the qualities predominates without the presence of the others, then life comes to an end: "Dencke wenn im Winter, wenn es also kalt ist, solte die Sonne weggenommen werden, was da für eine Kälte und gantz rauhe und harte Finsterniss würde; da konte kein Leben bestehen" (*Aurora* xiii, 56).

4. Cf. Popp (1935).

5. Böhme's pronunciation of the postvocalic *r* in final position was probably nonsyllabic rather than uvular. Orthographically, though, the *r* signals astringency in any position. Böhme does not distinguish allophonic variants.

6. Böhme describes the experience in a letter to Caspar Lindner:

> In solchem meinem gar ernstlichen Suchen und Begehren (darinnen ich heftige Anstösse erlitten, mich aber ehe des Lebens verwegen als davon ausgehen und ablassen wolte)

> ist mir die Porte eröffnet worden, dass ich in einer Viertelstunde mehr gesehen und gewust habe als wann ich wäre viel Jahr auf hohen Schulen gewesen, dessen ich mich hoch verwunderte, wuste nicht wie mir geschahe und darüber mein Hertz ins Lob GOttes wendete ... Es eröffnete sich aber von Zeit zu Zeit in mir, als in einem Gewächse: wie wol ich 12 Jahr damit umging, und dessen in mir schwanger war, und einen heftigen Trieb in mir befand, ehe ich es könte in das Aeussere bringen: bis es mich hernach überfiel wie ein Platzregen, was der trift, das trift er: Also ging es mir, auch, was ich konte ergreifen in das Aeussere zu bringen das schrieb ich auf (*Sendbrief* xii, 7, 10).

Compare also *Sendbrief* x, 3, 7, 9; xii, 11; and *Erste Schutzschrift gegen Tilke* 28, 32, 33.

7. The astral part of the phenomenal manifold is beyond ordinary knowledge and common inferences about nature (cf. Thomas 1976:33ff.).

8. By *Fiat* Böhme means "das schaffende Wort GOttes, oder der Wille GOttes zur Schöpfung" (*Drittes Register der Theosoph. Materien* 184). It is the verbal "es werde, das Wort zur Schöpfung" (*Erstes Register* 19) and is described in *Drey Principien* viii, 5:

> Also muss man nun die Matricem dieser Welt mit den Sternen und Elementen nicht ansehen, als wenn GOtt nicht alda wäre seine ewige Weisheit und Kraft hat sich mit dem Fiat in alle Dinge eingebildet, und ist Er selber der Werckmeister; und in dem Fiat sind alle Dinge herfürgegangen, ein iedes in seiner Essentia, Kraft und Eigenschaft.

Cf. *Drey Principien* v, 28; xiii, 47; xiv, 74.

9. Böhme rephrases the idea in the following chapter:

> So wir nun urkunden des Menschen Leben in Mutterleibe,

von seiner Kraft, Rede und Sinnen, und von dem edlen hochtheuren Gemüthe, so finden wir die Ursachen, warum wir so ein lang Register haben vor diesem von der ewigen Geburt gemacht. Denn die Sprache, Sinnen und Gemüthe haben auch einen solchen Urkund, wie obgemeldet von der ewigen Geburt GOttes, und ist eine theure Porten (*Drey Principien* xv, 27).

10. Böhme summarizes the functions of the sensory counsellors:

In Summa, ihrer sind darum 5 in dem fürstlichen Rathe, dass einer dem andern soll Rath eingeben, und ein ieder ist einer sonderlichen Qualität; und der zusammen=gefügte Geist, der sich aus allen Kräften gebäret, der ist ihr König oder Fürst, und sitzet im Kopf im Hirn des Menschen; und im Engel in der Kraft ans Hirns Stelle auch im Kopfe auf seinem fürstlichen Stuhle, und exequiret dasjenige, was durch den gantzen fürstlichen Rath ist beschlossen worden (*Aurora* v, 39).

11. *Buchstabengelehrte* approach the names of external objects from the standpoint of conventionally accepted semantic features. Böhme attacks those readers who remain on the *Buchstaben* 'alphabetic' surface of his writings, blinded by their own erroneous manipulations of the letters.

12. *Buchstaben zelen* 'counting the letters', commonly referred to as cabalistic gematria, does not interest Böhme. The paradigmatic extent of the finiteness of numerical interpretation is too time-consuming and intricate. Böhme's prophetic urge does not allow him time to explore in detail this ancient science. Cf. Scholem (1974).

13. Böhme includes under the words *seltsame Dinge* 'curious things' the distance believed to exist between the planets. Physicists of his time place Jupiter 7,875 miles above Mars (*Aurora* xxv, 76), Mars 15,750 miles from the sun (*Aurora* xxv, 76) and

Saturn somewhere between Jupiter and the stars (*Aurora* xxvi, 11).

14. The lily is the sign which marks the new-born spirit within (*Letzte Zeit* i, 30) and the communion with Christ (*Gelassenheit* 46). When compounded with *Zeit* 'time', *Lilien-Zeit* refers to the end of the physical world (*Clavis* 253). The fictionalized novels of Böhme's life (Mikeleitis 1943; Spunda 1961) elevate the symbol of the lily to a secret password among the persecuted Böhmenites.

15. *Mercurius*, like the *Vater Unser* of Chapter I, visually attempts to describe a dramatic sequence. Böhme says:

> Mercurius begreiffet alle vier Gestalten, wie das Leben aufgehet, und hat doch seinen Anfang nicht im Centro, wie Phur, sondern nach dem Feuer=Blitze, als die herbe, harte, finstre Gestalt erschrickt, da sich die Härtigkeit in die weiche Schärfe verwandelt, da der andere Wille, als der Wille der Natur, welcher Angst heisset, entstehet, da hat der Mercurius seinen Urstand: Dann Mer ist das zitternde Rad, gantz erschrecklich, scharf und giftig, feindig, welches sich in der Herbigkeit im Feuer=Blitz also nimt, da das grimme Leben entstehet. Die Sylbe Cu ist der Druck ausm strengen ängstlichen Willen des Gemüthes der Natur, der ist aufsteigend und will oben aus. Ri ist die Fassung des Feuer=Blitzes, welches im Mer einen hellen Ton und Klang gibt: dann der Blitz machet den Klang; also wird der Salz= Geist der Schall und ist seine Gestalt grieslicht, gleich dem Sande: und hierinne entstehen Stimmen, Hall und Lauten, also auch das Cu der den Blitz begreiffet, so ist der Druck gleich als ein Wind, der über sich stösset, und gibt dem Blitze einen Geist, dass er lebet und brennet: also heisset die Sylbe Us das brennende Feuer, welches mit dem Geiste immer von sich treibet; und die Sylbe Cu dringet immer auf dem Blitz (*Dreyfach* ii, 42).

Notes 173

CHAPTER IV

1. Man's passage through the fall (embodied within the form of Adam) brought his angelic astral existence to an abrupt halt. The human form is produced through a divine will toward manifestation, a force which cannot express itself fully within the astringent-laden composition of animals, plants and minerals. The original man (Adam), while engrossed in divine contemplations, had little need of bestial procreation since elemental matter was of little significance to his relation with the divine. Through delusion with matter, Adam's *Gemüt* identified itself with the elements, and in an overwhelming attempt to transcend this attachment, Adam and Eve expressed themselves within bestial procreation. Böhme does not lay blame on Adam, rather views the process as an irreconcilable human accident. Without Adam's falling into matter, there would be no Christ. Cf. Hildegard von Bingen *Wisse die Wege* (1954) for the earliest description of Adam's passing through the magnetic elemental matrix.

2. The terms nominative (God in himself, beyond manifestation), accusative (God as an extension of himself into matter, yet separated from himself) and dative (the created object resulting from a self-conscious effort of the accusative) are terms which best describe the mystical observations of linguistic syntax. While many established religions argue among themselves over the verbal semantics (McNiell 1966:50), Böhme's astringent world concentrates on substantive interaction. Units of interrelated meaning structure the shape of his uniquely contrived world, a world derived from another unseen and unmanifested corpus of meaning. The verbal matrix separates the unseen nominative from the seen accusative.

3. The noun *Wirckung* (+Mystical Nominative) is unseen; the verbal *wircken* is the matrix, and its manifested reflection is the *Gewircke* (+Accusative). The manifested abstraction *sonderliches*

Gewirck is *das Ausgesprochene*, both cleverly reflecting the temporal marker +Past.

4. Böhme pays lip service to the names of the holy languages, languages which have little to do with his linguistic theory. The question as to whether Böhme knew Hebrew, or knew of Hebrew, and the possible effect of this knowledge on his theory of language will be treated in the final portion of Chapter V. His linguistic nationalism, though, gave Grunsky (1940) good reason to see the shoemaker as the "Schöpfer einer Germanischen Philosophie des Willens."

5. Although Böhme mentions the number 72, he carefully derives the sum from the internal and external zodiac (6+6) in combination with other 6+6 sequences:

> Weil dann die 12 Zahl zwey Reiche halten, mit doppelter Zahl, als ein englisches und menschliches, iedes in sechs Zahl, dass es zwölf zusammen ist; so haben die Zwey Reiche noch andere zwey sechs=Zahlen an sich, als das Feuer, das Reich des Abgrundes, und die Luft, das Reich des Viehes, und aller irdischen Wesen. Das hat auch iedes am Centro sechs Zahl, nach den sechs Planeten irdisch, und nach den sechs Planeten feurisch; dass macht nun zusammen vier=und=zwanzig Zahl: Das sind die vier=und=zwanzig Buchstaben in den Sprachen, daraus urständen sie. Und siehet man, wie die Zunge Gutes und Böses redet, Himmlisches und Teuflisches, nach den zwey Quellen der Buchstaben, wie das ihre eigene Namen bezeugen, nach der Natur=Sprache. Wann man nun diese Zahl nach der Dreyzahl, dreymal vier=und=zwanzig zehlet, als sich dann die Dreyzahl also eröffnet mit dreyen Reichen und Personen, und nach der Dreyzahl alles dreyfach ist, und nach den Creaturen zweyfach, so hat man zwey=und=siebenzig Zahlen: Das bedeutet und sind die zwey=und=siebenzig Sprachen, und bedeutet Babel, eine Verwirrung und ein Wunder (*Dreyfach* ix, 67, 68).

Böhme's internal justification of either Biblical or theological ideas (72 created human languages), rather than prove that the *Natursprache* was composed of 72 languages, each with 24 alphabetic letters (Schulze 1959:25), agrees with the sum total of the statements about the *Natursprache (nach der Natursprache)*. The alphabetic number 24 corresponds to the numerically derived 24. The statement *Und siehet man, wie die Zunge Gutes and Böses redet, Himmlisches und Teuflisches, nach den zwey Quellen der Buchstaben, wie das ihre eigene Namen bezeugen, nach der Natursprache* 'Take notice how the tongue articulates both good and evil, astral and earthly (devil-like), according to the two sources of the letters, which the names themselves attest, according to the language of nature' calls for close linguistic analyses according to the rules of the code, rather than an external historical equation with commonly accepted ideas.

6. *Sendbrief* iii, 3 (October 24, 1619) and iv, 28-31 (November 14, 1619) reveal the busy Böhme travelling widely within German-speaking areas. The various dialect areas which "verdrehen sich fast alle 5 oder 6 Meilen" undoubtedly impressed upon his mind the necessity for a linguistic transcendence within all forms of every spoken language. Since anger, wrath and war seem to be everywhere, Böhme's reliance on the *Signatur* reveals a reason behind linguistic disharmony: the *Poli oder Höhe* 'geographical positions' of the language areas are ruled by different *Eigenschaften* 'characteristics', different *Signaturen*.

7. Böhme's reliance on the word *Tetragrammaton* as an acoustical shell is quickly realized upon consideration of the technical aspect of the cabalistic term:

> The tetragrammaton YHVH—the "lost word"—was above all others the "saving" name in the tradition of Israel; it is known as *shem hameforash*, the "explicit name," the one, that is, of which every consonant reveals and symbolizes one of the four aspects or fundamental degrees of divine all-reality. It is also called the "complete name" and the

"synthesis of syntheses" because it includes all other divine names, each of which, by itself, expresses only one or another particular aspect of the universal principle; it is called the "unique name" because it is for the "unique people," and more especially because of its incomparable spiritual efficacy, in that it gives the possibility of direct actualization of the divine presence (*shekhinah*) (Schaya 1974:145).

Cf. Scholem (1974) for detailed information on the nature of the tetragrammaton JHVH.
    8. From Luther (1545).
    9. See also *Mysterium Magnum* xxxi, 7-9; xxxii, 5, 7-9.

CHAPTER V

1. The *Tabula Principiorum, Von Gott und Von der grossen und kleinen Welt. Gestellt durch Jacob Böhme, Sonsten Teutonicus Philosophus genannt. Zu Amsterdam . . . 1682* does not incorporate the diagram into the text. It appears on a fold-out sheet attached to the beginning of the work. Franckenberg designed the chart according to the textual citations of the *Tabula Principiorum*, a chart which unhappily falls short of the visual semantic intricacy he is capable of within his own writing. Franckenberg's *Raphael oder Artzt-Engel* (1636) overflows with semantically unified diagrams: *Gott* is

GOTT	A		Selbständiges	Wesen	o	G Gut	Gemütt
O Vater	L S	AE W	Gnädiger	Wille	d	U Water	Wasser
T Sohn	E I	I	Allwissendes	Wort	e	T Sühne	Sonne
H Geist	I N	G	Allmächtiges	Würcken	r	T Geust	GeIste

See also *Raphael* 4, 5, 6, 7, 11, 17, 18(!), 21, 22, and 44(!). The structuring effect of Franckenberg on Böhme has never been analyzed, since Franckenberg has always been assumed to have been Böhme's fanatical disciple.

2. *Gewirckete* is a manifested accusative derived through the verbal matrix **wrk* 'to do, effect' and reveals the +Past marker *ge-*. The Son is the product, the comprehensibility of divinity (mystical nominative) within matter.

3. *Einfasslichkeit* < *einfassen* 'to grab within, to border, to enclose within a perimeter'. Böhme's term for the paradigmatic extent of nature.

4. *Ichheit* is the repository for the accusative *Gewirckete* 'that which has been done' and the *Einfasslichkeit* 'perimeter of created

matter' within humanity. It is man's conscious self-awareness. Self-consciousness *Ichheit* 'I-ness' occurs only within matter; outside of matter there is only divine consciousness.

5. See *Aurora* viii, 41ff., where Böhme discusses the interactions between astringency and sweetness, an interaction which dynamically pulls and pushes the astral qualities into their *Einfasslichkeit* as a material sheath of a flower. Cf. Konopacki (1977: 39-41) for a detailed discussion of the Aurorean flower.

6. Gichtels (1730) noticed a similar derivation, since the *Clavis* 16 is marked with a reference to *Tafel* 19.

7. The original Silesian text shows no *H*:

Wer was Habel/ ein scheffer/ wer war Henoch/ und Noa/ ein feltige leute/ wer war Abraham Isaac. Jacob. viehe hirten waren Sie . . . (*Aurora* ix, 3).

8. The intrigue-ridden first meeting has been fictionalized by Mikeleitis (1942:307ff.) and Spunda (1961:348), and although amusing, Böhme's saying "Trotzdem ich hätte das Buch [Mysterium Magnum] latein schreiben sollen . . . Warum hat man mich diese Sprache nicht gelehrt" (Spunda:348) is unacceptable fantasy. A more accurate account is Peuckert (1961:147-59).

9. Cf. Benz (1936), Borst (1958) and Kayser (1930) for attempts to localize Böhme within the Tower of Babel argument. As mentioned in note 5, Chapter IV, Böhme's involvement with *Babel* reflects his own striving toward transcendent freedom, rather than any scholastic involvement with the thought of the times.

10. Böhme's relativizing the Hebrew words *Jehovah, Adonai, Immanuel,* and *Tetragrammaton* into his linguistic system appears to be condescending toward the oriental animal, the foreign, non-Germanic element in his own corpus. That it has been given a human heart, the source of divinity within the human body, reflects Böhme's growing acceptance of esoteric Eastern traditions, once thought to be dangerous, but now easily accepted as

human. I suspect closer relations with Eastern thought through the agency of Abraham von Franckenberg, an accomplished linguist of the times.

11. Cf. Peuckert (1967).

12. Cf. Kluge (1975:856) and Wright (1966:231).

13. Franckenberg's introductory cosmology in *Raphael* employs the *Wollen/Wallen* distinction: "Also fassete Er nun in diesem seinem Vorsatz, einen innigen zu sich selbst gekehrten Willen, oder geistliches Wallen und aufquällen" (*Raphael* p. 2, line 2). Franckenberg seems to have understood Böhme's nominative > verbal-accusative distinction. Note the shift from the present to the past tense derivation in the following:

> ... Und welcher stieg auf ein subtiler Dampf, oder geistlicher RAUCH und Nebel ... Deme folgete der GeRuch, und die Entzündung, so da war ein Göttliches übernatürliches FeUR (*Raphael* p. 3, line 9).

14. The sequence *O. JAH.* is the most puzzling linear sequence in all of Böhme's writings. Although he describes his meaning (*Fragen* 2, 8), close semantic relationships with a syllabic reversal *JAH. O* (>*JEH+O* [vaH]) are likely. Böhme knew of right to left orthography, and judging from Franckenberg's deep interest in the vocalic sequence *IAH (JAH)*, and the growing involvement in the *JAH/NEIN* distinction, Böhme may well have been on the way toward accepting the structure of the Hebrew language into his linguistic explications. His untimely death during the *177 Fragen* leaves the modern reader with nothing but speculation on this point.

15. *Annehmlichkeit* 'a *Wesen* which can be grabbed, held, perceived within its material boundary' is similar to *Einfasslichkeit*.

16. *Inmodelung* 'to bring into form' Lat. *modulus* > OHG *modul* > NHG *model*, verb *modeln* 'to create according to a pattern'. *Inmodelung* infers interiorization of this process within the *Gemüt*.

17. As seen in note 1, this seems to be Franckenberg's sole purpose. Position and linear flow of the eyes across the printed page compact the diagram into a multidirectional message.

18. Böhme's argument with the cabalists of his day has been consistently equated with his involvement in the movement. Similar argumentation has aligned Andreae with the Rosicrucians, a fact which the Rosicrucians deny, but which literary scholarship feels justified in supporting. For Böhme's supposed cabalistic involvement see Huber (1971) and Schulze (1959).

19. The word *Iesus* (VVCVC) is far less astringent than the word *Drachen* (CCVCVC), which shows a dental stop + the astringent *r*. *Jesus*, at best, is only a sibilant hissing through manifestation, rather than a materially bound astringent dragon.

20. In addition to answering the *177 Theosophic Questions*, Taylor includes isolated passages from the following Böhme translations: *The Aurora or Morning Redness; The Three Principles of the Divine Essence; The Threefold Life in Man; Fourty Questions of the Soul; The Incarnation; The Great Six Points; A Brief Summary of the Earthly and Heavenly Mysteries Contracted and Comprised in Nine Texts; Of the Divine Vision or Contemplation; Signatura Rerum; God's Election of Grace; Baptism and Lord's Supper;* and the *Mysterium Magnum*. He makes no effort to include those passages in Böhme's writings which speak directly about linguistic matters.

21. See Alphabetic Index of this work.

ALPHABETIC INDEX

Böhme's unique readings of linguistic transcendence within the structure of language, the written letter, are not an arbitrarily designed means of codifying thought, but rather a haphazard method of remaining mystically involved with unravelling the serious consequences of astringent compaction. Although a shorthand guide to recognition of the ever-present matter-bound centripetal force and the ever-present spiritualizing centrifugal aspirations contained within the fabric of matter, Böhme abandons the reader at precisely the point where *Begreiffligkeit* terminates and reascension in *Geist* begins, withdrawing to the secret confines of the *etliche wenige*. His phonologized yearnings for Spirit encapsulate into one statement: if the breath stream is in any way modified, directed, deflected off or through articulators, it is astringent (to greater and lesser degrees) *Begreiffligkeit*. If the breath stream is unobstructed, it is *Geist*. He categorizes the descent into words into an equally basic principle of case relationship: the mystical nominative verbalizes itself within the matter of an accusative object (*Gegenwurf*), that is, *Geist* becomes *Begreiffligkeit*. All letters and all words can and do reflect this theosophically semanticized grammar.

A

The *A* is the opening between the gums which allows the encapsulated *Geist* "Raum ... nach seinem Gefallen" (*Aurora* xix, 91). Labial opening allows the word to express itself within created nature. Böhme later is unsure about the *A* since it has no characteristic brand of astringency. He settles on calling it *Anfang*, ascribing to it the feature of temporality, although it exists beyond the astringency of the consonants, hence beyond time.

It later structurally highlights the threefold *I*, which whirling through space forms the *A*, the *E* and the *N* (*Tafel* 9).

B

The *B* receives little attention other than being labelled as a labial stop (*Aurora* viii, 74). He includes it within the ranks of astringent manifestation calling it the *äussere Regiment* 'external regiment' (*Dreyfach* xvi, 40).

C

The *C* first appears in the *Drey Principien* where Böhme employs it to signify centrifugal expansion. He says the syllable *-cu-* (*Mercurius*) is "mit der Herbigkeit nicht zu frieden, sondern erhebet sich und auffsteiget" (*Drey Principien* i, 13). Later in the same text, Böhme posits the vowel *u* with the feature of +upward ascent, indicating that the *C* may carry little meaning other than astringency. He mentions its presence in the word *Iacob* (*Mysterium* lii, 41) where it signifies astringency. In *Tinctur* the *C* assumes the shape of the curved *I* (*Tafel* 30).

D

Böhme notices that the *D* is labiodental, produced with the back portion of the velum in the +low position. It is a voiced stop (*Aurora* xviii, 70), hence astringent. He reintegrated the *D* into his argument in the *Tafel*, where we see it swirling spherically as motion within a cross-like *T*. The swirling sphere is represented in the round "body" of the letter; the vertical downstroke is the cross at rest.

E

The *E* is briefly mentioned in the *Aurora*, where Böhme notices that the tongue is not required in its production: "Es braucht sich aber die Zunge zu der ersten Sylben Er nicht, sondern sie schmäuget sich in den untern Gaumen hinein, und verkreucht sich als vor einem Feinde" (*Aurora* xviii, 69). The tongue fears the astringent-laden *R* rather than the ineffective *E*. As with the *A*, Böhme equates the *E* with a word beginning with that letter, *Erniedrigung* 'degradation into matter' (*Drey Principien* xxii, 87). Böhme later calls it the angel (from *Engel*) (*Mysterium* xxxv, 51) as well as unity (from *Einheit*) (*Clavis* 14).

F

Böhme identifies the *F* as a labial fricative (*Dreyfach* xvi, 33), describing the labial closure as the result of the upper gums and teeth pressing onto the lower lip (*Dreyfach* v, 102). Like the *S* and the *SH*, it hisses into manifestation (*DSR* ii, 13).

G

Böhme mentions the *G* only once in the entire corpus, where it is a palatal closure reflecting voice within manifestation (*Aurora* xviii, 60).

H

As seen, the *H* is relatively unimportant in the earlier works, where it passively accepts whatever is placed into it (*Dreyfach* xvi, 33). It eventually symbolizes *Aushauchung*, an important link between the astringent-ridden consonantal obstruents and the astral origins of the nonobstruent vowels. Böhme incorporates the *H* into the name JeHsus to stress his brief association with matter.

I(J)

The *I* always represents Jesus (Iesus) (*Mysterium* xxxv, 51), and is an expansion of the cross-shaped *T (Tafel* 29, 30).

L

The lateral *L* affords the *Geist* room to exit from the mouth into manifestation. It is considered nonobstruent in nature, although it does offer a groove over which *Geist* slides out of the mouth into *Begreiffligkeit*.

M

The *M* receives much attention within the corpus. It is understood as a voiced, nasal, labial stop (*Aurora* xviii, 48) which assumes the function of serving as a wall, or matrix, which holds the expanding *Geist* within the mouth, away from external manifestation. The *M* serves to delineate the astral nonmanifested plane from the physically manifested. It is synonymous with *Himmel* (*Drey Principien* xxii, 85).

N

Böhme identifies the *N* as a voiced alveolar closure (*Aurora* xviii, 67; xix, 110) in the same functional category as the *M*. It is a wall which forces the vibrating *Geist* to exit through the nose (*Aurora* xviii, 72). Böhme later incorporates the shape of the letter into the structure of the threefold *I* (*Tafel* 9) as well as calling it the "Ausfluss des lautenden Geistes" (voice) (*Tafel* 29). Its variant, the *NG* signifies astringent destruction removed from divine unity (*Aurora* xviii, 53, 56).

O

The *O* attracts Böhme's attention in the *Dreyfaches Leben* (1620) where it assumes the feature of finality (+Omega). Böhme later uses it to represent the heart, the center, and the Son within the boundaries of a circumscribed manifestation (*Mysterium* xxxv, 50; *Tafel* 9). The spherical shape suggests the —boundary feature, since it "ist die Circumreferentz des dreyfachen I, als die Geburt der Stätte GOttes in sich selber" (*Tafel* 9).

P

The *P* appears described in only one citation where Böhme notices that it is a labial stop, hence astringent (*Aurora* xviii, 89).

R

The *R* is the most astringent of all the human sounds, trembling in the gums (*Aurora* xviii, 71), lending the mother tongue its linguistic depth. It remains a phonological constant throughout the entire literary corpus. Böhme pays homage to it in *Tafel* 29, 30.

S(SH)

The *SH* appears described from the perspective of the raised apex allowing the breath to pass over the dorsum through a dental closure (*Aurora* xviii, 57). Böhme describes it as a dental fricative (*Aurora* xviii, 88) which through hissing (*Aurora* xviii, 100) signifies the interaction of a molecular confrontation within matter (*Drey Principien* xviii, 17). The simple *S* signifies the purification bath (*Dreyfach* xvi, 35).

T

First noticed as hard pounding (*Aurora* xix, 84-86), Böhme notices that it is voiceless. It comes to represent the crucifix-shaped *T*, a derivative of the threefold *I* (*Tafel* 30). It becomes the "Tau oder Aufthun der Einheit, als das + des dreyfachen I ein Grund zum Hauchen" (*Tafel* 29).

U

The *U* signifies an upward gliding toward the astral realms of heaven, both vertical staves pointing away from earth (*Drey Principien* xxii, 84). It signifies the upward ascent of Jesus back into *Geist* (*Drey Principien* xxii, 87). Böhme notices its low dorsal position (*Dreyfach* v, 88), referring to this letter (as all vowels) as *Geist* (*Mysterium* xxxv, 50; *177 Fragen* 2, 7). When doubled, he notices the +voice feature (*Dreyfach* xvi, 33).

WORD INDEX

Abgrund, 145
Ada, 124
Adam, 118
Adonai, 28, 137, 147
Ängstlichkeit, 151
(das) Aeussere, 86
Alphabeten, 111, 112, 131, 159
also, 27, 32
am, 6, 20, 25
Amen, 28, 38
Anfang, 6, 7, 8, 20, 21, 25, 115
Angst, 35
anziehen, 65, 75
Ararat, 129
auch, 27, 32
auf, 27, 32
auf(f)steigen, 43
ausgesprochen (das Ausgesprochene), 6, 12, 71, 108, 114
ausgesprochenes (Wesen), 6, 12, 28, 36, 69, 73, 134
ausgesprochenes (Wort), 97, 103, 104
Aushauchung, 106, 114, 119, 122-24, 138

Barmhertzig(keit), 6, 10, 11, 18ff., 24, 61, 65
Begierlichkeit, 147
Begreiffligkeit (begreifflig), 2, 13, 14, 15, 41, 42, 49, 86, 94, 112, 137, 146, 154, 158
Beweglichkeit, 147
Bild, 70
bildlich, 149
Bildlichkeit, 152
Bitterkeit, 11
Brot, 6, 26, 27, 34
Buchstaben, 91, 110, 112, 114, 116, 131, 137, 150
Buchstabengelehrten, 60

Cain, 122

Cainische Kirche, 110
Centrum, 98
Centrum zur Wiedergeburt, 54, 55
Chaos, 89
Christus, 61, 67, 68
Creatur, 29, 102
crystallinisch, 121

dein, 27
Demuth, 93
Doctores, 59, 109
Drache, 153
Druck (einen schnellen), 7, 21, 73

Eden, 117
Einfasslichkeit, 138
Einheit, 138, 154
einleiben, 134
einsprechen, 103-06, 108
Empfindlichkeit, 147
Engel, 99, 115
entzünden, 43
Erden, 6, 11, 24-25, 33, 119, 120
erheben, 43
erlöse, 28, 37
erscheinen, 51
Erscheinung, 92
Esau, 130
Essentien, 56, 66, 69
etliche wenige, 152
Etwas, 85, 119
Evä (Eve, Hevä), 118

Feindig, 151
Feuer, 147
Fühlung, 57
führe, 28, 36

Gaumen (obern), 21
Gegenhall, 83
Gegenwurf, 148

Word Index

geheiliget, 27, 30
Geist, 2-4, 13-17, 49, 57, 58, 74, 86, 131, 133, 154
Gelassenheit, 90-92, 95
Gemüt(h), 54ff., 81, 83, 84, 93, 122, 133
geschehe, 27
Geschöpf, 51-53, 58
Gesicht, 97
Gestalt, 78, 115
Gestaltniss, 78, 79, 83, 86
Gestorbenen, 120
Gewirck, 105
Gewirckete, 138
gib, 6, 27, 33
Gott, 6, 7, 22, 23, 25
Grimm, 37
(das ewige) Gute, 98, 102, 103, 154

Härte, 148
Hall, 78, 79, 82, 110
Ham, 128
Hanoch, 123
hauchen, 106, 145
(erstes) Haus, 12
Henoch, 127
Herbigkeit, 11
Herrligkeit, 39
heute, 27, 34, 35
Himmel, 6, 8, 20, 23, 25, 27-29, 32, 46ff., 56, 61, 63, 64, 75, 104, 120
Höle, 7
Höllen=Porten, 14
Hülse, 77, 80, 83, 109, 117

Ichheit, 138
Icht, 145-46
Idea, 149
Imagination, 70, 75, 76, 91, 111, 121
Immanuel, 61, 64, 65
Impression, 103
in (im), 27-29
Inmodelung, 149
Irad, 123, 127

Jacob, 130, 131
Jah, 148-49, 153
Jammerthal, 62, 68
Japeth, 128
Jared, 127
Jehovah, 116, 141ff., 146, 149, 152
Jesus, 61, 66, 67, 115, 122, 132

Kenan, 127
Klang, 36, 80
komme, 27, 30, 31
Kraft, 31, 39, 51, 97, 138, 140
Kunst, 60

Lamech, 124, 128
Leib, 53, 74, 87
Liebe, 147
Lilien, 63
Lust, 139

Magistros, 110
Mahalaleel, 127
Mahujael, 123
Maria, 61, 62, 133
Materia, 45
materialisches (Wasser), 47
Matrix, 44, 48
Meer, 48
Meinheit, 124
Meister, 81
Mensch, 61
Mercurius, 42ff.
Methusael, 123, 124
Methuselah, 127
Monstrum, 152
Mund, 55, 78

Nacht, 8
Naema, 126
Name, 27, 29
Natura, 69

Word Index

Natur=Recht, 26
Natur=Sprache, 2, 80, 111
Naturwerdung, 29
Nein, 148-49, 153
Nichts, 85, 119, 145, 147, 154
Noah, 128

Principien, 41ff.

Qual, 35, 148
Qualitäten, 89

Reich, 27, 30, 39

Salitter, 21, 22, 104
Schärfe, 148
schallen, Schall, 16, 56, 147, 148
Schatten, 52, 53, 65, 122, 127
schuf(f), 6, 12, 22, 25, 71ff.
Schuld, 28, 35
Schwätzer, 159
Scientz, 139
Seele, 29, 45, 85
Selbheit, 90-93, 95, 123, 130
sensualische Sprache, 107, 112, 114, 116, 117, 131
Sem, 128
Seth, 126
Signatur, 53, 76, 77, 83, 90, 108, 122
Sohn, 138
sonderlich, 105
sondern, 28
sprach, 7, 13
Sprache (sensualische), 107, 112, 114, 116, 117, 131
das Sprechende, 89, 104
sprechendes (Wort), 88, 103, 104
Stachels=Reibung, 43
Stachlicht, 151
Sterben, 120
Stimme, 29, 78, 110
Streit, 68

Substanz, 52
Sulphur, 44, 45, 84-86

Tag, 6, 15-17
täglich, 6, 27, 34
Tetragrammaton, 28, 116
Teuvell, 6
Thieren, 58
thirisch, 87
Tinctur, 140ff.
tönen, 58
Tubalkain, 125
Tugend, 140
turba, 129

Übel, 28, 38
und, 6, 25, 28, 36
Unruh, 35
uns, 6, 28, 36, 37
unser, 6, 27, 28, 36
(den) Unsern, 141

Vater, 27-28, 115, 138
Vater Unser, 26ff., 39
verlass, 28, 35, 36
vermischt, 61
Vernunft, 92
Verstand, 56, 109, 129
Versuchung, 28, 37
verzücken, 127

Wasser, 47, 120
(heiliges) (crystallinisches) Wasser, 47, 120
(materialisches) Wasser, 47
werde, 27, 30
(ausgesprochenes) Wesen, 6, 12, 28, 36, 69, 73, 134
(das) Wesen Gottes, 4
Wesenheit, 33, 34
wie, 27
Wille(n), 3, 27, 29, 31, 69, 138
willen/wallen/wollen, 31, 138, 145, 154

Word Index

wircken, 32, 105
Wirckung, 105
Wissendschaft, 139
Wort, 15, 49, 74, 134, 158
(sprechendes) Wort, 88, 103, 104
(ausgesprochenes) Wort, 97, 103, 104
Wortes=Fassung, 64

Zilla, 124
Zeit-Geister, 99
Zerbrechlichkeit, 48, 59
Zorn, 148

BIBLIOGRAPHY

Bastian, Albert. 1905. *Der Gottesbegriff bei Jakob Böhme.* Kiel: Dissertation.
Benz, Ernst. 1936. *Zur metaphysischen Begründung der Sprache bei Jacob Boehme.* Euphorion 37. 340-57.
———. 1951. *Die Sprachtheologie der Reformationszeit.* Studium Generale 4. 204-12.
———. 1959. *Der Prophet Jakob Boehme: Eine Studie über den Typus nachreformatorischen Prophetentums.* Wiesbaden: Franz Steiner Verlag.
Bharati, Agehananda. 1976. *The Light at the Center: Context and Pretext of Modern Mysticism.* Santa Barbara: Ross-Erikson.
Bingen, Hildegard von. 1954. *Wisse die Wege. Scivias.* Salzburg: O. Müller.
Blau, Joseph L. 1944. *The Christian Interpretation of the Cabala in the Renaissance.* New York: Columbia University Press.
Böhme, Jacob. 1955. *Sämtliche Schriften.* 11 vols. Edited by Will Erich Peuckert. Stuttgart: Fr. Fromann Verlag.
———. 1960. *The Aurora.* Translated by John Sparrow (1656). Greenwood, S.C.: Attic Press.
———. 1974. *Aurora oder Morgenröthe im Aufgang.* Edited by Gerhard Bartsch. Leipzig: Reclam.
———. 1978. *The Way to Christ.* Translated by Peter Erb. New York: Paulist Press.
Bornkamm, Heinrich. 1925. *Luther and Boehme.* Bonn: Marcus und Weber.
Borst, Arno. 1957. *Der Turmbau von Babel: Geschichte der Meinungen über Ursprung und Vielfalt der Sprachen und Völcker.* Stuttgart: Anton Hiersemann.
Brooke, Kenneth. 1955. *An Introduction to Early New High German.* Oxford: Oxford University Press.
Brown, Robert. 1977. *The Later Philosophy of Schelling: The*

Influence of Boehme on the Works of 1809-1815. Lewisburg: Bucknell University Press.
Buddecke, Werner. 1937. *Die Jakob Böhme Ausgaben: Ein beschreibendes Verzeichnis.* Göttingen: Häntzschel & Co.
———. 1963. *Die Urschriften I.* Stuttgart: Fr. Fromann Verlag.
———. 1966. *Die Urschriften II.* Stuttgart: Fr. Fromann Verlag.
Buddecke, Wolfram. 1972. *Die Jakob Böhme Autographen: Ein historischer Bericht.* Wolfenbütteler Beiträge I. 61-87.
Daube, Anna. 1940. *Der Aufstieg der Muttersprache im deutschen Denken des 15. und 16. Jahrhunderts.* Frankfurt a. M.: Verlag Moritz Diesterweg.
Deussen, Paul. 1922. *Jakob Böhme: Über sein Leben und seine Philosophie.* Leipzig: F. A. Brockhaus.
Dornseiff, Franz. 1925. *Das Alphabet in Mystik und Magie.* Leipzig: B. G. Teubner.
Eco, Umberto. 1976. *A Theory of Semiotics.* Bloomington: Indiana University Press.
Felgenhauer, Paul. 1640. *Das Büchlein Iehor, oder Morgenröthe der Weiszheit. Von den drey Principiis aller Dinge, die immer sein mögen, dadurch die grossen unnd viel Geheimnüssen beydes in Gott . . . klar erkant werden . . .* Gedruckt im Jahr Christi 1640. Im Jahr der Welt, 5870.
———. 1650. *Sphaera Sapientiae in Ostio Aperto: Die Sphaer oder Circkel der Weisheit in einer Offenen Thür: In welcher die bisher verborgenen Geheymnüssen entdeckt und offenbaret werden . . . In Sieben unterschiedenen Capitulen dagezeigt . . .* Gedruckt im Jubeljahr, nach Christi Geburth 1650.
Franckenberg, Abraham von. 1639. *Raphael oder Artzt-Engel. Auff ehmaliges Ersuchen eines Gottliebenden Medici. A. S. Auffgesetzt von H. Abraham von Franckenberg, Equite Silesio, im Jahr 1693 (i.e. 1639). Jetzo aber durch zuthun guter Hertzen und Freude verlegt, und ans Licht gebracht.* Zu Amsterdam, Gedruckt bey Jacob von Felsen, wohnhafft in der Utrechtschen Gasse, am Reguliers Marckt 1676.
———. 1651. *Gründlicher und wahrhafter Bericht von dem Leben*

und Abschied des in GOtt selig=ruhenden Jacob Böhmens, dieser Theosophischen Schriften eigentlichen Autoris und Schreibers. In Sämtliche Schriften. Vol. 10. Edited by Peuckert. 1-31.

Götze, Alfred. 1967. *Frühneuhochdeutsches Glossar.* Berlin: Walter de Gruyter.

Grunsky, Hans. 1940. *Jacob Boehme als Schöpfer einer germanischen Philosophie des Willens.* Hamburg: Hanseatische Verlagsanstalt.

———. 1956. *Jacob Boehme.* Stuttgart: Fr. Fromann Verlag.

Halevi, Shimon. 1974. *Adam and the Kabbalistic Tree.* London: Rider and Company.

Hankamer, Paul. 1960. *Jakob Böhme: Gestalt und Gestaltung.* 2nd ed. Hildesheim: Olms Verlagsbuchhandlung.

———. 1964. *Deutsche Gegenreformation und Deutsches Barock.* 2nd ed. Stuttgart: J. B. Metzlersche Verlagsbuchhandlung.

———. 1965. *Die Sprache: Ihr Begriff und Ihre Bedeutung im Sechzehnten und Siebzehnten Jahrhundert.* Hildesheim: Olms Verlagsbuchhandlung.

Hartmann, Franz. 1929. *The Life and Doctrines of Jacob Boehme.* New York: Macoy Publishing Company.

Heckel, Hans. 1921. *Geschichte der deutschen Literatur in Schlesien: Von den Anfängen bis zum Ausgange des Barock.* Breslau: Ostdeutsche Verlagsanstalt.

Hegenicus, Ehrenfried. 1669. *Send=Schreiben, wegen Sel. J. Böhms Talent und dessen Schriften, auch seiner Erkentniss des Grundes der Natur, nebst zweyer Görlitzer Bürgermeister Zeugnissen vom Autore.* In Sämtliche Schriften. Vol. 10. Edited by Peuckert. 53-96.

Heller, Arno. 1964. *Die Sprachwelt in Jakob Böhmes Morgenröte.* Innsbruck: Dissertation.

Hoffstein, Robert. 1975. *The English Alphabet: An Inquiry into Its Mystical Construction.* New York: Kaedmon Publishing Company.

Horodezky, Samuel Aba. 1912. *Mystisch-religiöse Strömungen unter den Juden in Polen im 16.-18. Jahrhundert.* Leipzig: Gustav Engel Verlagsbuchhandlung.

Huber, W. 1971. *Die Kabbala als Quelle zur Anthropologie Jakob Böhmes.* Kairos 13. 131-50.

Jecht, Richard. 1924. *Jakob Böhme: Gedenkgabe der Stadt Görlitz zu seinem 300 jährigen Todestage.* Görlitz: Selbstverlag des Magistrats der Stadt Görlitz.

Kämmerer, Ernst. 1971. *Das Leib-Seele-Geist Problem bei Paracelsus und einigen Autoren des 17. Jahrhunderts.* Wiesbaden: Franz Steiner Verlag.

Kayser, Wolfgang. 1930. *Böhmes Natursprachenlehre und ihre Grundlagen.* Euphorion 31. 521-62.

Kluge, Friedrich. 1975. *Etymologisches Wörterbuch.* 21st ed. Berlin: Walter de Gruyter.

Kobers, Tobiä. 1624. *Von der Kranckheit, Absterben und Begräbniss des sel. Autoris Theosophi, an die Edlen Herren von Schweinichen.* In Sämtliche Schriften. Vol. 10. 40-52.

Kocher, Kurt E. 1975. *Jakob Böhme: sein Werk und seine Aussage.* Dannstadt-Schauerheim: Heko Verlag.

Konopacki, Steven A. 1977. *Frustration and Promise: Jacob Boehme's Language Theories in the Aurora oder Morgen Röte im Auffgang.* Ann Arbor: University Microfilms.

Koyré, Alexandre. 1929. *La Philosophie de Jacob Boehme.* Paris: Librarie Philosophique J. Vrin.

Luther, Martin. 1974. *Die gantze Heilige Schrifft (1545).* München: Deutsche Taschenbuch Verlag.

Martensen, Hans. 1949. *Jakob Boehme: Studies in his Life and Teaching.* Translated by T. Rhys Evans. London: Rockliff.

McDermott, Robert. 1975. *Indian spirituality in the west: A bibliographical mapping.* In Philosophy East and West 25, No. 2. 213-40.

McNiell, John T. 1977. *The History and Character of Calvinism.* London: Oxford University Press.

Melzer, Friso. 1946. *Unsere Sprache im Lichte der Christus Offenbarung.* Tübingen: J. C. B. Mohr.

Mendels, Judy. 1953. *Jacob Boehme's 'R'.* JEGP liii. 559-62.
Mikeleitis, Edith. 1942. *Das Ewige Bildnis.* Berlin: Georg Westermann.
Monzo, Julio Navarro. 1931. *La actualidad filosófica de Jacobo Boehme.* Buenos Aires: Editorial Mundo Nuevo.
Moulton, William. 1952. *Jacob Boehme's Uvular 'r'.* JEGP li. 83-89.
Penny, A. J. 1912. *Studies in Jacob Böhme.* London: John M. Watkins.
Peuckert, Will Erich. 1956. *Pansophie.* Berlin: Erich Schmidt Verlag.
———. 1961. *Das Leben Jakob Böhmes.* In Sämtliche Schriften. Vol. 10. 1-240.
———. 1967. *Gabalia: Ein Versuch zur Geschichte der magia naturalis im 16. bis 18. Jahrhundert.* Berlin: Erich Schmidt Verlag.
Popp, Karl Robert. 1935. *Jakob Böhme und Isaac Newton.* Leipzig: S. Hirzel.
Prophet, Mark. 1974. *Studies in Alchemy: The Science of Self-Transformation.* Los Angeles: Summit University Press.
Quint, Josef. 1953. *Mystik und Sprache: Ihr Verhältnis zueinander, insbesondere in der spekulativen Mystik Meister Eckharts.* DVJS 27. 48-76.
Schäublin, Peter. 1963. *Zur Sprache Jakob Böhmes.* Winterthur: P. G. Keller.
Schaya, Leo. 1974. *The Universal Meaning of the Kabbalah.* Baltimore: Penguin Books.
Scholem, Gerschom. 1974. *Kabbalah.* New York: Quadrangle.
———. 1974. *On the Kabbalah and Its Symbolism.* New York: Schocken Books.
Schulze, W. 1959. *Jacob Boehme und die Kabbala.* Judaica 11. 12-29.
Schwarz, Wolfgang. 1970. *Pico della Mirandola und Jakob Böhme: Oder der spielende Gott.* In Schlesische Studien. Edited by Alfons Hayduk. 113-18.

Secret, F. 1964. *Les cabalistes chrétiens de la renaissance.* Paris: Dunod.
Seligmann, Kurt. 1971. *Magic, Supernaturalism and Religion.* New York: Pantheon Books.
Solms-Rödelheim, Günther. 1960. *Die Grundvorstellungen Jakob Böhmes und ihre Terminologie.* München: Selbstverlag.
Spunda, Franz. 1961. *Das mystische Leben Jakob Böhmes.* Freiburg im Breisgau: Verlag Hermann Bauer.
Stam, James H. 1976. *Inquiries into the Origin of Language: The Fate of a Question.* New York: Harper and Row.
Steiner, George. 1975. *After Babel: Aspects of Language and Translation.* New York: Oxford University Press.
Steiner, Rudolf. 1942. *Results of Spiritual Research: Jacob Boehme.* New York: Rudolf Steiner Publishing Company.
Stewig, Christiana. 1953. *Böhmes Lehre vom innern Wort in ihrer Beziehung zu Frankenbergs Anschauung vom Wort.* München: Dissertation.
Stoudt, John. 1957. *Sunrise to Eternity: A Study in Jacob Boehme's Life and Thought.* Philadelphia: The University of Pennsylvania.
Suares, Carlo. 1970. *The Cipher of Genesis: The Original Code of the Qabala as Applied to the Scriptures.* London: Stuart and Watkins.
Taylor, Edward. 1691. *Jacob Behmen's Theosophic Philosophy Unfolded; in Divers Considerations and Demonstrations . . . Also, the principal treatises of the said author abridged. And answers given to the remainder of the 177 theosophic questions . . . left unanswered by him at his death.* London: T. Salusbury.
Thomas, Edward E. 1976. *Grail Yoga.* Hankins, N. Y.: Grail Books.
Trier, Jost. 1931. *Der deutsche Wortschatz im Sinnbezirk des Verstandes: Die Geschichte eines sprachlichen Feldes.* Heidelberg: Carl Winters Universitätsbuchhandlung.
Vetterling, Herman. 1923. *The Illuminate of Görlitz or Jakob Böhme's Life and Philosophy.* Leipzig: Markert and Petters.
Völker, Ludwig. 1972. *Gelassenheit: Zur Entstehung des Worts in*

der Sprache Meister Eckharts und seiner Überlieferung in der nacheckhartschen Mystik bis Jakob Böhme. In Getempert und Gemischet. Göppinger Arbeiten zur Germanistik 65. 281-312.

Waldemar, Charles. 1959. *Jakob Böhme der schlesische Mystiker.* München: Goldmann Verlag.

Wehr, Gerhard. 1975. *Jakob Böhme in Selbstzeugnissen und Bilddokumenten.* Reinbek bei Hamburg: Rowohlt Taschenbuch Verlag.

Wentzlaff-Eggebert, Friedrich Wilhelm. 1944. *Deutsche Mystik zwischen Mittelalter und Neuzeit.* Berlin: Walter de Gruyter.

Weissner, Cornelius. 1651. *Von des sel. Jacob Böhmen Sanftmuth, Demuth und Freundlichkeit, it. von dem Examine zu Dresden, in Gegenwart Churfürstl. Durchl. und acht der fürnehmsten Professoren.* In Sämtliche Schriften. Vol. 10. Edited by Peuckert. 32-40.

Wright, Joseph. 1966. *Historical German Grammar.* London: Oxford University Press.

Yates, Frances A. 1978. *The Rosicrucian Enlightenment.* Boulder: Shambala.